Gender and the Negotiation of Daily Life in Mexico, 1750–1856

THE MEXICAN EXPERIENCE | William H. Beezley, *series editor*

SONYA LIPSETT-RIVERA

Gender and the Negotiation of Daily Life in Mexico, 1750–1856

UNIVERSITY OF NEBRASKA PRESS | Lincoln & London

Publication of this volume was assisted by a
grant from Carleton University.
Library of Congress Cataloging-in-
Publication Data
Lipsett-Rivera, Sonya, 1961–
Gender and the negotiation of daily life in
Mexico, 1750–1856 / Sonya Lipsett-Rivera.
p. cm. — (The Mexican experience)
Includes bibliographical references and
index.
ISBN 978-0-8032-3833-6 (pbk.: alk. paper)
1. Mexico—Civilization—18th century.
2. Mexico—Civilization—19th century.
3. Mexico—Social life and customs—18th
century. 4. Mexico—Social life and
customs—19th century. 5. Mexico—Social
conditions—18th century. 6. Mexico—Social
conditions—19th century. 7. Sex role—
Mexico. 8. Space—Social aspects—Mexico.
9. Human body—Social aspects—Mexico.
I. Title.
F1210.L575 2012
972'.02—dc23
2011045564

Set in ITC New Baskerville by Bob Reitz.

For my son, Jason José

Contents

Illustrations

Preface and Acknowledgments

This book is certainly not what I envisaged when I began the research. I started thinking about women and violence while going through packet after packet of documents simply classified by year in the Archivo Judicial de Puebla. Because there was no catalog I looked at a lot of documents that had no relevance to the project that I was finishing at the time. I encountered the case of a woman complaining of unjust imprisonment despite her husband's violence. The story had all the elements of an eighteenth-century soap opera and I was hooked. I began discussing the connection between women and violence with Mexican friends and family. One theme came up over and over: that many Mexican women sought out this abuse because it was proof of their husbands' or lovers' affection. I was not convinced and the documents certainly do not corroborate this belief. In the many court cases that I read for this book, I found strong and resilient women who refused to conform to a societal model that would make them into these eager victims. In the end it was not this research question that remained front and center in the final product, but I hope that this message is not totally obscured.

Because I was finishing other projects, this monograph was long in gestation and it took twists and turns not contemplated when I first started it. There were several seminal moments that altered its course. First, while looking at an exhibition of western art in a Fort Worth gallery, Lyman Johnson and I conceived of the idea of a book on honor. The resulting anthology led me into honor studies and a perspective on colonial societies that altered my outlook considerably. It also allowed me to work with Lyman, a great friend and incredibly perceptive historian. The next moment occurred when Bill Beezley came to Carleton and talked to my class. He drew diagrams of a Mexican house and an American house and explained how the spatial configurations differed. It all made sense to me and I began to look at my material differently. Finally, when I read Pieter Spierenberg's essay on eighteenth-century Amsterdam men and weapons I began to think about criminal documents in a totally different manner. These three moments of inspiration allowed me to forge a study that is very different from what I had first contemplated, but I hope it is more inspired than what I had originally planned.

With generous support from the Social Sciences and Humanities Research Council of Canada I began research in several Mexican and Spanish archives and libraries. The staffs in the Archivo General de la Nación in Mexico City and the Archivo Judicial de Puebla were particularly helpful and supportive. I cannot thank them enough for little kindnesses and big favors. The head judge of the Archivo Judicial del Tribunal Superior del Districto Federal gave me permission to examine the colonial and national documents in the court basement and it was one of the strangest and best experience of my research life. I also worked in Spain at the Biblioteca Nacional and the Archivo General de Indias, whose staffs were courteous and obliging.

I spent a lot of time in Mexico City, always with my lovely

in-laws, Francisco Rivera Aguilar and the late Amalia Ayala Figueroa. They made me feel welcome, fed me delicious food, and told me many wonderful stories. I also want to thank all my brothers and sisters-in-law, who also made and continue to make any time I spend in Mexico more delightful. Fidel and Toña, Raul and Engracia, Jaime and Salome, Estela and Luis, Teresa and Jesús, as well as Marisela, Guadalupe, and all their wonderful children are indeed a kind and welcoming extended family. Sergio Rivera Ayala continues to be a good friend and his intellectual influence is definitely present in this work. In Puebla I often stayed with my good friends Rosalva Loreto López and Francisco Cervantes Bello, who not only shared their home with me but also their passion for history. Pilar Gonzalbo Aizpuru gave me many opportunities to present my burgeoning ideas at El Colegio de México—a chance for feedback that was invaluable.

I have benefited from the friendship of many people in our field including Linda Curcio-Nagy, Anne Rubenstein, Don Stevens, Colin Coates, Megan Davies, Susan Schroeder, Stafford Poole, Ann Twinam, Fritz Schwaller, Deborah Kanter, Susan Deeds, Susan Kellogg, Ann Blum, Martin Nesvig, Linda Hall, Jeffrey Pilcher, Lyman Johnson, Bill Beezley, and, most of all, the late Elinor Melville, who was both an inspiration and a very dear friend. Some friends helped beyond the call of duty; Javier Villa-Flores read this manuscript twice and provided the most helpful suggestions and critiques. I also wish to acknowledge the comments of the anonymous readers, whose words helped me beyond measure. Christine Rivas also read all my chapters and assisted with illustrations. Her comments as well as Maureen Mahoney's helped refine the argument and avoid confusion. There are also many fine people in my university who make my work life pleasant and inspire me with their example and their ideas; David Dean and Susanne Klausen are not just good friends but intellectual companions. I am also grateful to Jennifer Evans, Janet Siltanen, Joanna Dean, Patrick McGraw, Andrew Johnston, Peter Gose, John Osborne, James Miller, and Bruce Elliott for their support. By his excellent example of incredible productivity, Antonio Cazorla Sánchez pushes me to excel and both his and Celine Bak's kind hospitality provided many a delicious respite. I also very much appreciated the constant help and advice of Bridget Barry, Ann Baker, and Heather Lundine at the press. Despite all this magnificent assistance, errors have undoubtedly crept into this work, and they are my responsibility.

There are friends who have nothing to do with academia but whose mere companionship is vital to any exercise: Anne Clark McMunagle, Neil Farish, Diane Marleau, Claire Heistek, Katherine Zielonka, Oswaldo Lazzuri, Tina Dubé, Louise Stattler, Caroline George, and Simone Williams. They all gave me wise counsel and helped maintain my balance. During some difficult times I gained much peace of mind through riding horses, and for the many rides I thank Walter Kahrer, and, although they would prefer carrots, I also thank my lovely equine friends—in particular Shatzi, but most of all Melville. Finally I need to acknowledge my family. My parents, Fred and Elizabeth Lipsett, stimulated my curiosity, encouraged me to spread my wings, and rescued me whenever I fell. My son, Jason José, is also an inspiration and a tremendous source of joy and pride. Despite the fact that books are not his thing, I dedicate this book to him.

Gender and the Negotiation of Daily Life in Mexico, 1750–1856

1. Negotiating Daily Life

How does culture affect the way that individuals interact both with their surroundings and with others? That is the question that is at the center of this book. In our daily lives, we relate with both our physical environments and with other people in manners that are culturally determined. That our interactions are the product of our cultural backgrounds is made obvious when we travel to a different place and struggle with unfamiliar cityscapes and body language. The mysteries of a foreign environment highlight how much we have a comfort zone within our own surroundings. Humans not only receive messages from the buildings and the people who form their milieu but they also shape these elements in order to conform to their worldview. There is a continuous loop between the creation of a particular architecture — both of spaces and people — and then the messages that are imparted to residents; that is to say, people build cities that correspond to their ideas about rank, morality, and honor, and then those who live in this environment will function within these constraints. As a result, their living arrangements will reflect the overall pattern. In the large cities of Mexico, for example, the wealthy and most honorable resided on the upper floors, and young people were educated into a body language that was acceptable within these spaces.

Take for example the rules of conduct that young people of the elite classes were supposed to put in practice when they entered a room. First, after climbing the stairs to the upper apartments, one should never enter the interior rooms of another person's residence without alerting the servants or after knocking loudly or repeatedly at entrances. After opening the door softly and greeting all the people in the room appropriately, the next major step was to choose a seat. It was not acceptable to simply sit down in the nearest armchair or perch on another piece of furniture. Rather, the newcomer had to make numerous calculations about the hierarchy of the hosts and the guests and then choose a chair, or, in the case of a young lady, a cushion that corresponded to her place within this ranking.[1] One could not, for example, take a seat that was superior to that occupied by a person of higher rank. How does one calculate the status of a chair? It was an equation that had to do with the height of the seat as well as its position in relation to the door and the interior of the room. The higher the chair and the nearer to the interior, the higher it was in the hierarchy of furniture.[2]

Mexicans filled the spaces where they resided with messages about morality, honor, and hierarchy. It was not only their homes that operated within these frameworks but also their very persons. When any young people entered a residence following the aforementioned etiquette, they did not just have to make judgments about chairs but they also needed to make their body conform to the rules of politeness and deference. In this way, spatial understandings as well as body language worked together within the overarching construction of honor.[3] It was not just young elite men and women who had to learn rules about spaces and bodies; rather, men and women of all ranks entered into this dance of deference and jockeying for position that happened in homes, courtyards, the church atrium, the market, taverns—just about anywhere people congregated.[4] These were the written and unwritten rules for gender in the negotiation of daily life.

Etiquette, Power, and History

History is not just about great men, wars, and revolutions; it is also about the subtle aspects of more ordinary matters. But the mundane and the grand are also related. In order to understand Mexico and Mexicans in the past and the present, it is necessary to appreciate the fundamentals—what made people tick. Etiquette is a way into these mental processes; it provides a starting point or a guide to understand the rules that governed behavior. In particular these rules show how people were expected to interact with particular spaces and how they were supposed to control their bodies. For Alejandro Cañeque, it was etiquette that provided Mexicans with a kind of "mental map to guide their behavior" but also supplied the framework for power struggles at the highest social levels. When individuals fought over whether they could sit on a chair (as opposed to a bench) or use a velvet cushion to soften a hard wooden seat, they were battling in symbolic realms that were not less real even if they did not lead to physical violence.[5] These skirmishes were a way of sublimating what could have led to blows. Power struggles occurred daily not just for elites but also for plebeians; they were present in everyday conflicts over hierarchy and reputation and at times did lead to violence. As Diana Taylor writes, "embodied practices" are a means of "transmitting knowledge"; that is to say, it was the ways of doing things that allowed the nonliterate to transmit their information.[6] It is by exploring the way that Mexicans negotiated their daily lives—how they behaved and interacted with their environment and with each other—that it is possible to build a more comprehensive understanding of Mexican history in general.

On a day-to-day basis the aspects of life that most preoccupied people were not the political machinations of generals or politicians but whether they could make a living, whether others accorded them the respect that they deserved, whether they were safe from an abusive husband, whether their wives and children would obey them; in short, the minutiae of daily life. When either witnesses to a crime or accused of a violent act, Mexican men and women expressed all these concerns to judicial officials; but, in addition, they spoke about how their housing arrangements affected them or how their surroundings mediated their lives. They also told about the ways that they interacted with other people based upon an understanding of the body that was particularly Mexican. It is by reading these court files, with an eye to the details that reveal how people understood their surroundings and their fellow residents, that historians can provide a cultural reading of the way that Mexicans handled the small decisions of their everyday lives.

Walls and body parts might seem unmovable and unchangeable but, in fact, over time and across cultures, individual perceptions of both do alter. If both a person's place within a room and their body language explains power relations, to comprehend these aspects of daily life it is necessary to capture what space and body meant to people in central Mexico in earlier times. This book explores the value systems that governed Mexican mentalities of the period in order to portray the ephemeral daily experiences and interactions of the people and to illuminate how gender and honor systems governed these everyday negotiations. Historians can approach such a problem either from a top-down perspective or one that is more mundane; that is to say, by reading manuals written by authorities and usually members of the elite or by exploring what people actually did.

Both approaches have their value but also their limitations. By only reading manuals any scholar's vision would be clouded by ideals and lack the nitty-gritty of life on the streets; on the other hand, by only reading of the day-to-day interactions, one lacks perspective on the overarching structures that directed these experiences.

This book reflects an attempt to blend these two approaches using the lessons on etiquette and morality that upper-class Mexicans would have been expected to learn as well as the records of crimes committed by men and women that reveal the ways that these lessons filtered down into the lower classes. Books on morality and etiquette from periods well before the years under study were used because these manuals provided the foundations for ideas about politeness as well as spatial and bodily relations.[7] Such ideas did not spring up overnight at the beginning of the eighteenth or nineteenth centuries but rather were formed over a long period of time and were remarkably unchanging. Valentina Torres Septién shows that nineteenth-century etiquette manuals still used the same models for conduct that Erasmus had proposed four centuries earlier.[8] The manners books and morality treatises allow me to describe the foundational structures of Mexican culture and society in terms of the ways that people interacted both with their built environment and with each other.

Violence as a Source

Although many different kinds of sources were used, the vast majority of the material for this book derives from court cases produced by judicial officials. There is one exception to this rule: ecclesiastical divorce cases that were administered by the Catholic Church rather than secular courts. What all these incidents have in common—whether secular or not—is that they involve violence. Historians have long acknowledged violent acts within past societies and have focused on episodes such as riots, rebellions, or wars for their studies; however, centering interpretation on violence itself does pose some methodological problems. One of the fundamental difficulties is that because violence is usually an aberration, how can it be used to paint a picture of any society? It is important to make a distinction between different kinds of violence. As Jennine Hurl-Eamon points out, in past societies certain kinds of violence were socially acceptable.[9] In many instances, when individuals are aggressive they often seem to lose control; they are said to not be themselves. How then can such acts be symptomatic of a culture or a people?

Duels were one of the first areas in which historians began to make a connection between the formulations of violent acts and a particular culture. Because it was the elites who fought these contests and they wrote manuals about the etiquette of duels as well a commentary and even, eventually, political debates, it was relatively easy for historians to understand the rules underlying these fights and relate these back to particular societies.[10] For plebeians, such a task was not so easy; the lower classes tended not to write rulebooks nor did they leave diaries and personal accounts of their boxing matches or knife fights. If the literate elites deigned to notice such plebeian fights, they would not have bothered to analyze them or to describe them in the kind of detail useful to historians; they dismissed them as another sign of lower class perversity. Luckily for historians, the courts recorded plebeian violence when it came to their attention, such as when bystanders called in the guard or when the all-too-frequent deaths or severe beatings required judicial action. Witness accounts become the major source for historians of plebeian violence. These often rich descriptions provide details regarding the buildup to actual blows, the role of audience and settings, and the way lower-class men and women understood the rules and rituals of combat.

Historians such as Robert Shoemaker, Thomas Gallant, Robert Muchembled, and Pieter Spierenberg note that while plebeian violence often seemed senseless and confused to elite observers, it followed its own internal logic. These historians note that when men engaged in fisticuffs or knife fights, they followed rules; these conventions might not have been obvious to people of another class or society but the participants and bystanders all followed the same playbook. If a fighter deviated from the rules spectators would intervene because they considered such an aberration to be unfair.[11] These rules for violence only worked because everyone involved ascribed to a system of honor; they fought to defend their honor but they did so in ways that were accepted and that followed established rituals and conventions because they behaved honorably.

The fact that honor systems applied to the lower class as much as to the elite in Latin America is a relatively new argument, but it is central to understanding the ways that people organized their lives.[12] Within Latin American and more particularly Mexican historiography, William B. Taylor was an unselfconscious pioneer in these types of studies. Without articulating his analysis in as pointed a manner as the previously mentioned historians, this author used a sample of acts of violence to try to understand village life in different Mexican regions. He looked for patterns and recognized what later historians would call "scenarios" or "mise-en-scène" for plebeian violence. Taylor introduced the notion that when people fought they followed certain patterns; one in particular that is particularly evocative is that of the "fighting words."[13] He writes that in the period leading up to brawls, men habitually engaged in insults and bravado — these were the lead-up to a fight and part of the ritual participants and observers would have recognized and understood.

These cues were the equivalent of the formal challenge that elite men would have given if insulted. Pierre Bourdieu describes how opponents had to read each other's body language: "each move triggers off a counter-move, every stance of the body becomes a sign pregnant with a meaning that the opponent has to grasp."[14] The culture of the fight and its mise-en-scène is recognizable enough to make its way into one of Gabriel García Márquez's novels, *Crónica de una Muerte Anunciada* (*Chronicle of a Death Foretold*), in which the protagonists do everything to signal their intention to fight to the death, hoping that someone will intervene to stop them.[15] What historians of plebeian violence have discovered is that, in the absence of manuals that spell out the rules of engagement for fights, they can uncover the rules by a deep reading of trial transcripts. They look for patterns that point to the rules that the lower class understood and enforced within violent acts; from this understanding of patterns it is possible to make sense out of what seems, at first glance, to be simply senseless, chaotic violence.

What ties these historians together as a nascent school of history is that they examine plebeian violence not from the point of view of law or criminality but by charting the patterns that lower class men followed when they engaged in conflict. As Spierenburg states, when scholars had previously looked at the fights between members of the lower class, all they had seen was "a heap of senseless violence."[16] By following what commonly led to a fight, historians can outline the values that were fundamental to plebeian society, that is, what was worth fighting over and what standards did they live by? Once engaged, men chose weapons that were class specific—in some cultures a knife, in others their fists. The only way to decode the rules governing such plebeian confrontations is to engage in a very detailed reading of the narratives written down by witnesses to fights and also those of the participants.

With such a "close reading" it is possible to approximate the "inner logic" that governed plebeian violence and determine what acts plebeians considered aberrant and unacceptable.[17] The choice of weapons was often driven by a class culture. Spierenberg shows, for example, how middle-class residents of Amsterdam eschewed knives because they were associated with plebeians and carried sticks to keep the riffraff away from their person and avoid engaging with a knife fighter.[18] The way that these opponents fought was also set out in popular understandings. In many cultures when one person had cut the face of another, that signaled the end of the conflict. These popular rules and the patterns underlying them also allow the historian to gain insights into the culture of the body. For example, as Spierenberg notes, a common pattern of ritual degradation occurred to the head, but for women, a common form of humiliation was to be stabbed in the buttocks.[19] What historians grasp from following the outlines and frameworks within which plebeian men fought each other is that these were not random conflicts but ones that operated according to rules, rituals, and traditions. Within seeming chaos there was order and this is where the notion of a scenario of violence is useful.

The scenarios of violence allow us to perceive plebeian codes of conduct—the kind of etiquette that was equivalent to elite notions but never written down in manuals and rulebooks. They also permit historians to get a sense of the values and culture of the plebeian class. The scenarios of violence might be superficially similar but they varied across culture and time, so that the kinds of knife fights that Gallant describes for nineteenth-century Greece are not the same as the conflicts that Spierenberg describes for eighteenth-century Amsterdam.

The concept of scenarios of violence is useful because it allows historians to get at the ways that ordinary people acted out their culture and how they interacted on a daily basis. Where this school of history has been lacking is in the inclusion of women in their analysis.[20] It has been easier in many ways to study solely masculine violence because the records reflect a preponderance of male fights; the sheer abundance of sources is attractive. In addition, society has traditionally considered female violence even more of an aberration than male violence, whereas men's assaults toward women fall into another category of analysis—usually that of domestic or sexual violence. What Hurl-Eamon's work and the current work show, however, is that female violence as well as cross-gender violence also follow certain patterns and that scenarios of violence can also be constructed in order to extend the methodological and analytical framework and deepen our understanding of culture and gender relations in past societies.

This form of analysis is extended by examining how people not only interacted with each other but also with their built environment (buildings and cityscapes) and bodily culture. Using the rich details from testimony in court cases, certain elements reveal the norms for polite conduct as well as what was considered rude. This work relies heavily on manuals of etiquette that provide the rules of good manners from a top-down perspective but also essentially supply a type of skeleton for norms of behavior that were altered by the lower classes and made their own. Just as it is hard to look at women without including men, it is hard to understand plebeian culture in isolation. Plebeians cannot be studied separately because they not only lived cheek and jowl with the elites but their culture was both shaped by and often derived from elite culture. (At times, lower-class culture also influenced elite culture.) These elements were part of the symbolic culture that governed Mexican life; they were the intangible elements that made individuals act in certain ways. People believed, for example, that women out at night were wanton not because of anything these women were doing or wearing but rather because of the symbolism that the night represented for Mexicans, and how the dark mediated and sexualized spaces that were innocent during the day.

Frenzied violence and passions do not seem to make sense. It is the patterns within this confusion that allows scholars to decipher the logic behind the frenzy and the logic within the mayhem. While attacks may have seemed senseless or random to an outside observer, to those who formed part of the culture they followed an accepted script. These confrontations made sense to plebeians, and bystanders recognized the various parts of the attack; further, as shall be seen in future chapters, bystanders at times intervened to stop the ensuing assault. Observers could follow the logic of violence because they recognized the pattern; they knew the grammar and the syntax of violence within their own culture. In part, the configuration that violent acts followed came out of usage and the repetition of acts, but it was also formed within a structure of beliefs surrounding not only their physical bodies but the spaces in which they lived. Because of the symbolism attached to both space and body, an assault behind a closed door was different from one in the countryside and a blow to the head was different than a cut to the face.

All these elements conveyed messages that people within the culture could read and understand without reflection, though historians can only perceive these same messages through painstaking analysis of criminal documents. Not all people acted out their violence in the same way—they followed their cultural norms. It is within these norms that we can discern their culture and their codes of conduct. Further, within the accounts of violence, we can find out many details of everyday life. Witnesses often recount elements of the circumstances that would not otherwise be recorded, such as the ways people looked or did not look at each other, or the ways that they greeted each other—essentially small details from their lives.

Honor Systems

The underlying structure that guided and organized the way that people interacted with each other but also with their environment was predicated on honor. Despite the apparent simplicity of this value, it had complex layers of meaning and was significant in multiple ways for middle-period Mexicans. It was a fundamental part of social relations of both the elite and plebeians. Honor as a field of study developed in the 1960s and first attracted anthropologists Julian Pitt-Rivers, J. G. Peristiany, and Julio Caro Baroja, who studied primarily rural peasant societies in the Mediterranean.[21] Their pioneering work established the ways in which honor systems structured people's lives in terms of their hierarchical relations but also in terms of their sense of self-worth. Taking their lead from these works, scholars have examined the way honor worked within a whole range of places very distant from the Mediterranean in terms of both geography and culture.

What the explosion of honor studies has shown is that honor was not particularly a Mediterranean belief system but rather one that was fundamental to most premodern societies. Nevertheless, although the fundamentals of honor were a constant, its actual mechanisms vary according to time and place; the way it was implemented and defined was situational. Scott K. Taylor argues quite correctly that people reacted to challenges to their honor in myriad ways—it was less a code than a rhetoric.[22] Honor evolved from an ancient regime type of ranking system into one that incorporated notions of citizenship. It also had different connotations for rural as opposed to urban settings. Despite or perhaps because of its nuances and alterability, it was a thread that ran through daily experiences for men and women in middle-period Mexico. Honor as an analytical framework is similar to gender: it is simply present—and inextricable from the fabric of life.

Honor had two integral parts: status and virtue. That is to say, an individual had or gained honorable standing either because he or she was born into a noble or high-ranked family or because of their actions particularly in terms of either bravery or uprightness. The Spanish language actually has two words for honor—*honor* and *honra*—that encapsulate these dual aspects of the term. *Honor* was conferred upon a person who was born into a family already among the ranks of the honorable; they could be noble, or simply well-respected among their peers.[23] The parents of such an individual were supposed to be married at the time of birth in order to impart the full value of honor—that is to say, an illegitimate birth tarnished honor, but as Ann Twinam demonstrates, this stain could be repaired.[24] This kind of honor by birth or family connection was supposed to be limited to the upper classes of Spanish and Mexican society. From a top-down perspective it was a value limited to the elite, but from the vantage point of the plebeians, it existed in their ranks as well.

It was not a kind of honor that elite members of any society would recognize when they observed the lives of the poor, but among those who populated the tenements and villages of middle-period Mexico there was a subtle ranking that conferred honor upon those in certain families. These were people who had traditionally been leaders and were more comfortably off than many of their neighbors. This slight gradation of honorable status can be seen in the conflicts between storeowners and some of their customers or between leading families and those who tried to join their household. Those who felt their honorable status being challenged either by unruly conduct or by the possible inclusion of say an immoral or lower status daughter-in-law would often resort to insults followed by blows.[25] Both elites and plebeians jockeyed to either maintain or improve their ranking within their local society; it was just the forms that these struggles took that were different.

The honor conferred by virtue, or *honra,* was attainable by all simply by acting in ways that demonstrated morality and, at times, piety. This was a more democratic form of honor; in theory it was available to both elites and plebeians. Once again, however, the people in the upper echelons of society were not likely to recognize the poorer classes' morality, often conflating and confusing relative poverty with an inherent immorality. The ways that individuals could demonstrate their virtue differed by sex. Men showed their honra when they performed feats of bravery, served as soldiers in campaigns, were good craftsmen, or proved their honesty.

For women, this aspect of honor was tightly bound up with sexuality. Therefore, their reputation was tied to their chastity as maidens and then their loyalty as wives and discrete respectability as widows. Although this aspect of honra was directed at women (since aggressive and promiscuous male sexuality enhanced rather than harmed male honor) it was intertwined with male honor as well. When a daughter, a sister, a wife, or a mother acted in ways that their contemporaries found depraved, their exploits did not just stain their own reputation but also that of the men in their lives who were supposed to control them. It was an attack not only on male honor but also on the very masculinity of their husbands, brothers, or fathers. In this way, male and female honor were connected. There was also a certain crossover of values in regard to the quality of honesty. Female vendors also benefited from a reputation for honesty, and it is clear from various studies that among the poor, honesty and honor were vital because plebeians depended hugely upon an informal network of lending and credit that only functioned if all were trustworthy.[26] The tensions that arose from a refusal to operate within this microsystem of borrowing and lending showed up in a conflict between an aunt and her niece, both of whom sold food in Puebla de los Angeles. When María Soledad Martínez ran out of *atole* (a hot drink thickened with ground corn) and asked her niece to lend some, the niece refused.[27] María

Soledad Martínez was outraged at this rupture in the give-and-take credit system between market sellers and proclaimed that she too would refuse any future favors. She was not only inconvenienced but also highly insulted; it was a slur on her honor—an imputation that she could not be trusted to return the favor—and it led to a violent skirmish between the two women.

Gender played a contradictory role in honor; there was certainly a double standard when it came to assessing men's as opposed to women's sexual honor. Whereas women derived their honra or virtue from restraint and purity, men obtained more credit and status when they were promiscuous. The same men who might be Don Juans in other bedrooms would, however, be diminished if their wives or sisters acted in the same way. It was in this way that honor was a household value; the conduct of one member of the household was intertwined with that of the others.

Traditionally scholars thought that it was a male prerogative and role to defend the household's honor and more particularly that of the women within the family unit. More recently historians have noted that women frequently not only defended their own honor but also that of their household.[28] Women's aggressiveness in these matters was channeled either into lawsuits over insults or more directly into blows and fights. Such violent behavior among women who wished to protect their reputation was common not just in Mexico but in many other parts of the world. Women kicked people out of their houses when they behaved badly and threatened to bring the household reputation into disrepute; they went to court to demand apologies or fulfillment of marriage promise; they attacked other women who accused their husbands of rape; essentially they defended not only their personal honor but also that of the people associated with them. At times it was women, not men, who took the lead in these matters and who were more aggressive in their vindication of reputation.

Honor and Mexico

Mexicans who testified in the court cases referred to their own personal honor or to concepts related to honor numerous times. It was clear from both the many actual mentions of honor but also from the descriptions of situations in which it was obvious that honor was the force that directed them, that honor was a value central within Mexicans' lives. It was a guiding framework for their conduct and their interpersonal relations. It gave them rules for how to behave in particular spaces and how to control their bodies in order to take their place in the hierarchy and to either be deferential or daunting. If honor was simply a Spanish import, it would not have had such a hold upon the Mexican psyche. Instead, because honor was not just a Mediterranean introduction but rather a value system that was also present among the indigenous people of central Mexico, it became a shared, syncretic value system.

The Nahuas—indigenous peoples of Central Mexico who speak Nahuatl and share similar religions and cultural frameworks—did not have an equivalent word for honor, per se, although they had comparable values. Their society was hierarchical to the extreme and they also valued honesty as well as modesty for women, including female virginity at marriage (something that not all indigenous societies believed to be important). Scholar Alfredo López Austin writes extensively about the way that the Nahuas instilled "the concept of honor" in their children, including an emphasis on moral purity that was associated with nobility, a bodily submission to those of higher ranks, and the creation of a "hierarchical environment."[29] The underpinning beliefs for the hierarchy, ideas of morality, or even for body language that the Nahua embraced were very different from those of the Spanish. But the result of the contact and intermingling of these two peoples was that they developed a shared culture of honor. The Nahuas' underlying ideas were lost in colonial and nineteenth-century Mexican culture, but the culture of honor became stronger because it was derived not just from Spanish ideas but also from that of the indigenous people. The resulting honor system became a vital foundational structure that guided social relations in Mexico.

Honor, Space, and Body

Honor was not exactly something that was tangible or could be measured in pounds or inches, but rather it was an ephemeral quality that people tried to make more present through physical elements such as their clothes, their homes, and their deportment. It is here that there is a connection to be made among honor, space, and body. There was an aspect of honor that was related to the subtle boundaries that people erected around themselves. One of the most important boundaries was what Edward T. Hall describes as being "surrounded by a series of expanding and contracting fields."[30] These fields operate like personal bubbles; they are an extension of the self that are common to all living beings. Robert Muchembled equates this personal space with an extension of the ego; he also shows how men used bodily functions such as defecation and urination to extend their personal space but, in addition, they also used their dogs as a type of sentry guarding their personal space.[31] James Farr notes that the assertion of boundaries between people was conveyed through the body: "[boundaries] found their way into the words and actions of the middle and lower classes and articulated an order within which these people maneuvered to advance their interests."[32]

The setting of boundaries implied rankings and hierarchies, according to Richard Boyer; these were "degrees of hegemonic consciousness" that were expressed bodily though gestures and rituals. Boyer argues that there was "an axis of hierarchy, sloped between higher and lower points for unequals, flattened for peers."[33] There was even an implicit spatial metaphor within honor by which people were placed in categories of "high" or "low" that corresponded with their blood or lineage.[34] As will be discussed later in this book, Mexicans categorized spaces along both vertical and horizontal axes; thus grouping qualities as well as spaces along notions of "high" and "low" was consistent. Infringing upon these intangible borders either with actual blows or insulting words was an attack upon honor and self. Both the body and the home were representations of honor and thus it was through the aegis of honor that violence surrounding space and body can be understood.

Honor in Daily Life

Honor was a central part of Mexicans' emotional and intellectual culture. It guided their conduct and their assessments both of themselves and of those they met. But honor was not solely about hierarchy and virtue (although these values were very important); it also shaped people's body language and the way that they acted upon other peoples' bodies and with the spaces in which they circulated. Returning for a moment to the young man or woman entering a room from the beginning of this chapter, it is possible to make the connection between honor, bodies, and milieu. The calculations that this young person had to make upon entering the room were all related to honor. First, he or she had to gauge the relative rank of all the people in the room; their status was derived from many elements but it operated within the honor system. Then the young persons made their body language conform to their place within this collective; that is to say, they had to lower their heads, and, if male, doff their hats, if female, perhaps curtsy and generally take their place in bodily language with the exactly correct amount of deference and respect. Their behavior was related to the horizontal and vertical axes of honor. Horizontally, the center was considered the most honorable and most moral part of the room, and therefore chairs in that part of the area had the highest honor quotient. The other axis—the vertical—can be seen not only in the way the young persons held their body but also in the relative height of each chair—that is to say, the higher the chair the more honorable it was, and the person sitting in the highest chair was to be the most honorable and highest status person in the room. It was in this way that both spaces and bodies were organized according to the system of honor. These two aspects of daily life are the central focus of this book. Although honor will be an organizing thread throughout this study, the focus is primarily on space and body in the negotiation of daily life.

Chronology and Region

The period covered in this book—1750 to 1856—corresponds loosely to what historians call the middle period. It represents a break with traditional chronologies of Latin American history that always ended at the Wars of Independence or other such political events. Here a relatively new terminology—middle-period Mexicans—is used to refer to the people under study. Although this term might seem confusing at first, it is less clumsy than forever referring to "Mexicans from the late colonial and early national period."

The choice to examine Mexico in this period was, to some extent, a practical one driven by the availability of documents. The criminal documents that were central to the work really only became abundant by the middle of the eighteenth century, and cutting off the research at the time of independence would have made this a short study indeed. Yet, it also made sense to see what continuities there were between the colonial and the national period. Expanding the period of study into the nineteenth century reveal subtle changes that reflected the new political ethos of the young republic. That goal, however, was spectacularly unsuccessful and the study, therefore, is not about change over time but rather about a very stable set of ideas. This aspect stems from the choice of topic—space and body—because when other subjects for this same period have been examined (e.g., how people understood the devil in their daily lives, or the status of mothers), considerable change was revealed.[35] In fact, it is quite striking how little the big political events of the day entered into the documents studied. It was almost as if the Wars of Independence, the American invasion, the first elections—all of which had enormous impact upon the nation—were happening somewhere else. There were indications of change within the documents but they were not part of the foundational structures; the changes tended to be the length of people's names, the choice of alcoholic drinks, the migration of peoples, the accuracy of time cited, how addresses were given. All these elements do, in fact, reflect important alterations in the fabric of Mexican life, but not those affecting their notions of space, body, and honor.

It was not possible to study the entirety of Mexican territory for this project and thus the regional scope of the study was limited. Two major cities were chosen: the capital, Mexico City, and its provincial neighbor, Puebla de los Angeles, for deeper analysis (see map 1). As a result, these areas feature more prominently in this book. The reach extended into an area around these two cities to cover some of the towns within an area that could be easily reached from Mexico City, and thus was able to include small villages and the countryside as part of the study in an attempt to give some indication of how people conceived of the concepts of space and body in both cities and small towns. Many of the choices were dictated by the availability of documentation and the ease of work in particular archives. Work in the Archivo General de la Nación in Mexico City and the Archivo

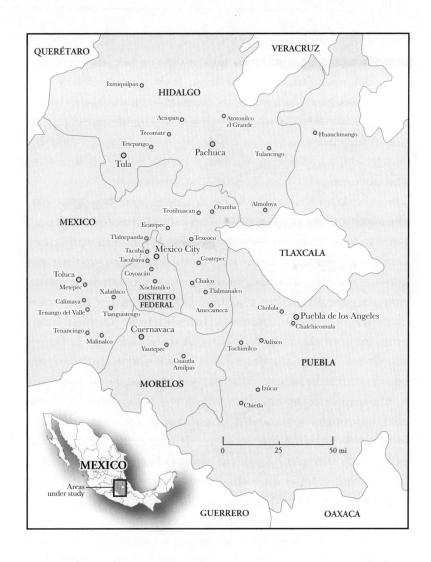

Map 1. Central Mexico at the Turn of the Nineteenth Century

Judicial de Puebla in Puebla was privileged because these institutions were familiar to me from previous research. When Lee Penyak gave me a guide to the Archivo Judicial del Tribunal Superior del Distrito Federal, it was possible to expand to these collections.

The Documents

The sample for this book was organized around one principle: violence that involved women. This included assaults of many types in which women were the victims, but also in which they were the aggressors. Crimes were studied according to the categories at the time, including murder, attempted murder, assaults, wounds, rape, seduction, marital mistreatment, and insults. Judicial records that touched on crimes but were not considered criminal were also reviewed; the ecclesiastical divorce petitions usually included a long description of the marriage that included acts such as beatings and attempted murder. These were particularly interesting because, unlike the documents from the criminal courts, they showed a longer picture of a marriage and were not focused on one incident. The research for this book began with an idea of women as victims of violence; as it turned out, the documents show that women were also quite willing to fight back and to take matters in their own hands, attacking other women and even sometimes their husbands. Nevertheless, the sample was chosen according to a principle, and thus it colors the work even though men appear as much as victims of violence as aggressors in this book.

The presence of men in this research became as important in explaining the lives of middle-period Mexican women as many other elements were. The lives of men and women were simply too intertwined to separate out one sex, and thus although the research for this study was predicated around women, the result is much more inclusive. Many studies of masculinity, especially in regard to violence, center on fights between men. Because of the sample choice, this book focuses on the attitudes that men exhibited with women, sometimes with other men as an audience and sometimes simply with their wives or lovers. As a result, while this book reveals how gender played a role in the conceptions of space and body for Mexicans, it also provides insights into masculinity and femininity in middle-period Mexico.

The people affected by or involved in crimes of violence in middle-period Mexico included members of a variety of social groups reflecting both race and social class. The sample was more inclusive in terms of class than race: both the poorest of the poor, whose clothes were barely rags, as well as men and women with the honorifics of don and doña, who lived in vast apartments in the luxurious buildings in the downtown. The very top of the social spectrum—the titled nobility—was missing because they kept themselves out of trouble. Names in this period were important indicators of rank and class: the poorest people generally had quite simple names, maybe only a first name, whereas the higher status people often had several last names. For this reason names are not shortened after a first mention. It is important to give the historical actors their full name. There is also a practical reason for this course of action: at times the plebeian actors all had similar names; thus the more ways to distinguish them the better. The spellings that were present in the documents were used, even if those seem archaic. The kinds of crime, acts of violence, and conduct did vary somewhat according to social hierarchy but there were uncanny resemblances that cut across class lines.

In the colonial period, most persons who testified in any capacity had to provide information about themselves such as their names, marital status, racial designation, age, where they lived, where they were from, and sometimes profession and address. Not all witnesses provided this complete list of specifications, but it was fairly common. Practices changed after independence and the corresponding files were more cursory and to the point, although more abundant. The racial designation, especially, disappeared from the documents. In the cases in which racial designation prevailed, however, it becomes clear that the sample was mostly limited to certain groups. Race is a tricky category in these documents but, according to the way that witnesses self-identified, it is clear that the sample was composed mostly of people of indigenous descent and Spanish heritage. In some ways this frequency is not surprising since both formed large groups within Mexico. But Africans and people of African descent were also represented in large groups, especially within the big cities of the sample. This is another puzzle that historians will have to ponder. What is clear is that much of the violence was internal to discrete groupings; that is to say, indigenous peoples tended to fight with others of their race; creoles or Spanish men were inclined to hit wives of their own ethnicity; and plebeian women usually fought with others of their class. Violence did cross class and racial-ethnic lines, but when people from different groups confronted each other there were additional tensions that made these incidents really stand out from the rest of the documentation.

Organization of the Book
Because this book is organized around two major concepts — the relationship of Mexicans to space and bodies — it also has a natural division into two parts with three chapters about space and three about bodies. It starts with a chapter that examines the way Mexicans conceived of their cities and their surroundings. Mexican cities followed a pattern; they were organized on a grid around the central plaza. Mexicans attached moral values to spaces, and thus the center was considered most honorable and was occupied by honest people; the peripheries were less prized and those who lived there were tarnished by association. The

countryside was very much outside of center and therefore considered dangerous and sexualized. This construction of space provided a horizontal grid into which individuals could be slotted. Because many buildings had several stories, Mexicans also had a vertical axis in which the most honorable lived in the upper reaches of buildings and the poorest had their residences at the bottom. These connections allowed Mexicans to pigeonhole the people around them, though these were not static identities. Historians have begun to analyze the ways that people interacted with space and have found that space was a determinant of violence. These links between space and violence allow us to gain a deeper insight into the ways that Mexicans interacted and acted upon the spaces in which they lived.

Houses were a vital part of the way that Mexicans defined themselves as moral beings. Chapter 3 discusses how women particularly used the concept of *recogimiento* to classify themselves as honorable and sexually pure. At the same time, enclosure within the house was also imposed upon women. Husbands expected their wives to negotiate this enclosure but were often angered by their wives' absence and thus they tried to enforce recogimiento. But being enclosed was not always safe for women—it often led to beatings and sexual assaults. The main door was the most potent signifier of morality and proper behavior. To maintain respectability, doors had to be open during the day (thus allowing scrutiny) and closed at night (blocking off dishonest visits). The threshold was also very important in the way that Mexicans approached their homes; it was a liminal space associated with the house but not entirely of the house. It was from the threshold that people observed and commented on the world, but also from there they insulted or were insulted. The threshold also was a demarcation between inside and out, and its negotiation—to enter or not—was fraught with tension. The interiority of Mexican architecture provided the language to associate individuals with an honorable or honest status and it was this code that Mexicans negotiated on a daily basis.

Chapter 4 shows that it was not only interior spaces that held significance for Mexicans. They moved between interior and exterior—sometimes willingly and sometimes unwillingly. Pushing a person out of one's home was a statement about their morality and honor and thus a profound insult. It was important to control internal spaces especially in terms of who was admitted to this inner sanctum. Such access could be used to enhance a home's respectability or to humiliate, as in the husbands who brought their mistresses home. Privacy was not common, even in the large houses of the elite, where servants could at times be relied upon to intervene in marital squabbles. In the more common tenements, neighbors and caretakers played an active role in rescuing abused women. At the same time, neighbors and bystanders could just as well serve as an audience, especially for the kind of exemplary violence that many husbands meted out to their spouses. They took their wives into a primarily male space—the countryside—where *montes* (scrubland) and *barrancas* (ravines) were often the setting for beatings, rapes, and murders. This external space was an area that, like the street within cities, sexualized women and made them even more erotic in their demeanor. The night had a similar effect upon spaces and those people who were found there.

Unlike the built environment, bodies generally come in one model. But despite this relative uniformity, there is enormous variety in the cultural and social construction of the body—that is to say, how different peoples have conceived of bodies. Chapter 5 examines the ways historians and sociologists have analyzed these conceptions of the body and relates these ideas to violence. The body served as a central social metaphor to organize hierarchy and thus its component parts took on additional symbolism within Mexican society. Because of its central position in the bodily metaphor of hierarchy, the head was the receptacle for honor. Heads were either held high or lowered, adorned or uncovered, to show respect or authority. Hair was more than an extension of the head's authoritative position; it had its own magical symbolism but it was also a way to express identity in terms of gender, ethnicity, and morality. Clothes and body language were also vital in expressing women's decency but also in shielding them when they left the protective enclosure of their homes and moved through the sexualizing influence of the streets. The symbolism of each element of the body determined the kinds of patterns that were evident in the violence described in the further chapters.

The rules of civility were not just written down in manuals but also developed by plebeians by observing the elite's practices and by common cultural understandings. These rules could be used to indicate respect but also turned upside down to humiliate. Chapter 6 is an examination of the patterns of attacks that centered on the head and the face primarily but also upon "the hidden parts"—the vagina and the penis. The theme that governs the patterns is that of hitting at the body as opposed to pulling at it. Husbands followed a formula to reassert their authority by hitting the wives' heads with any object available. These were domestic incidents that can be contrasted to the pattern of cutting the face, in which the root motivation was sexual. The victims of face-cutting were usually mistresses who tried to rebut their erstwhile lovers or women who rejected a man's advances. Eyes and mouths could also be used aggressively when staring or spitting. Many such acts were the equivalent of provocative words. Finally, groups often meted out violence against women's vaginas by hitting, scratching, and assaulting with sticks, bones, or stones in a form of punishment for sexual activity. Although not as common, men and sometimes women grabbed other men's genitals as a form of humiliation.

Aggression toward the body followed different patterns and logics; there was a syntax for these acts that was connected to the symbolism associated with bodily parts. Chapter 7 examines the ways that clothes and hair had similar roles in the constructions of social identity through the body. Both elements were extensions of the body but also at its boundaries. In addition, both hair and clothes were central to social ranking and also individual character. Clothes also had an economic value because they either had to be made or, more often, purchased or rented. Attacks on dress therefore were also assaults upon a person's financial well-being. Haircutting was not so much an economic crime but one that could not so easily be repaired — it took time to grow back. Both also were intimately tied to sexuality: clothes as a prelude to seduction and marriage, and hair as a form of seduction in of itself. Pulling at hair and clothes were strategies that borrowed from the actions of officials; they were acts designed to restore authority and honor but also to humiliate. These actions also inherently affected the body's position thus acting on the body in an indirect manner.

The ways that Mexican men and women jockeyed for position within their homes and families and on the streets was second nature to them. Just as when we circulate within our own environments we don't have to ponder about how to adjust our bodies or react to the spaces through which we circulate, middle-period Mexicans knew how to engage with others and how to behave properly according to their station. Of course, what was normal and acceptable for middle-period Mexicans would be shocking conduct in the twenty-first century. Plebeians borrowed elements of the rituals that they observed officials practicing; they not only learned to bow their bodies but also how to grab at hair and clothes or to drag away their wives in order to perform exemplary punishments. They also developed bodily messages of reprimand that were particular to wives or mistresses and they acted out their frustrations in regard to spaces such as homes, streets, atriums, or doors. They learned what to expect according to their environment and they reacted to their milieu but they also created it; they acted out in relation to the grammar and syntax of violent acts. What seems to us a complicated dance of action and reaction was simply to them the normal negotiation of daily life that they could perform without hesitation.

2. Space and Mexican Society

Mexican men and women lived in particular spaces, a kind of microenvironment that surrounded them, shaped their daily lives, and defined who they were. Individuals created personas by controlling their built environment as much as possible. Wealthy urbanites, for example, chose to live in the upper floors of their buildings to emphasize their superiority.[1] Less prosperous Mexicans showed their moral natures by making sure that the doors to their houses or rooms were closed or open at the appropriate moment in the day. As well as the positioning of rooms, they had to ensure the morality of decor—for example, paintings or images that graced their walls, the ostentation or simplicity of furniture, and, finally, the company they kept inside their residence. They were acutely conscious of the moral and hierarchical implications of the built environment and their interaction with this architecture. Mexican housing was defined by an interior orientation that was associated with morality, but even inside these residences the decor and furniture had moral and hierarchical implications. The space through which Mexican men and women traveled on a daily basis in their work, leisure, or worship had potent significance that changed depending upon many factors. There was an architecture that was particular to Mexican cities and towns. Mexican housing arrangements were imbued with ideas of morality and honor that were derived from both Spanish and Nahua traditions. Buildings and cities provided a framework for space, but they are not one and the same. The architecture was the skeleton that encompassed and helped to create spaces and thus gave them meaning.

Interactions with other people were also defined within spatial understandings. Thus, not only did Mexicans seek to define themselves through their built environment but they attached meaning to others because of their spatial situation. As a result, passersby would consider a woman who left her house to do errands in the day as correct in her behavior, but one who tried to accomplish the same task after dark was tarnished simply by being out after dark—the space changed at night. Her presence in the streets at night was not considered appropriate and so her being there made her vulnerable to "justified" attacks. Any dealings with other people had to be accomplished with care to respect the spatial hierarchy in what Christine Stansell aptly terms the "geography of social life."[2] Spaces were a backdrop for human interactions; they could be active or passive, conducive to violence or not.[3] An active space could be one in which an aggressor would have an audience. For example, many Mexican women attacked others in front of their local church at the end of mass when there was a guarantee of spectators for any exemplary violence. Other places were simply a spot where passions erupted but often had no audiences. Places held symbolism that was particular to the culture—for example, in the Mexican countryside barrancas were the most common site of violence against women. In addition, taking a wife to the monte was an act imbued with a highly violent, punitive imagery.

But the most pernicious transformation of space that Mexican women had to deal with was the sexualization of exterior spaces. When women left the domestic enclosure they had to contend with the fact that they entered into a masculine world — one in which they became eroticized.[4] Some consideration must be given to ideas and theory regarding the role of space in people's lives and how Mexican cities and homes were organized and conceptualized.

[place + space]

Ideas about Space

People are constantly engaged in a dialogue with the spaces around them; they receive multiple messages from their built environment. Buildings can inspire fear and awe. They can make people feel small or big. Individuals feel comfortable or overwhelmed by their surroundings. According to Michel de Certeau, space "is composed of intersections of mobile elements." He contrasts space, which is not fixed, to place, which is static. Space also has the capacity to be read and appropriated.[5] Space can be imagined; something ephemeral happens in which people associate places and buildings with qualities, values, or even just belonging. Leonardo Fabricio Hernández argues that late colonial Guatemalans developed their own concept of neighborhood that had nothing to do with the boundaries of parishes but rather with either certain families or particular buildings.[6] These people defined and imagined the space in which they lived rather than accepting the official boundary lines.

Historians have begun to pay more attention to the roles that space played in the lives of people. Space was not a static or mute player in people's existence and actions but rather influenced men and women and molded their behavior. Children learn an understanding of space in their early years and they apply this knowledge later as they interact with their built environment. People absorb what spatial forms are acceptable in their

Space – not fixed – appropriated
place – static (fixed)

33

formative years; they learn to screen out certain information and to lay out their rooms, their homes, and their cities in ways that are culturally determined.[7] Cities and houses reflect both the cultural background but also values that emerged from that experience.[8] Architecture, therefore, can be seen as an extension of the accepted norms of space that people teach their children. Beyond the larger picture, probably the most important building in our lives is our residence; homes are charged with symbolism and have deep meaning for residents. Homes can be seen as a metaphor where their spatial structure underpins the social relations that they reflect.[9] The built environment of central Mexico carried messages about morality and hierarchy that were part and parcel of both Spanish and Nahua culture. As a result, the people living within these spaces understood their social place with reference to both their location within the urban grid and where they actually lived within buildings.

Gender and Space

Spaces can also have a gender component. Buildings in some past and present cultures actually have a gender division designed into the structure, but beyond that the different domestic and work roles that women and men play can designate certain areas within a home as either male or female.[10] Moving outside the home, cities also have been gendered spatially.[11] In Mexico, houses were feminine areas whereas the street and the countryside were masculine. The act of walking, according to de Certeau, is "a process of appropriation," thus it is perhaps simply because men were more present in the streets and countryside that these spaces became masculinized.[12] The street was a dangerous area for women, one in which they were sexualized. Doña María Justa Satiturne y Summáraga complained, in 1782, that because of her husband's laziness, she was forced out into the dangerous streets of Mexico City to go to work.[13]

Licenciado don Christoval Gutiérrez de Hermosilla protested that because of his wife's poor character, his children spent their days in Mexico City's streets "at risk of bad company."[14] María Guadalupe Hernández was caught by the night watchman in the streets of Mexico City at two in the morning and arrested. She tried to explain her presence but the officials decided to investigate her life and customs—essentially whether she was a moral woman.[15] The idea that homes were oases of morality and order meant that the street, in opposition, was a location of disorder and immorality.[16]

There was a strong class element to this dichotomy, since those who worked were forced to be in the streets for all sorts of reasons. Men generally had to leave the house for many tasks but often even if they worked in their living space (in an *accesoria*, for example), their tasks spilled out into the street. Women, who in an ideal world were supposed to stay in the home, had to leave their living spaces to buy supplies, fetch water, do the laundry, work in fields, and gather foodstuffs outside the city limits, as well as many other tasks. The streets were, apart from a work space, also a location of sociability, where people met, chatted, drank, courted, and often made love.[17] In the eighteenth century, as metropolitan and local elites began to try to impose a more orderly vision upon plebeian Mexicans, the image of the street as distasteful—in the eyes of the upper classes—was accentuated.

Gender also played a very central part in this dichotomy since society expected women to be associated with and rooted in the home. A lot of the moralist literature as well as the ideas of the ancient Nahuas emphasized the parallel lives of husbands and wives, with the man leaving the house to work and the woman remaining within the household. Yet in all practicality this idealized vision was impossible.[18] Men imposed the notion of women staying home and out of the dangerous immoral streets,

gender parallelism + complimentarity

however, when husbands complained that their wives were not home when they should have been and when women suffered sexual attacks ostensibly because they were in the streets. For women, the streets became a space with highly charged sexual content, and when they left the confines of their homes they risked being tarnished by this sexualization. Mexicans reacted to this dichotomy of order-disorder and home-street by pushing any perceived source of disorder into the street; they thus cleansed their homes and kept their households part of the moral center that characterized their worldview.

Traditionally, women's spaces within cities were more circumscribed because their roles in the labor market were more limited. When women moved into "male" spaces such as the streets they had to use strategies to protect themselves, such as being accompanied and having modest dress and body language. But despite such tactics, when women went into the "male" streets their presence in an alien territory sexualized them. By being "out of place" women put themselves in a situation of vulnerability. There were unwritten rules for space — who belonged, who did not — and these were not entirely gender based. For example, people could violate these informal regulations by misbehaving in a formal setting, by inappropriate dress in a place of worship, or by violating gender norms. Spaces were also mediated by time — night made places more dangerous and those who moved through these areas were "asking for trouble."

Space and Violence

The built environment in which people lived was not only coded with culturally specific messages but as a spatial context it also became an actor in their lives. J. Carter Wood suggests the notion of "geographies of violence." He proposes that the spatial contexts in which people lived could both produce and construct violence — that is to say, violence was molded into certain forms by the setting, but in addition there was also a connection made by those involved to the basic tenets of that culture.[19] The kinds of places where working-class people lived provide many examples of the ways that spatial context might lead to violence. The density of habitation, for example, brought individuals into constant contact and made people share resources and services—which led to friction over such "common resources, boundaries, privacy, borrowing and noise."[20] Working-class people naturally fought to keep rights that flowed from their control of space, and this battle was all the more important if they had little room to call their own. But rights defined by space were not solely the preserve of the poor because essentially these rights were about ranking and hierarchy. The wealthy also struggled to maintain a position within certain spaces; for example, as several historians have shown, when they fought about seating at bullfights or place in a procession.[21] These skirmishes were not just the elite's foolish spats but rather a way to ensure their place in the social ranking and their access to official positions and wealth. Such combat over place and social position happened in spaces where the working classes or the elites met and mingled.

The built environment provided for spaces of sociability where people worked or where they indulged. There were places where people were supposed to congregate (the church, the market, the *pulquería*) but others where people simply were likely to meet (the courtyard of the typical Mexican building, the street corner, the *fandangos*, or at parties in people's homes). These places could often be very crowded and so individuals jostled for position and to ensure their rights in the hierarchy. People sought to preserve and protect what Wood calls their "spatially relevant rights." There were actually rules within what might have seemed to be chaos, and when those rules were breached, it could lead to insults or violence.[22] In addition, these places

provided an audience for any scripted kind of violence. The
crowds were important as witnesses for whatever jockeying over
position occurred and the acts themselves were often a spec-
tacle geared to the witnesses.[23] Boyer adds that not all audiences were equal: a group of observers made up of neighbors
and friends had more "power" than strangers. It was the "in-
sider audience," as Boyer terms it, that had a collective memory for a person's reputation and honor. [24] In Mexico, churches
were just such an excellent place, especially at the end of mass
when people's attention could turn to secular matters. The setting shaped the kinds of events which transpired—for example, the kinds of violence in a pulquería (a type of tavern where
fermented cactus sap was served) were usually different from
what happened in a home or in a market.[25] In pulquerías, violence between men and women tended to be an extension of
domestic tensions, whereas marital problems rarely seemed to
be played out in the market and violence at church seems to
have been between groups of women rather than across gender
lines. Conviviality did not only occur in such structured environments as taverns and churches but also on a more informal
level. The typical Mexican architecture meant that people met
in the courtyards at the center of each house or building; within cities, they would meet at street corners but also at the fountain when they fetched water.

Concepts of Privacy
Mexican housing did not provide a stark separation between
public and private spaces: people spilled out of their rooms and
workshops into courtyards and streets; they kept their doors
open so that all might see into their lodgings; what was interi-
or was also visible to the exterior in many cases. Like many other working class communities that have been studied, "the private was often very public."[26] In our modern conceptions many

acts of violence occur in private — these clashes depend on seclusion. But the idea of intimacy of space or privacy is a modern invention.[27] The concepts of privacy and domesticity first
appeared in Europe in the eighteenth century, according to Witold Rybczynski, and in Mexico a century later, according to Pilar Gonzalbo Aizpuru.[28] It would be easy to assume that middle-
period Mexicans thought that a closed door meant private, but
the ideas that our society takes for granted were not necessarily
an accepted reality in past times.[29] In fact, people did use spatial understandings in ways that heightened the impact of violence; that is to say, they were conscious that a slap to the face
in a public place, in front of an audience, was more humiliating than one without any witnesses.[30] To make the distinction
(which can be important because the notion of public-private
has an impact on human behavior), it is useful to remember
that space is not just bricks and mortar but is also a creation
of imagination. Different spaces are conceived or imagined by
the associations made with that place; for example, the home
is associated with women, the street is a place for violence.[31] In
Mexico these definitions were fluid: the street could be a place
of conviviality but could just as quickly turn into a place of violence. Husbands at times dragged their wives very openly and
in front of audiences out of their houses and into the countryside — playing on both public and private conceptions of what
was permissible in gender relations. Mexicans had their own
notions of what constituted private versus public space, and
these conceptions changed according to time, class, and gender, among many other factors.

With such fluidity between inside and outside, public and
private, it is hard to imagine that the Mexican home might be
considered a preserve of family domesticity, especially for the
working classes. Yet Mexicans had a conception of home; it was
a place that had to be respected and defended.[32] The home

was, for most Mexicans, an "imagined space": a place that was not so much a solid construction as an idea. For Mexican men, especially, but for women, too, it evoked a sense of territoriality. The way that Mexicans most often expressed this sense of boundaries about their homes was through a defense of its morality and its honor. The values of the home were almost synonymous with those associated with the household, so an attack on the actual building was often interpreted as a slur on the morality of those who inhabited it. In Coyoacán, a small town very close to Mexico City, don Cristóbal Télles Xixón evoked this feeling about his home. He denounced the conduct of señor Clemente Rincón, who burst into his house "without respecting the jurisdiction of the house of an honorable man, that I am, and of my honorable behavior and the rights that I enjoy as a result of this honorable behavior." Señor Clemente Rincón's actions were all the worse because don Cristóbal Télles Xixón was not home — only his wife was there — and thus señor Clemente Rincón's disrespect for the territory (home) of another man was particularly egregious.[33]

Male authority also was expressed by control over the home. Thus Marcelo Cortes explained why he picked up a sword and wounded Antonia Josefa when she declared "I give the orders in my house."[34] Other men showed a different attitude: contempt for a household. In one case, Juan Guerrero broke all the dishes and ripped his wife's clothes whenever he returned to his lodgings, and Marcos Paz took all his lover's belongings.[35] The attitudes of Mexican men and women toward their home were manifested in their actions. Part of the way that Mexicans demonstrated the decency of their household was to make sure that they could be seen, that is to say, although the orientation of Mexican architecture was to the interior, they kept their doors open in the daytime to show that they had nothing to hide — that they were open to scrutiny.

Inside and Outside

The connection between outside and inside, interior and exterior was a daily reality for Mexicans. Their spatial context did not stop at the front door but rather was part of a continuum—the streets, the market square, the church atrium, the courtyard in their buildings—all were part of their domestic world. But, especially when they lived in smaller communities, they were also influenced by the natural world around them. People not only charged their urban architecture with symbolic messages but also the countryside at their doors. As Amos Rapoport reminds us, residences do not exist in isolation from the city or town, but rather must be considered as part of a system that connects the house, the inhabitants' lifestyle, the city, and even the landscape.[36] For Mexicans, the countryside was filled with danger and was also a sexualized space akin to the street. Some of these ideas were derived from the ancient Nahuas, who believed that invisible creatures lived in the areas outside city limits and that these beings could attack those who ventured into those regions. They also considered roads, woods, and streams to be hostile places that would imbue those who ventured near them with evil that was equivalent to sexual transgressions. In addition, according to the ancient Nahuas, women who ventured into these places could be easily seduced.[37]

The Spanish in colonial Mexico had a similar view, albeit for different reasons. For them, urban living was counterpoised as an area of order, justice, and piety, as opposed to the countryside, which was alien and occupied by potentially violent people.[38] The sexualized nature of these parts of the landscape around Mexican cities and towns remained part of the mindset of the inhabitants well into the colonial and early national periods. Men who encountered women on their own in the countryside and raped them often evoked the devil as a metaphor to explain their sexualization of even very young girls.[39]

Men often harassed women in the woods and scrubland outside villages; these were liminal areas, full of danger and erotic content. Ravines were also an important space where men usually dumped the bodies of women they had killed or took their wives to punish them for sexual transgressions or just offenses against the marital bargain.

Space was not and is not a simple passive backdrop to human life and actions. It is a factor in the way that people negotiated their daily lives; it defined who individuals were as well as their households. The built environment as well as the natural surroundings that Mexicans witnessed every day was charged with symbolism that provided them with suitable places for certain acts and gave men and women an indication of how to behave either properly or disrespectfully. Both elite and working-class Mexicans were in a constant dialogue with their spatial context; they had to adapt their conduct in relation to what they saw and experienced around them. The elites had codes of conduct as elaborated in etiquette manuals and undoubtedly drilled into them by servants and parents. Plebeians were equally mindful of the proper way to behave in different settings. The particularities of the way that urban and rural Mexicans interacted with their surroundings were very much connected to the way that Mexicans constructed and organized their municipalities and their lodgings. The next section includes a description of the way that Mexican cities and homes were laid out, which will provide a more tangible context for the ideas described so far in this chapter and for the incidents recounted in the following chapters.

Cities and Towns

The cities and towns of central Mexico followed certain patterns—principally they were organized around a central plaza that provided a core to the municipality.[40] From this plaza,

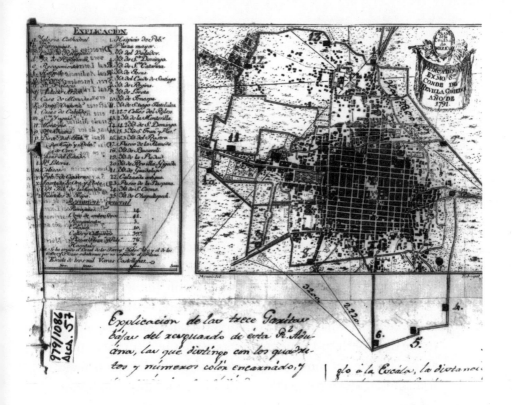

1. Plan of Mexico City with its sentry boxes, 1791 to 1816. By Fabregal, engraver, and José del Mazo y Avilés, master. Source: Archivo General de la Nación, Alcabalas, vol. 57, fol. 36b. This map shows how Mexico City was centered on the *Zócalo* or main square, with intersecting streets on a grid plan. Notice also how this orderliness breaks down on the edge of the city.

streets extended in straight lines to form what are usually described as a checkerboard pattern. This blueprint, typical to Hispanic cities of the Americas, was an architectural manifestation
of the order that cities were supposed to represent.[41] It was, according to Valerie Fraser, what the Spanish conquerors believed
cities should be like rather than what they knew in their home-
towns in Europe.[42] It can be seen very clearly in figure 1, a map
of Mexico City showing a core area from which major streets intersect in an orderly fashion. The houses of greatest value and
prestige were located closest to this central plaza, which encompassed the most important structures such as the church or cathedral, as well as governmental and commercial buildings.[43]
Originally when Spanish conquerors rebuilt Tenochtitlan into
Mexico City they conceived of this central area — the *traza* — as
reserved for Spaniards and as an orderly, safe region in contrast
to the disorderly indigenous parts outside the artificial boundary.[44] This idea of center being associated with the Spanish was
transmuted into a connection with status, morality, and honor.
Because Latin American colonial societies were fundamentally
organized along hierarchical bases, the spatial arrangement of
the cities and towns was also imbued with ranking. Charles F.
Walker states that "the use of space [w]as a key social and cultural marker."[45] Within Mexican cities each parish and neighborhood replicated this framework of core and periphery between the central plaza and surrounding streets.

This spatial organization implied a horizontal axis of ranking that also had moral overtones.[46] At the city center many of
the most prestigious houses were occupied by one family and
their servants. Further out, similar buildings were divided into
residential and commercial uses with different classes and occupations coexisting. On the city's periphery, residences were
smaller mostly composed of small houses and *jacales* (huts or
small houses made from adobe).[47] Structures that were further

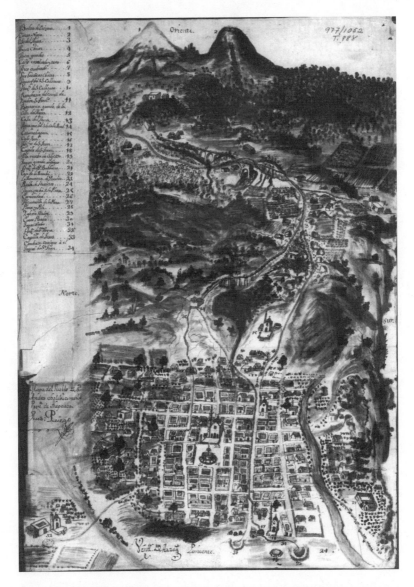

2. Plan of the village of San Andrés Chalchicomula in Puebla, by Buenaventura de Arze. Source: Archivo General de la Nación, Tierras, vol. 888, exp. 20, fol. 26, 1764. Notice the same centeredness on the main square as in the map of Mexico City, as well as the orderly quality of the core area of the village. In this example, the orderliness not only breaks down on the edges of the town but also the countryside infiltrates and invades the peripheries.

away from the urban core were less desirable and therefore those who lived in these buildings were lower ranked and assumed by the elite to be less decent and honorable. This sense of core and periphery can be seen in figure 2, a plan of a smaller village in Puebla called San Andrés Chalchicomula. The central plaza is clearly marked by the predominant fountain and church. The blocks around the plaza seem orderly with straight streets on right angles. Further way from the core, however, the houses are less impressive and no longer obey the rules of the checkerboard pattern. Here the countryside is more present with more vegetation, fields, and the attendant disorder. The world of nature, or the monte, is close by, represented at the top and the right-hand side of the plan, where there are hills and ravines—all open spaces in which urban order did not prevail. Bernabé Cobo followed this logic of core equating morality and honesty when he lauded Lima for its orderly city center while lamenting the less orderly quality of the city's peripheral areas. He made the connection between the lack of regularity of the neighbor-hoods on the edge of the city and those who lived there: indigenous people and Afro-Peruvians.[48] The very neatness of the central streets was a "metaphor for the orderliness and civility of the people who live within it."[49] Thus the converse was also true for those streets that did not live up to this model. These sentiments are echoed in the words of Juan Tejado Bonifacio when he petitioned ecclesiastical officials for a divorce. Of his wife's choice of living accommodations he stated: "She lives on her own in a house near the city gate on the plaza with a great deal of freedom and in such a way as to cause scandal."[50]

The connection between living on the edge of the city and poor morals was also present in Mexican mind-sets. The mayor of San Buenaventura de Cuaxomulco in the area around Cuernavaca expressed very similar attitudes toward Juan de los Santos alias Escalante and his friend Miguel Antonio. These two men were thieves and of no use to the community since they did not pay tribute. The mayor linked their rejection of social utility and community participation as well as the moral standards to where they lived: "*Because* they make the periphery their home and residence" (emphasis added).[51] Clearly, there was a very potent link in the minds of contemporaries between the city center and the qualities of order and morality as well as the periphery being the site of disorder and immorality. This connection was then extended to encompass the city core's inhabitants and permeate them with qualities that were class and race driven but expressed in terms of choice of residence.

The ordering of housing implied that there was a spatial arrangement of areas that were instilled with morality (and therefore, residents who were honorable and honest) and areas further from the center that were commensurately less moral and less honest. The sense of core and periphery was a strong part of the heritage of ideas about cities that came not just from Spain but also within Mexico. The Nahuas considered the city core as an intrinsically ordered and therefore moral space, whereas the periphery was fundamentally chaotic and immoral.[52] Residential patterns corresponded, in some way, to this idea, with those living closest to the core—the plaza mayor—defined as the most honorable and moral. The other source of this core-periphery dichotomy came from Islamic ideas. According to R. Brooks Jeffery, Islamic society "is defined by concentric layers of centrality" that places the home as an individual center that is then extended to a larger district.[53] This notion of morality as attached to the city's central part was part of the horizontal framework that defined the inhabitants of different parts of cities. The prestige of living in the city core lasted throughout the colonial period and well into the nineteenth century. In Spain the elites only began to move to suburbs in the 1840s, and in Mexico City the upper classes began to move into new

3. La Casa de Alfeñique in Puebla. Photo by Elizabeth Lipsett. Built for the Morales family in 1791, this house is typical of elite homes, with multiple stories and an imposing exterior. The owners would have lived on the top floor.

suburbs to the city's western parts in the 1850s.[54] It meant that
the built environment was infused with symbolic values that
could be read by the distance from the city core. It was only
when the elites chose to move away from the city's center that
its prestige diminished.

Hierarchies of Housing

Urban Mexicans classified their lodgings according to many
variables and they had a vocabulary to describe every category of housing. Each living space had a name that described its
relative size, location within a building, and status within the
hierarchy of residences. The most obvious way in which these
different types of housing varied was size, with the largest residences in the prized area closest to the core or central plaza.
The range of housing choices descended in size and luxury in
areas further from the city's central core. In the district around
the central plaza or city core, the most common type of residence was the *casa*, or house (this is sometimes translated as a
mansion). It was at the top of the hierarchical ranking of housing and consisted of a building occupied by one household: a
nuclear family or an extended family as well as its staff (servants
and sometimes slaves). Figure 3 shows such a house in Puebla, the Casa de Alfeñique, which was built in 1791. Note that it
has three stories with windows and balconies facing onto the
street. At times, other families who were related to the owners
by blood or work arrangements might share the house. Usually
these casas had more than one floor, depending upon the resources of the residents and their status. Figure 4 provides both
the façade and the interior plan of a large two-storied house.

Generally, the house was entered through a *zaguán* (breezeway) into a central patio around which there were spaces used
by servants or for storage.[55] The house on the Calle de los Gallos
had two deep zaguanes that opened onto patios. In the central

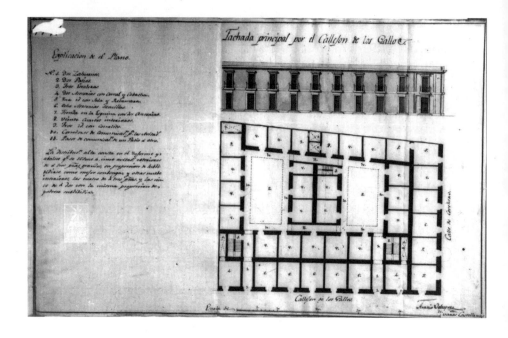

4. Plan of a casa in the Calle de Gallos in Mexico City, 1799, by Antonio Velásquez. Source: Archivo General de la Nación, Bienes Nacionales, Leg. 1719, cuadro 5, fol. 31. This house plan shows how houses were organized around the central patio, replicating the way that cities were arranged around the central square.

Mexico City parish of Santo Sagrario these large houses represented only 5 percent of lodgings.[56] The *vivienda* was a form of housing ranked below the casa; it represented a shared space within a building, although the sizes of such lodgings and their place within a building varied considerably. Some had many different rooms and might be compared to an apartment, although the more modest viviendas were little more than a room. Some of these dwellings even had specialized rooms such as the *sala de sillas* (chair room) and a *sala de estrado* (dais usually associated with women).[57] The kind of resident who lived in this type of lodgings also ranked lower than those in the casa. Yet the viviendas are not to be confused with *cuartos*, or rooms, which were one of the simplest forms of lodging and the type of housing used by the vast majority of urban residents. The cuarto consisted of one room in which entire families resided. Few had their own facilities like kitchens and generally all services were shared in the building. The most fortunate of cuarto residents had access to a shared latrine called *communes*; in addition, a location near the water pipe was considered so valuable a commodity that it cost more to rent or buy.[58] Generally the cuartos had windows and doors that opened onto the courtyard or patio.

The *accesoria* was a space that had its orientation toward the street—that is, unlike the other forms of lodgings its door and windows opened onto the street. The house plan in figure 4 shows different kinds of accesorias facing onto streets on two sides. Figure 5 shows more accesorias, again on two sides of the building. The accesoria was used primarily for work, either as a commercial space, for storage, or as a workshop, but these spaces were frequently also used as living spaces. Sometimes there was an interior division forming a *trastienda* (an area beyond the division) and occasionally a stairway allowed the residents to walk up to a kind of loft above the commercial space.[59] At times Mexicans used accesorias primarily as a residence, but it

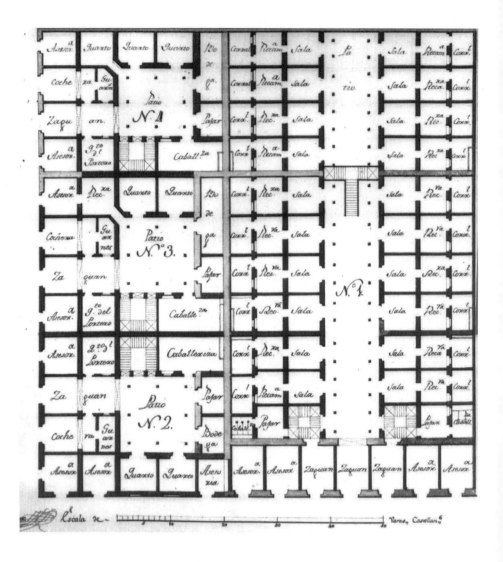

5. Plan of the ground floor of a house owned by the Colegio de San
Pedro y San Pablo in Mexico City, 1788, by Ignacio de Castrera, architect.
Source: Archivo General de la Nación, Monte de Piedad, vol. 2, fol. 338.
This building consisted of viviendas to the right and some smaller houses
arranged around three patios to the left. Note the accesorias at the front of
the building with doors opening onto the street.

must have seemed unpleasant because they were isolated from the sociability of neighbors and the shared services within the building. There were also two other forms of habitation that were not mentioned in this documentary sample: the *covacha*, a space under the stairs, and the *entresuelo*, a space between floors at the level of the stair landings. These two were the lowest of the low in terms of quality and status of housing. Generally fashioned out of adobe, they were so small as to afforded absolutely no privacy despite often being inhabited by large extended families.[60] The vast majority of the population did not have more than a room in which to live; in Mexico City 68 percent of the population lived in either a cuarto or an accesoria.[61] Each type of lodging placed its inhabitants within a ranking of space and social status that was both horizontal (city grid) and vertical (upper or lower floors).

Hierarchy within Houses

In addition to the moral symbolism attached to the horizontal grid, the city also held a very important vertical axis. Rosalva Loreto López notes that in colonial cities, different parts of buildings had higher or lower values depending upon whether they were part of the upper reaches or the lower floors. The most elevated parts of the edifices were of greatest value but also greatest desirability—even going as far as being termed "the noble floor."[62] R. Douglas Cope shows this connection in his use of ecclesiastical rent books, where he found that the percentage of persons with the honorific don or doña was higher for rentals costing above one hundred pesos annually and therefore were located in the upper floors.[63] The bottom levels were also rented as commercial space to artisans or businesses at street level.[64] In practical terms this pattern translated into a practice of richer, socially elevated families living on the upper floor of their own houses while lodging servants on lower floors and renting rooms to poorer families on even lower floors. This contrasts with the pattern in Anglo-Saxon wealthy houses where the servants were in the highest rooms—the attics—or the lowest rooms—the basements—and the masters had living and sleeping quarters in the intermediate floors.[65] The importance and social symbolism of living on the upper floors was highlighted for elite residents of Lima after the earthquake of 1746. In the rebuilding process, enlightened thinkers tried to outlaw upper floors because they were structurally vulnerable. Lima's elite fought back, arguing that "they had the social right and perhaps even obligation to rise above the city's lower orders." Living on the upper floors of their mansions was "a key marker of their respectability."[66]

Among the smaller residences classified as viviendas there was a distinction made between *viviendas altas* and *viviendas bajas,* or high and low dwellings. Mexicans considered the higher ones more desirable and also of higher rank; they were located principally in the northern sector of Mexico City's core, which contained larger buildings with more floors available than in other parts of the city core.[67] Of course, there were practical reasons for why the upper floors were more desirable. The rooms in the top floors had more access to natural light and air and they were at a greater distance from the sounds, smells, and scandals of the street.[68] Cope reminds us that colonial Mexicans "treated public thoroughfares as private garbage dumps" and that most public areas—plazas or streets—had mounds of refuse piled in them.[69] Thus, the desire to keep a distance from such sights and smells was quite reasonable. Rooms at street level were generally cold, wet, and poor in air quality; they did not often have access to water or natural light. In Mexico City these rooms often flooded during the wet season.[70] Most houses in the city center were socially heterogeneous, being divided into different forms of habitation such as single rooms, accesorias,

viviendas, and jacales.[71] This coexistence across class lines was
not uncommon in Mexican cities but it always followed vertical
lines of ranking: the poor lived in the lower reaches whereas the
rich had their residences in the upper floors. The symbolic import of this vertical axis was also taken up in the disposition of
internal and exterior architectural elements of these buildings.

Core and Periphery in Housing

These large, multistoried structures in the central part of cities presented an imposing face to the street. There were, however, breaches in the daunting façade: thresholds, stairs, and
windows all provided points of contact. Communication with
the exterior world was generally made through barred windows
that "transmitted a symbolic message of privacy" and through
the zaguán—a kind of massive wooden door that opened into a
high-ceilinged passage or room that served as the halfway point
between in and out for the building.[72] The largest zaguanes, for
the wealthiest of families, were big enough to allow the passage
of a horse and carriage. Their design also was more or less imposing in order to indicate the rank and quality of the persons
living beyond the door.[73] The door, according to Henri Lefebvre, "heralds the reception to be expected."[74] The threshold defined the territory of the home; it separated interior and exterior, thus permitting the important moral distinction of those
within and those outside.[75] These elements—windows and en-
tryways—symbolically represented not just the access points of
a building but also moral dimensions of those who lived within.[76] Because they were on the border between the external life
of the streets (with all their immoral disorder) and the moral
interior realm, doors and windows were highly potent as moral signifiers and often taken up by authors commenting on morality. Windows and doors allowed communication with the
street but could preserve a safe place, one that was still part of

the moral interior. Mexican women often used the threshold as a vantage point for their contact with people outside their residences. Mexicans interacted with this symbolism on many levels.

Contact between people was not only organized around internal and external spaces but also occurred within the buildings themselves. Generally, the larger residences were organized internally around patios—a kind of inner plaza that was exposed to the elements and provided light and air for the interior space. Rooms opened onto these patios, as did the zaguán and some of the accesorias.[77] Preconquest houses were also patterned with a central patio.[78] Several of the more lush patios had fountains and water basins.[79] The patio was surrounded by a portal of arches supported by stone and plaster columns; these were a kind of frame for the space. Patios served as a space of domestic sociability where residents could meet and in many cases, they functioned as a continuation of workshops.[80] The patio also served to provide an interior orientation for the buildings, which made it the core of the residence.[81] Within these buildings about one-quarter of the space were areas where people circulated or could congregate such as hallways and patios.[82] These buildings were not places of social isolation with people shut away in their rooms or apartments but rather places in which people had to coexist in close proximity. Some Mexican houses also had a *corral* (pen for livestock) that might have performed a similar spatial function as the patio. Mexican cities and villages were often full of livestock but the corrales also were an open space where people at times went out to sleep or to get some privacy.[83]

The vertical axis that defined hierarchy was also present in these interior elements and was very much symbolized by the staircase, which Loreto López describes as a "structural element of social differentiation."[84] Cañeque emphasizes that stairs were critical points of formal contact "at which the hierarchical relations between hosts and guests could be measured by the point at which the hosts decided to greet their guests. The higher up the hosts met the guests, the lower the status of the guests."[85] Etiquette required well-bred Mexicans to greet extremely distinguished guests at the street-level door and accompany them up the stairs into their receiving rooms; less important visitors could be welcomed at the head of the stairs. Upon departure, they could simply leave their guests of honor at the head of the stairs. Other less important callers simply made their way into the interior parts of the residence with due deference.[86] The stairs, clearly, represented a method to differentiate the different classes of people who entered the residence. In his nineteenth-century book of etiquette, Manuel Diez de Bonilla provided a code for politeness in receiving guests in which stairs played a major role.[87] Because they naturally divided and provided access to the upper floors, they were a barometer of social class within the building's vertical axis. Residents of the lower floors at times were aware of events in the upper reaches, but they seemed distant to them. When interrogated about events in the house where she served, the *portera* (caretaker) Preciliana Aguilar reported that she did not know what had occurred because it all happened "in the higher reaches of the house."[88] This witness was clearly aware of the vertical differentiation within buildings. Stairs, apart from being the structural element that allowed for verticality, also were a kind of frontier.

The large residential buildings were symbolically classified both horizontally (within the core-periphery axis) and vertically within their interior. But, for the vast majority of urban Mexicans, their share of residential space was a room that they rented for about two pesos a month. A study of central Mexico City shows that in 1790, 98.57 percent of residents rented their lodgings.[89] Families slept in one room and shared any other communal services in the edifice.[90] The number of individuals who comprised a family could be quite high. For example, a 1753 census of Mexico City showed that twenty-two people forming an extended family occupied one vivienda. In 1790 a family of fifteen lived in the same space.[91] About 1 percent of these rooms had a dual usage of work and living space; some could also be used for storage or rented out as hotel rooms. Although most rooms looked onto the central patio and their doors opened onto a corridor or hall that was common to all the residents of that floor, accesorias represented a different type of room. They were constructions that usually had direct access to the street, sometimes contiguous to the building but often simply with a different orientation—one that was toward the exterior, not the interior. They were generally used solely for commercial purposes either as a store or a workshop. But some Mexicans both worked and lived in accesorias. Because of their outward orientation and consequent isolation from the sociability of the internal patio, women who lived in accesorias were more vulnerable.[92] The kind of habitation that accesorias represented tarnished the female residents and allowed men to justify sexual attacks as a result.

Core and Periphery in Rural Mexico

The built environment of smaller towns and villages replicated the patterns of the larger and more studied cities of central Mexico in some ways. Although the size of the municipality was not as extensive and the actual buildings were not as imposing or large, the model of central plaza as the symbolic center—along with its panoply of church, municipal buildings, and commerce—remained a constant. One way that this prototype was expressed in the more rural environment was that disorderly women tended to be identified as living in locations on the edge of town or in an adjacent part. Women who lived close to the border between town and countryside also seem to have been more vulnerable to attacks within their houses.

The horizontal grid that existed in large cities such as Puebla de los Angeles and Mexico City was expressed in an alternate way, making women either outcasts or rendering them exposed when they were far from the core.

The daily experiences of living in such settlements also brought people into contact with the countryside in a much more direct manner than in larger cities. Men and women had to leave the confines of the built environment for work in the fields, travel to another town, to collect plants, to go to market in other towns, and herd animals, among many other tasks. When they did so, they entered into a liminal space — one that was clearly part of the periphery. In some senses this peripheral space was the equivalent of the city streets: both were sexualized and so just as city women were subject to sexual attacks when out in the streets, men often assaulted or harassed women when they were out in the fields or the monte — perhaps because, according to Steve Stern, generally Mexicans considered the monte a male preserve, dangerous for women but acceptable for prepubescent girls. [93] In addition, husbands often made a show of taking their wives out to the countryside, frequently to the monte, in order to discipline them. Of these symbolic places none seems to have had as much impact as the barranca. Men dumped female bodies in ravines, tried to kill their spouses by throwing them into ravines, attacked them near ravines. The barranca was the place used by Mexican men to show their contempt for women; it held incredible potency as the antithesis of the moral core at the town center; it was a place of violence and danger where the devil might appear.

Although the smaller towns and villages did reproduce a type of horizontal grid, the vertical axis that was so important in the city was not usually present because there were fewer of the large mansions that had several floors. Nevertheless, rural Mexicans did not live as isolated nuclear families. Many of the homes in villages were, like the buildings of the city, arranged around a courtyard. This patio was a space of both sociability and work. It was the place where women took their weaving and some of the cooking preparation, and in some cases, where male artisans practiced their trade. The rooms that surrounded this courtyard usually faced inward and so the home still had an inward orientation that provided a kind of moral compass centered on the patio. In many of the documented cases, different related families lived in the rooms that circumscribed the courtyard. The family residential arrangements were cross-generational and interrelated; several generations lived together. This pattern meant that the close scrutiny by neighbors afforded by the kinds of living arrangements that was present in the cities was very much a fact of life in smaller polities as well. Apart from family members, neighbors also intervened in loud disputes, so the rural home was certainly not one of isolation but rather one that existed within a family and community structure.

How a House Should Be

Because of the great variety of types of housing in Mexico, ranging from simple rooms to palaces, no single prototype of how a house should be could fit all these various sizes and levels of lodgings. In the most prestigious homes there were multiple rooms, each with its own function. The stature of those who lived in such houses was reinforced by a room called the *salón del dosel*, or throne room, which was used to display royal portraits. Only the nobility were permitted to have such a room in their lodgings. They would also have an *estrado*, a kind of dais-like platform where women congregated and received their friends, as well as a chapel and various other rooms for receiving guests. In Mexico City's mansions and those of other principal cities, there was more than one interior patio around which rooms were concentrically arranged.[94] In the largest mansions the principal patio was located toward the street. The back patios were reserved for service functions and were not as elaborate or lushly decorated. The functions of the rooms also replicated this pattern with the living room, estrado, rooms for receiving, and music all located to the front of the building; rooms where servants worked or lived, such as the kitchen, their bedrooms, the stores, and the latrines were all located at the back of the building.[95] Even poorer houses and tenements were arranged around a patio, so, while less ostentatious, these residences also maintained the interior orientation. This type of building remained a constant in Mexico even after independence when architects were influenced by the Industrial Revolution and other trends. Colonial-style homes continued to be the norm because political and social upheaval prevented much innovation or new construction until the last quarter of the nineteenth century.[96]

There was a rule of etiquette for conduct in these mansions, which assigned higher honor to different locations within the house. In a sense, the operating principle replicated the architectural orientation of the house by emphasizing the interior as the most honorable place. The interiority of Mexican architecture was founded on this principle, making the most interior and private rooms the most imbued with honor. This was an adaptation of the horizontal axis of urban values. In addition, the vertical axis was also reproduced: the higher the room or apartment, the greater the prestige and therefore honor. But this was also expressed within the interior receiving rooms, where a visitor would have to try to judge upon which chair to sit based on how far into the room's interior the chair was placed and also its relative height.[97] A nineteenth-century etiquette manual reinforced the association between interior and honor when its author advised that the head or most honorable position at a dining table was the most interior one facing the door. In addition, there was a practical reason why the interior position would be that of most prestige—it was also the one of greatest comfort, because, as Diez de Bonilla reminds his readers, the opposite position meant being next to the door and exposed to its opening and closing, the wind, and the traffic associated with guests coming and going.[98]

These prescriptions for proper behavior and etiquette applied, of course, only to larger more elaborate lodgings, but the respect for interior spaces was not something that poorer Mexicans took lightly. The working class had their own sense of propriety and decorum that involved respect for their living space. Sergeant Miguel Ortiz, for example, explained how he never tried to take his girlfriend out of her house because it would represent a "lack of respect for her parents."[99] He equated respect for parents with respect for their living space. Many of the incidents of violence that form the sample for this book involve working-class people ejecting or attacking those who acted in a manner considered disrespectful toward the people and the space.

Morality was, however, one quality that could be expressed in all living spaces. The moralists had prescriptions that applied mostly to the wealthy possessing more elaborate homes, but some of their ideas seem to have filtered into the consciousness of the poor. Doctor don Manuel Rossell asked his readers to examine the condition and demeanor of their houses: in order for a living space to reflect the residents' own morality, they had to reduce the quantity of furniture and decoration; they should avoid having paintings, sculptures, or tapestries that were pornographic; and they should have only art that represented sacred stories taken from the Bible.[100] He may have been reacting to an increase in the amount of furniture found in homes, which began in the eighteenth century.[101]

What or who the heads of household decided to allow into their house was an important moral consideration. Rossell called for a simplicity within homes that resembled the kind of plainness that was required of women who wanted to show their morality with their clothing and conduct. This injunction—for home and body—was more aimed at the wealthy who could overdecorate their living spaces. In fact, as Loreto López shows, rich families demonstrated their religious values by extensively decorating their houses with religious paintings. In addition, some rich houses in Puebla de los Angeles were designed in such a way that their private chapel's cupola could be seen from the street—a clear external as well as internal demonstration of their faith and, by extension, the morality of their homes.[102] But even the poor demonstrated their piety by decorating their houses with pious etchings, engravings, and sometimes paintings.[103] Rossell also advised to carefully choose which persons would be admitted into the house; in a sense, he was equating the moral content of adornment with that of individuals.[104] Father Gaspar Astete advised his readers that "their house should be like religion; with daughters who embraced silence, abstinence, and piety."[105] He also emphasized that chastity should prevail in a house by refusing admittance to vain, talkative men or flattering women whose lives revolved around gossip and fashion; these were suspicious individuals indeed.[106] Reading books of chivalric adventure and romance was another activity that was of great sinfulness and the equivalent of bringing a blithe young man into the house.[107] The purity of the living space meant not just a simplicity and wholesomeness of decor but also the maintenance of a space free of bad influences derived from human examples.

The principles that these moral authorities expressed were also conveyed in the form that Mexican architecture followed, in particular its interiority. As previously mentioned, Mexican houses generally looked onto interior patios. The wealthier, however, had windows and small balconies that looked out onto the street—these represented a break in the moral armature of Mexican houses and were a danger to women's character and purity specifically. One of the constant refrains of the moralist literature was the hazard that windows mostly and sometimes balconies were for the souls of young women. Astete compared women who sat in windows in order to see and be seen to Jezebel.[108] Another moralist, Juan de la Cerda, wrote that parents should enclose their virginal daughters so that they could have no contact with men and he warned parents against allowing daughters to stay in windows to look at the outside world, which was the same, according to him, as allowing these young women to be in the street.[109] Mexican archbishop Francisco Lizana y Beaumont also equated the street with sitting at windows; he advised that beautiful women who either stayed at their houses' windows or strolled around in the streets were sinners.[110] There are numerous other references to windows in the books of morality that provided advice to parents of the period; they particularly focused on mothers and daughters since the onus fell on these family members to ensure the sexual purity of the household.[111] In reality, there are few references to windows in the Mexican criminal documents studied.[112] These references to windows and balconies in the moralist literature are important, however, because they demonstrate that the prevailing interiority of Mexican architecture had a moral component that was breached in the windows. The absence of reference to windows in the sample is explained by the fact that most of the documentation deals with lower class Mexicans who would not have had windows at all or at the very least would not have had windows that looked onto the street. Instead, the working class equivalents of the window were the threshold and the door. These were the moral signifiers for the plebeian Mexicans.

Gender and Homes

Apart from the gendered quality of the morality associated with housing, there was also a gender component to Mexican homes.

Whatever the living arrangements of middle-period Mexicans, there was an expectation that work was divided according to sex: living quarters were connected to women, whereas the outside world was a male environment.[113] Martín de Córdoba writes clearly on this subject: "[A]ccording to philosophers, in the domestic and household regimen, the work of men and women is divided. That of the husband is to work outside the house whereas the woman works inside. It is natural for the woman to always be at home." He goes on to link the women's place in the home to her role in serving her husband.[114] This connection is important because the gendering of home as feminine was a major part of the way that Mexicans conceived of their spatial context but it also implied that women who left the domestic enclosure were not subject to their husbands. It was the source of a great deal of tension between Mexican women and men because working-class women had to leave their living quarters for all sorts of reasons. But it also helps to explain the sexualization of streets. If the house was a feminine space, then the street was a masculine area.

When women left the house, they were in rebellion against their assigned role in the house and therefore they were not good women. Padre Fray Baltasar de Arizmendi expresses this sentiment exactly in his sermons when he urges women to emulate the Virgin Mary by enclosing themselves in their homes and thus renouncing the temptations of the devil.[115] Astete also takes up the Virgin as a model for young women in order to elevate the notion of recogimiento — a kind of life of seclusion — for young women.[116] The idea of recogimiento pervades the moral literature but it also appears in the court documents. Women claimed this virtue when they reported a sexual attack; they clung to it even while the fact that someone had attacked them made a mockery of their attempt at seclusion. Nevertheless, this notion of seclusion and the sexual purity or chastity that it implied was central to the way that Mexican women tried to define themselves both in their conduct and their relationship to their lodgings.

Conclusion

The messages in the built environment of Mexican towns and cities were unequivocal. A house was not simply a place to live but rather a space that defined who you were and how you were allowed to function socially. Lodgings defined morality and ranking. Hierarchy was manifest in the housing's actual location within the city and its relative proximity to the center; the horizontal grid worked to classify those who lived closest to the core as highest ranked and most moral and those on the periphery as the lowest in status and the most dubious in terms of honesty. The actual architecture of individual houses also carried messages of rank and honor. For example, the doorway or zaguán was larger and more imposing for houses lodging persons of high rank. The interiority of buildings and the lack of activity at windows (which needed to be barred and shut) was also an indication of the moral nature to the residents. In effect the design of Mexican houses held many moral signifiers that were often conflated with rank and identity. The vertical axis of Mexican buildings simply reinforced this pattern with the upper classes residing at the top and those at street level having a more lowly status. Thus, it would have been easy to say who a person was by looking at where they lived.

This understanding of the way that the Mexican built environment spoke to people in the middle period provides a glimpse of the relationship that men and women had to their spatial context. It affords an entry into the way that middle-period Mexicans defined the spaces around them but also how these spaces defined them. Next is a consideration of the realities of interaction within spatial contexts and demonstrated in the actions of Mexican men and women, especially in their acts of violence. The tensions that people felt and acted upon in their contacts with other people were influenced by their surroundings. But, in addition, their setting also played a role in determining the kinds of actions that were appropriate. Mexicans also sometimes used elements of the built environment as proxies for the people who lived inside which reveals the moral signifiers of Mexican architecture in practice.

3. Behind Closed Doors

As Mexicans moved through their built environment, they most naturally and unconsciously read the messages that the architecture and its manipulation conveyed. This process was not necessarily a deliberate practice but more than likely it was happening instinctively in their thoughts. Etiquette manuals explain the thousands of little decisions about rank and precedence that were supposed to be made by those in the upper ranks, but such adjustments of position and attitude were also the norm for lower-class Mexicans. Some of these negotiations were around their homes. Mexican men and women were conscious of the ways that both their lodgings and the way they interacted with their households indicated their moral stature to others around them. In essence, they were aware of the ways that the moral signifiers of the house worked in practice. Mexican men and women had unspoken rules about different parts of the house but, in particular, the door was a vital way for them to demonstrate their morality. Thus they made decisions every day about when their door had to be closed or open and they chose whether to stand at the threshold. The door was a very potent moral signifier: it symbolized the household's morality and its manipulation sent all sorts of messages to neighbors and passersby. All these minute choices had moral implications that were weighed and considered and they appear in the court documents when the situation turned sour.

It is important to look past the theory into what the dichotomy between public and private meant for Mexicans in their daily lives as well as how enclosure operated for women. Mexicans interacted with all parts of their built environment but certain parts of their houses had more significance. It is important to know what doors and thresholds meant and how people related to these parts of the house in practice. In addition, it is important to answer the key question for Mexicans of the day: whether the door was to be closed or open, and at what time of the day. The symbolism of the open or closed door was related to the gendered notion of recogimiento, and although in theory it applied to the whole household, it was really directed at the moral nature of women.[1] This idea of the enclosure of women was further expressed by their presence or absence in their homes; husbands and lovers complained when "their" women were not at home when they arrived. The interiority of the Mexican house did not always succeed in enclosing women and thus led to tensions over gender roles within couples. Of course, this anxiety was connected to the perception in the prevailing culture of streets as places of danger and debauchery and so the dichotomy between houses-moral and streets-immoral meant that any time a woman was absent from her house, she was courting sexual adventures. In the fluid world of Mexican housing not much created separation between households and people congregated in courtyards, markets, pulquerías, on the streets, at church, and in many other places. The division between public and private was not clear-cut, yet Mexicans had a sense of when that dividing line was breached.

Doors: Open or Shut

Don Joaquín Moles, one of the authors whose books ended up in the Lafragua library in Puebla, expressed the connection between morality and doors very clearly and evocatively. In the tradition of these kinds of moral treatises, he told a story to put moral concepts in human terms. An old man, he wrote, asked him one day why he did not feel the combats of temptation and resistance in his soul. Moles answered, "[B]ecause you are like the great door of a large house." He went on: "[O]r more like the door in a tenement in which anyone can enter without the neighbors knowing. Your conscience is wide and does not protect you from what can enter, you feel nothing. . . . If you had the door closed to these thoughts then you would feel the battle that they waged to enter. If the door is closed then whoever wants to enter has to knock, but if it is open, then they come in without knocking. O unfortunate souls!"[2] For Moles, life was simple: you kept your door closed and your soul was safe.

Pedro Galindo, another moral authority of the time and prolific author, equated the door with the street, the window, and parties and dances.[3] This author brought a more gendered view of the door question by urging mothers to prevent their daughters from engaging in these activities. Historian Javier Villa-Flores reports another earthier usage of the imagery of a door to represent female morality. In a denunciation to the Inquisition, Sebastián Jiménez reported overhearing Melchor de los Reyes accusing his lover of being like the door of the church of the Macarena in Seville. Villa-Flores interprets this insult to mean that the woman—like this particular door—was open to all kinds of people and thus she was sexually promiscuous.[4] It is an example of using doors and their status (open or shut) as a metaphor for morality. Fray Luis de Granada compared doors to eyes "through which all the vanities can enter into our souls"; doors were meant to safeguard either the morality of the home

6. The main door of a large house in Mexico City. Photo by
Elizabeth Lipsett. This door was large enough to accommodate a
carriage. It opened onto the zaguán and then into the first patio.
Former mansion of the Counts of Santiago de Calimaya, built in
the eighteenth century. It is now a museum.

or the soul.[5] Clearly, the door was a potent symbol of morality, although in the lengthy description of etiquette in noble homes it is clear that most doors were closed and had to be approached with care (see figure 6). Doors in noble homes were also protected by layers of staff, the superior or upper location of the rooms, and the mere fact of having many rooms. This situation was not a reality for the vast majority of Mexicans who rented rooms and who had only one door that opened out onto a corridor and the internal patio typical of most Mexican buildings.

Plebeian Mexicans who lived close together in tenements or in the lower floors of more elaborate and desirable houses did, however, have rules governing their doors. These were not written down in any etiquette manuals but rather are revealed in the criminal documentation that records so much of the practice of everyday life. Gonzalbo Aizpuru writes that in Mexican cities the prevailing custom was to keep doors open during the day so that guests and passersby could see into the interior — the more intimate parts of the home. A lot of the activities such as cooking, eating, work, and socializing occurred in collective spaces such as the streets or the patios.[6] Urban Mexicans demonstrated their propriety by keeping their doors wide open in the daytime but shutting them at night. The open door during daylight hours showed that the household had nothing to hide and was open to scrutiny. Conversely, the closed door at night was an indication of respectability, that parties and similar events were not a regular occurrence for the household, and that the residents were not receiving disreputable guests.[7] The closed door at night was particularly important to women, who often expressed it as proof of their quality as *recogidas* or being enclosed and moral. Father Gaspar de Astete, a moralist, was the only author whose work was consulted who hinted at this schedule of morality around doors. He writes that widows must demonstrate their modesty in their houses and should not open the door for anyone at night or have guests at that time.[8] There is a kind of logic to this schedule: these were large cities with accompanying crime and violence, so a closed door at night made sense. The ideas surrounding the closed or open door were not entirely about security but rather were about morality and honor as well.

Finding a door closed during the daytime was disturbing for middle-period Mexicans especially if the person inside was a wife or lover. This situation immediately evoked suspicions. Andrea Salazar, a married woman of Puebla de los Angeles, suffered the consequences for her disregard of this rule. In 1856 she was in her room with her son, who was ill. Her *compadre*, Apolinio Fernández, was with her and the door was shut, apparently because her other children had closed it as they left the room. Her husband, Magdaleno Juáres, came home at around noon and, finding the door closed, pounded on it. When she finally opened it, instead of commiserating on his son's health, he beat her with a stick. In her defense, Andrea Salazar stated that although the door was closed, the windows were open. Her husband was not impressed with this logic; he was adamant that doors were only closed at night.[9] It is interesting to note that Andrea Salazar did not refute the notion that doors must be open in the daytime but rather tried to argue that the open windows were compensatory. Clearly, the rule enunciated by her husband was one that she understood though she was trying to evade and obfuscate. The link between a closed door and untrustworthy conduct was also expressed by Mexicans of higher stature than Andrea Salazar and her husband. Don Francisco Pila, a man whose honorific "don" placed him in a slightly higher category, was a member of Mexico City's merchant community. He had been married to doña María Ciriaca García for five years. When he came home to find the house closed with the door locked in the daytime, he was suspicious.

He told the authorities that it was the sign of an illicit affair.[10] Clearly this was a code that was understood across class lines; it was a very potent sign.

Conversely, having the door open at night was a similar sign of immorality although the implications were somewhat different. It was for this reason that Saturnino Zapata was so angry when he returned to his home in Puebla at 9:00 p.m. to find the door open. The argument that he had with his wife as a result was so severe that neighbors reported it to the authorities.[11] While keeping the door shut during the day implied that the woman of the house was conducting a liaison, at night the suggestion of immorality was more diffuse — it meant that people were free to enter and the only people who would do so at night were those of a dissolute nature. So the openness desired in the daylight hours reversed itself after dark, and what was a positive sign during the day was the opposite at night. The night itself acted upon space to make it peripheral, dangerous, sexualizing, and masculine.

It was especially important for women to be enclosed at night. Isidora Josefa, an indigenous widow in the small community of Otumba, was adamant that she and her daughters were recogidas in their home the night that Manuel Rodríguez broke down the door to her house and attacked her. Isidora asked that Manuel Rodríguez pay for the repair of her door and that he leave her alone so that she could "maintain myself in the state of honor that I have until now." Manuel Rodríguez's wife and her friends were incensed by the accusations, and their attacks on Isidora Josefa's person (and her door) will be examined later because they are rich in connotation. It is the description of Isidora Josefa's reputation that is interesting here. Jacinta Islas, one of the wife's friends, said that it was well known that Isidora Josefa was immoral and that she spent the nights in the streets and in fandangos, and that "her house was never empty of people."[12] The contrast between the two images is important. Isidora Josefa wanted the officials to believe that despite having had an illicit relationship with Manuel Rodríguez sometime in the past, she was a moral woman who kept to her house at night and was enclosed. It is key to note that Manuel Rodríguez had to break down her door in order to assault her. This image contrasts the one disseminated by Manuel Rodríguez's wife and friends, which was of a woman associated with the immorality of the street and parties and whose door was never closed, even at night.

Two other women recounted stories of attackers who broke or forced doors at night. In Cuautla Amilpas, a small community in Morelos, Andrea Antonia, a mulata wife of Francisco Morgado, was in bed at 9:00 p.m. when Ignacio Alvares broke down her door and said he had to sleep with her. She admitted to an illicit relationship with him nine months previous to the incident.[13] In the nearby village of Cuautitlan, Diega Martina García was alone at home because her husband was working on the drainage works in Mexico City. Josef Contreras, the *alcalde mayor*, arrived and, pretending to be drunk, forced the door. Luckily for Diega Martina García, her neighbors heard the commotion and helped her. She stated that Contreras had tried to rape her.[14] Would any of these women have reported the attacks if their doors had been open at night? They probably would not have done so because the implication would be too obvious that they were immoral women who were not enclosed at night. Reports of the rapes of women beyond puberty and either married or of marriageable age were not as common as those for young pubescent or prepubescent girls because the mere fact of being sexually assaulted was a stain on a woman's character.[15] Women who did report being raped had to be particularly adamant that they did not court the attack and thus they had to be especially emphatic about their honor and sexual purity. In all these cases, the closed door was symbolic of the women's recogimiento and therefore their honesty.

These women emphasized their morality even in the face of having had previous relationships with their attackers. But women were vulnerable behind closed doors for other reasons. Women, who lived either in the outer parts of town or in accesorias, were also more exposed to harassment; they had placed themselves outside the core either of the city or the building and therefore on the horizontal grid discussed in the last chapter. In the eyes of men and some women they lacked moral principles. One night at 10:30 p.m., María Florentina Díaz heard knocking at the door of her residence on the edge of Atlixco, a small town in Puebla. Some soldiers called her name and offered her a coin to have sex. She refused to open her door but they broke it down. Initially, according to her account, they said that they were arresting her. But they took her even further to the edge of the town of Atlixco, on the perimeter of the hill near the wide stairs, and they raped her.[16] The soldiers broke into her house in what would have been considered the middle of the night; they could justify such an act to themselves and others because she lived on her own on the edge of town—her morality was inherently suspect and she was vulnerable. They took advantage of this fact and also of their authority as men and as soldiers. Women in Mexico City were just as exposed when they resided in the outward-facing accesorias. When women put themselves on the periphery, either by living on the edge of town or going to the monte, by leaning out of windows or going into the street, they made themselves vulnerable and men believed that they were tacitly giving permission for a sexual encounter. Brigida Gómez, a coyote and a *soltera* (single, not virgin, therefore morally suspicious by race and by marital status already) was asleep with her friend, María Micaela, when at midnight someone knocked and said that she should open the door for

the night watchman. Unlike María Florentina, she was not suspicious and she opened the door. The night watchman entered,
asked for sex, and when she refused he raped her.[17] In both these
instances men took advantage of their positions and authority but they also targeted women who had placed themselves on
the outer edges of the horizontal grid of morality. Closed doors
meant nothing to these men because they did not respect the
women's morality; the men chose to ignore the symbolism of
the closed door.

Men did not only break down the doors of women living
alone, although probably these cases were more likely to enter
the documentary record. Incidents that did not involve violence
against women would not have fit into this book's sample. But it
is interesting to note the dynamics when a man broke down the
door because of a woman's actions when her husband was present in the home. This specific example stemmed from an encounter in the Plazuela de Pacheco in Mexico City. Simón Carranza overheard María Estefania Guebara talking to her sister
in Nahuatl. He asked what the word *cacachique* meant; they answered that it was black. Simón Carranza felt offended by their
definition and both scolded María Estefania Guebara and gave
her a blow. Nevertheless the women went home. María Estefania Guebara was going to bed; she was enclosed with her husband and child and probably felt safe when Simón Carranza
knocked at her door.

Here the accounts differ. María Estefania Guebara says that
when she and her husband refused to open the door, Simón
Carranza put his hand through a hole and opened it himself.
She was terrified; she grabbed her child and moved toward the
home altar. According to Simón Carranza the door was open,
so he entered and engaged her again, asking about her rude-
ness. She continued to be rude to him but hid behind her husband.[18] Without getting into the question of who was telling the

truth in the two accounts, there is something rather intriguing about this case. The woman in question makes sure that we know that her door was closed and that she was in recogimiento with her husband and child. The man, in contrast, told the authorities that the door to María Estefanía Guebara's house was open. They are both painting a picture of morality or lack of it; the door — open or shut — is a metaphor for the household's honesty and honor. The witnesses positioned themselves in the spectrum of reputation by this simple fact. The contrasting descriptions of María Estefania Guebara's movements once Simón Carranza had entered the house are also revealing of the house's dynamics. According to María Estefania, she moved closer to the home altar, an action that could be interpreted as religious in nature but also meaning a move to the moral core of the house and to a more interior and therefore more honorable part of the house. Simón Carranza's version of her movement differed slightly: he said that she hid behind her husband. His reading of the events was much more keyed to the husband-wife relationship — the one that counted for him.

Apart from the dichotomy of open or shut doors, there was actually a middle ground: the half-closed door. There were not many references to this halfway point, but in the context of the larger discussion it is worth noting this additional category. In one case, Severiana Figueroa, a married women who sold *pulque* out of an accesoria in Puebla de los Angeles, told the authorities that she had the door half-closed as always when she was sexually attacked.[19] The fact that she stressed the status of the accesoria's door is interesting here because it provides a counterpoint to the previous examples. Although it is not explicit, perhaps the door was not totally open because selling pulque was not an activity that was completely honest but it was not closed so as to not fall into the category of suspicious women. In addition, the fact that she was in an accesoria as opposed to a room inside a building made her more isolated and vulnerable, just as in the previous examples. The half-closed door was also an invitation to sexual assault in another example. When doña Antonia Sánches, a widow, left her ten-year-old daughter alone, Bernavé Pedraza came by. He asked the girl, Juana María, for a light for his cigar. She brought him into the kitchen where the door was half-closed. This action, it seems, was invitation enough, and he raped her.[20] In both cases the message of the half-closed door was interpreted as suspicious and as an incitement or at least a safe environment in which to sexually assault either an adult woman or a prepubescent girl.

The Symbolism of Doors

Because the message of open and shut doors was so potent, the doors of Mexican houses began to embody the message of morality. They stood in for the resident's honor and became a kind of metaphor. Attacks on doors had roots in Spanish tradition where "house-scorning" involved "burning, breaking, or otherwise defacing the door of someone's house."[21] Deborah Kanter, in her study of rural Mexico, recounts an incident when a man acted out his revenge by constantly dirtying his enemy's door with mud.[22] Such assaults on doors often stood in for other tensions. Mexico City resident María Josefa had once lived with Manuel Mendoza in an illicit relationship but then refused his advances. Manuel Mendoza then destroyed her door with rocks.[23] The door stood in for the person; where a man might not be brave enough to attack his former lover he could sully her reputation by breaking her door. The message was that she was a broken, corrupt woman.

In the case of Isidora Josefa, whose story was featured earlier, despite the fact that Manuel Rodríguez broke down her door at night when she was enclosed with her daughters, the broken door became additional proof of her immorality. After Manuel

Rodríguez had served his time in jail, his wife and some of her friends came to Isidora Josefa's house. Manuel Rodríguez's wife proclaimed—quite clearly for the audience that she and her friends had assembled—that she wanted to see the woman whose door had been broken. Her emphasis on the broken door, not the fact that Isidora Josefa was an adulteress, shows that the broken door held a symbolism that other middle-period Mexicans understood. The group of friends included an official's wife as well as his daughters—clearly the more connected and influential members of society in opposition to a widow of dubious reputation. The women then burst into Isidora Josefa's house, grabbed her, and cut off her braids. Haircutting was a well-recognized and perhaps even globally accepted means of branding a woman as sexually promiscuous. But the women did not stop there. They began to pull off Isidora Josefa's clothes with the intention of putting a chile poultice in her vagina. Such actions against women's bodies were not uncommon but it is the connection to the door that should be noted here. Every woman interviewed by the authorities after the fact returned to the question of the broken door. Their sexual insults—the cut braids and the chile in the vagina—all began because of Manuel Rodríguez's attack on Isidora Josefa's door, which stood in for the thwarting of their sexual relationship. And, in fact, at the end of all this tumult the officials were convinced of Isidora Josefa's immorality because it was Isidora Josefa who ended up locked up, not the women who attacked her.[24] It was not only her door that was broken but also her reputation.

The message imparted by a closed door at night was supposed to be clear to middle-period Mexicans, but some men chose to disregard its meaning. They did so when they believed that the woman behind the shut door did not merit their respect. Men either broke it down when they decided to attack these women or they attacked the door as a stand-in for the woman whom they wished to punish. When women lived in liminal areas such as accesorias or on the edge of town they took the risk that men would not acknowledge the symbolism of their closed door. The fact that they lived in certain ways either by their flouting of social conventions or simply because of where they lived on the horizontal axis evoked a different message—one of immorality and dishonorable status. Mexican men manipulated and massaged the closed-door message for their convenience. They were quick to point out an open door at the wrong time of day but they also broke down doors when it suited them. But women hung onto to this symbolism because the closed door at night was proof of their proper conduct. Thus they tended to give it more weight than their attackers did. It fits in with the message of interiority and enclosure that Mexican architecture imparted: it was an extension to that larger message of interiority as morality and sexual honesty.

The Threshold

The door was important as a moral signifier because it was the demarcation line between inside and out; between the moral interior and the rowdy street. There was no patch of grass or front garden that provided a kind of buffer zone in Mexican cities and villages—the walls of the house were directly adjacent to the street (see figure 7).[25] Therefore, while the door was a boundary, the threshold acted as a liminal space perhaps akin to that patch of grass in front of many American houses, where people are neither in nor out—and the threshold or the zaguán, in the case of larger buildings, could form a kind of safe zone.[26] The differentiation of inside or out was not as clear as the line of the threshold implied. Rather, it was a suggestion and it was up to the residents and potential guests to interpret as to when they actually passed into the moral interior or were still within the realm of the street. The etiquette books of the elite hint at this

7. Street scene in colonial part of Puebla. Photo by author. The buildings are immediately adjacent to the street leaving no buffer zone.

ambiguity. Different rules governed the reception of guests at the door, halfway down the stairs, or in receiving rooms. Such discrimination between the various ranks shows that for some the threshold came sooner than for others. Perhaps it is similar to the description of the honor of chairs: where the threshold actually was located was an equation that Mexicans calculated according to their rank relative to the building's inhabitants.

According to Lefebvre, the threshold is a transitional object, one that "has traditionally enjoyed an almost ritual significance."[27] The threshold held many meanings—it could be a space of sociability, where people could innocently communicate with the outside world without tarnishing themselves with its immorality.[28] The division between public and private was mediated on this boundary, but there was also a small bubble of semiprivate space in urban Mexico in front of the house and in rural villages at the back in the corral or *solar* (figure 8). These areas were morally attached to the residence so that people who wanted to insult a member of the household could do so in this space. The extension of the home into the street and the permeability of the threshold might be caused by the way that household or work activities constantly spread out into the street.[29] Because of this semiprivate status the threshold could be a place of violence, particularly verbal aggression, which at times escalated into blows. Laura Gowing finds that early modern women in London used the threshold to mediate the tension between the sanctity of internal spaces and the profane quality of the street.[30] Hurl-Eamon finds that Londoners used the liminal space of the threshold to accentuate the insult of their violence—for example, dragging householders out of their home.[31] The threshold escaped some of the moral content that the door had; it was a type of grey zone.

Although the moralists constantly rebuked women for sitting in windows to see what was going on in the streets (and to be

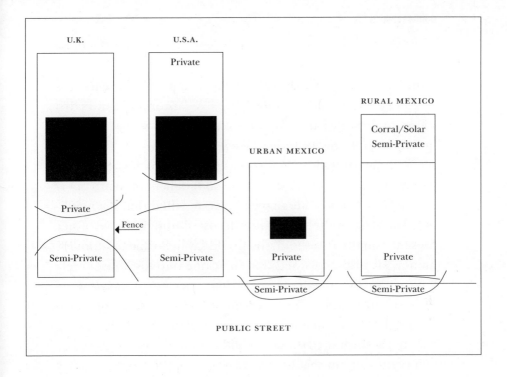

U.K.

U.S.A.

RURAL MEXICO

URBAN MEXICO

Private

Corral/Solar
Semi-Private

Private

Fence

Semi-Private

Semi-Private

Private

Private

Semi-Private

Semi-Private

PUBLIC STREET

8. Drawing of the concept of threshold. The two drawings to the left show this concept for the United Kingdom and the United States. They are taken from a drawing by Amos Rapoport in *House Form*. The two on the right represent a similar visual of threshold as well as public, private and semipublic spaces for both urban and rural Mexican houses.

seen), plebeian women especially seem to have used the door for this function. There does seem to have been a strong class element in where exactly women chose to position themselves to observe the world around them.[32] As historian Juan Pedro Viqueira Albán writes, "Young women of bad morals" lurked in doorways.[33] The attitude of licenciado Pascual de Cárdenas reeks of his contempt for a working-class woman when he describes the way she was always in the door of her house in a poorer neighborhood of Mexico City. He testified that his neighbor, María Samudio, constantly accosted him; because of her presence on the threshold, she would say hello and ask him for money. He also explained that she came into his house freely but that he did not enter her residence because it was *de vecindad*—in other words, it was too low class for his status as a professional. His explanation also shows how the threshold was negotiated according to status. He did not want to be tarnished by going into her household, but she was happy to enter his. They both understood the moral calculations that were implied by entering into someone else's interior space. When he was able, he moved away from this neighborhood to a more respectable part of the city but he still saw María Samudio around in the city streets—clearly her morality was of an inferior type and her behavior corresponded.[34] Although María Samudio's conduct may have seemed inappropriate to a man of some stature, it did not carry the same stigma among those of her own class.

Even among plebeian women, however, there was some tension over proper conduct in and around the doors to a building. María del Carmen Méndez was a caretaker for a Puebla house that belonged to don Manuel Durán. Clearly she felt that one of her roles as caretaker was to keep order. This preoccupation was not uncommon: caretakers often intervened when violence between couples escalated from a squabble to something more murderous. In the incident in question, however,

María del Carmen Méndez believed that some children who were playing in the patio area were making too much noise. She scolded them and told them to go into the streets to play. The children's mother got mad at María del Carmen Méndez and, according to the caretaker, the mother insulted her and hit the child that María del Carmen Méndez was carrying in her arms. The caretaker then closed the zaguán to avoid a scandal—apparently giving one of the raucous children a *puertazo* (hitting with the door), making her fall.

María del Carmen Méndez was clearly making a judgment about the rowdiness of children and whether it was appropriate for a space associated with an honorable man—don Manuel Durán. She had determined that their conduct was too noisy and boisterous and not "inside" behavior. The children's mother, however, held different views and provides an interesting analysis of which spaces of a Mexican building were "truly" interior. According to the mother, first of all, her children were only playing, which was acceptable. Second, she and her children were in the zaguán, not the patio, which meant that they were still in this liminal space—not really an interior area. Therefore, even if her children's play was disruptive, they were playing in an area where such conduct should have been tolerable. Anyone, according to the mother, could sit in the zaguán. According to her, it was a space that did not really belong to the building; it was public.[35] The status of the zaguán was not clearly defined; it was contested and subverted by various people. Even in a contemporary study Fernando Nuñez sees it as transitional and not a definitive space. He argues that it "creates a transition" so it is neither interior nor exterior. In the colonial period, the wealthy disembarked from their carriages in the zaguán, thus it served as a point to switch from one space to another and allowed a filtering of those entering. But even poorer Mexicans without carriages had zaguanes, so it had to retain its function without the mediation of ascending or descending from vehicles.[36] Again, it seems clear that a lintel did not mean a threshold. Instead, the threshold and the division between interior and exterior was a moveable line that depended to a great extent upon the relative ranks of those involved and their perceptions of the attributes of those involved and their place within the rankings.

Another Mexico City incident further illustrates the zaguán's liminal role. When Pablo Durán came looking for his lover, despite his inebriation and violent mood, he did not pass further into the building than the zaguán.[37] Clearly he felt the limitations of entering further than this liminal space allowed. In another episode in Xalatlaco, María Cayetana Saldíbar recounted how she and her mother took refuge from a threatening man who was following her on a mule; in this case, she and her mother went into a house and the caretaker closed the door, preventing the man and his threatening conduct from sullying her building.[38] The contradictory views of the zaguán and patio area highlight the tension over what was public as opposed to private but also the difficulty in defining these liminal areas. Several historians argue that the division between public and private is not always clear-cut nor equivalent to modern-day notions. The conflict described here also seems to have some of the class elements seen in the criticisms faced by María Samudio for standing in her doorway. Conduct that was acceptable for one class was not so for another, and these two interpretations of proper behavior tended to meet on the threshold.

Plebeian men and women were often found in their doorways; they could converse with other residents and they could keep an eye on the affairs of all their neighbors and the street traffic. Even in the countryside this practice was the norm. Doña Guadalupe Ortiz, a resident of the rancho de San Alejo, showed no reticence to admit that she was standing in the door of her residence at noon when she saw a man passing by of a certain description.[39] In fact, her powers of observation and memory were of use to the authorities in this case. Ygnacio Torrizes was standing on his threshold in Mexico City when a woman came by and began to insult his wife.[40] In Teotihuacan, Luciana María also incurred problems from a passerby when she was standing in the door of her house in the middle of the afternoon. She saw another woman, Marta María, walk by and she laughed. Marta María interpreted the laughter as an insult, and told Luciana María to mind her own business and go back inside her house. Luciana María believed that Marta María was making fun of both her and her husband's poverty. The two women came to blows over this misunderstanding, showing that standing in the doorway could also be a place of vulnerability.[41] María de Jesús Ramírez probably regretted being on the threshold in Puebla when her landlady came by. The landlady had been asking her family to leave; this time, however, the landlady insulted her, spit at her, and they ended up in blows.[42]

It is not clear why Ygnacio Torrizes, Luciana María, or María de Jesús Ramírez were standing in their doors, but Rita Trinidad did explain why she was in her doorway in Xochimilco at about seven in the evening. Along with her aunt, she was waiting for Nicolás Padillo to come by because she wanted to talk to him. The strategy of staying in the door rather than going to look for a man—someone else's husband—was safer and allowed her to remain in a space still associated with her home.[43] Gowing also makes this connection in her study of early modern London. The threshold, she writes, was "a crucial vantage point." Because English moralists, like those from Spain and Mexico, emphasized the need for women to stay within the house, it made sense for them to position themselves in the door when accusing another woman of licentiousness. By doing so, they still positioned themselves within the space of chastity and modesty: the home.[44]

Perhaps because of the regular habit of Mexicans to stand on their thresholds the area in the front of residences was a choice place from which to insult those who lived within. It was a place of interaction not just for those of the building but also for those who walked by. Although the threshold was the dividing line between public space and the private domain, this division was not so clear-cut. As discussed earlier, Mexicans expected some openness of the house in daytime and so the interior spaces were usually visible from the outside. In addition, the area in front of a door or threshold was associated with those inside; essentially there was an area of what Rapoport calls a semipublic domain in front of the house.[45] As such the space of the house extended into the street and allowed for associations with the household into the public domain.

Doña María de Herrera was insulted, she recounted, when she was passing by the house of don José Quevedo in Mexico City, his wife took some *naguas* (petticoats) out onto the balcony. The residents used the balcony for a purpose other than seeing and being seen but rather to make some kind of statement about the person walking by the house. Doña María de Herrera was quite clear that this act was directed at her and she was affronted. She later went back to don José Quevedo's house and with some friends, she began to insult don José Quevedo's wife from the area right in front.[46] This example represents the way that the threshold extended into the street. Clearly for those who walked through city streets, the area in front of a house was a place where the actions of those inside could stick to them and insult them but they could also avenge themselves by proffering insults in front of a residence. The threshold could extend into the street and created a semi-public domain.

Proper manners regarding this space in front of the house and on the threshold were important. María Josefa Castañeda discovered the problems associated with breaches of etiquette.

At 5:15 a.m. she heard a knock at her door in Mexico City. She opened it but saw no one. A neighbor walked by and greeted her. She answered but not very loudly and so he did not hear her words. This man took her apparent lack of greeting as an insult; he asked her if her mouth was full of shit. With this commotion, the neighbor's wife opened her door and joined in calling María Josefa Castañeda a whore. The couple along with another man pulled María Josefa Castañeda out of her house and beat her in the vaginal area with a bone.[47] In a similar case Captain Ramón de Riveros complained that doña María Josefa Paula Moctezuma came to the front of his house, threw rocks at the windows, and insulted his young daughter. Some neighbors came into the street to observe while others watched from their windows, which made this incident doubly humiliating.[48] This pattern points to the way that Mexicans perceived the threshold and area in front of the house. It was to some extent an extension of the household—insults in front of the house were still directed at those inside, as it was clearly understood that words spoken in the vicinity of the doorway were aimed to the residence. The semipublic domain at the doorway connected insults performed in the street to the household inside. It breached what should have been a private domain and extended it into the public domain.

Crossing over the threshold was an act that sometimes took courage; it represented breaching the dividing line between public and private and it meant embracing whatever values were represented by the household inside. It was probably done multiple times without any consequences or problems, but it could be fraught with tension as well. Doña Josefa Joaquina Estrada felt this anxiety when at around 6:00 p.m. she was on the way to her sister's house in Coyoacán and she met Bernarda Sala who was on the doorstep of a house. When Bernarda Sala offered doña Josefa Joaquina Estrada some pulque she felt that it would be rude to refuse—she had entered into the ambit of this other household and she did not want to offend its residents. She was right to be worried, however; Bernarda Sala was definitely not someone to be trusted. She promptly began to gossip and then insulted and hit doña Josefa Joaquina Estrada.[49]

In a similar example, Casiano Ortiz was wandering around the streets of the village of Malinalco with his friend Blas at around 8:00 p.m. when they heard singing and guitar playing coming from one of the residences. They went to the door and observed a party; people were drinking pulque and singing. After a while the people inside invited them in but they demurred, as they were not sure that it was a good idea. Casiano Ortiz and his friend were happy enough in the street observing but they were uncertain whether to join in. Their reticence insulted those who were inside partying; they understood the reluctance as an affront and one participant told them, "Your Worships can enter or if not, go to Hell."[50] The sarcastic honorific shows how Casiano Ortiz and his friend's conduct was perceived by those inside; they were acting as if they were too proper, too elevated to join in, and in doing so, they had breached the etiquette of the threshold. In another example of such a gathering, Clara Obando recounted how, one afternoon in Puebla, Mariano el Siego was passing by her house and she called him in to play his guitar. He did so and when the carriage driver and an official came to drink cane brandy with some women, they heard the music and asked her husband's permission to enter.[51] The threshold was the dividing line but the area in front of the door was also an extension of the household. Therefore, those who tarried in front of a door or house had to act in ways that were appropriate. Their actions could be either deliberately insulting or unintentionally so.

The habit of standing in the doorway could also make women vulnerable to abduction. Perhaps being on the threshold gave women a false feeling of security—that they were inside the sphere of their homes and felt the protection of home. María Guadalupe Suárez was standing in the door of the accesoria where she lived in Mexico City. Of course, like all accesorias, the room's doorway opened directly onto the street. José Chapin, a man with whom she had been having an affair but whom she was trying to rebuff, came by and saw her. He grabbed her, took her by the arms, and dragged her to the orations of the nights. According to her sister, José Chapin would come by regularly and whistle to her in order to get her to come out and join him. María Guadalupe Suárez resisted going with him and stayed in the house; she made herself vulnerable, however, by standing on her threshold. The day after the incident in question José Chapin came by again, this time at night. He knocked (since the door was closed) and when she refused to come out, he entered the accesoria and stabbed her.[52] The exposure for women was not only when they stayed on the doorstep but also when men waited on their threshold. This was the case for María Ciriaca when, in Mexico City, her mother sent her to the bakery after the orations of the night. She had to pass by the house of Ignacio, a man who had been trying to get her to engage in sexual relations with him with promises of clothes and money but whom she had refused. Ignacio was in the door of his house and seeing her he grabbed her by her shawl. He might have been emboldened by the fact that it was night—a time when "decent" women were not out in the streets. In any case, he forced María Ciriaca to accompany him to an alleyway and dragged her in a large, dark zaguán where he raped her, taking her virginity.[53]

The zaguán was more than just a threshold. Because of its size and depth, and definitely its dark corners, it was also the place for assignations and for meetings. It was the way into the moral interior of buildings but it was still a place where it was permissible to break some boundaries. In Mexico City, Guadalupe

Terrazas told court officials that Marco Peralta had been flirting with her for about four months. She paid him little attention. But, at about 5:00 p.m. one night her mother sent her to buy meat, and as she left her house, Marco Peralta was waiting for her in a zaguán near the butcher shop. He asked her to come into the zaguán with him. In her testimony before the court officials, Guadalupe Terrazas stated that she entered the zaguán only a little so as to avoid scandal but surely she understood the implications of her acceptance of Peralta's invitation. Marco Peralta took her movement forward into the zaguán as acquiescence and he dragged her in further. They then went to Tacuba Street and in the entrance (door) of the Alameda Park, they had sex, and he took her virginity.[54] Also in Mexico City, when María Leonarda Villegas was going to buy bread at about 7:30 p.m., a patriot soldier pulled her into a zaguán and raped her.[55] Francisco Pacheco and Dominga López also went to a Mexico City zaguán when they wanted to consummate their relationship. Then, when it was late, he took his love to an accesoria where they had intercourse three times and she lost her virginity.[56] Angela Olivares was only nine years old but was being courted by José Sirilo in Mexico City. One night he shouted to her from the zaguán to come out and open the door. Perhaps not understanding the implications of her act, Angela Olivares did so and thus allowed José Sirilo access to the house where he raped her.[57] In all of these instances the zaguán was a preliminary step on the road of courtship and sexual relations. It was not the moral space of the courtyard in which all was observed but rather a dark place of mysteries where loving fumblings could lead to more serious amorous activities.

Being Enclosed

The enclosure of women was intended to be a positive quality; it was supposed to ensure their chastity, their honor, and their safety. Most women who appeared in the court documents tried to claim this quality for themselves because it also gave them legitimacy when they complained of sexual attacks. But enclosure was not always positive for women. At times, a closed door was very sinister and more akin to detention rather than protection. The moralist Pedro Galindo recognized that in marriage, the relationship between husband and wife could change from tender, loving, and generous to one of shutting the wife in. The wife then became afraid of her previously kind husband "because he starts to enclose and tie her down with a thousand rules and laws up to the point of depriving her, simply because of his whims, and for no other reason, that she cannot look out of door to the street, that she cannot talk to her neighbors, nor visit her parents or relatives, even that she cannot go to mass."[58] Galindo recognized that what seemed desirable on one level—recogimiento—could be transformed into an oppressive control over women's movements. María Emma Mannarelli also finds that both Peruvian husbands and officials tried to lock their women away.[59] This tension over enclosing women and keeping them at home was related to the problems that arose between husbands and wives when wives were out of the house when their husbands returned home. Just as a closed door in the daytime could be suspicious, being enclosed in a room with a man during the day often meant some kind of violence for women—either a beating or rape.

Despite the fact that Mexican society accepted that husbands were within their rights to discipline their wives, neighbors, family members, caretakers, and even local officials would often intervene to prevent this violence from escalating. Therefore, husbands not only needed privacy but also the ability to close the door or even lock it. The power to create this kind of isolation would not have been as easy for residents of the crowded tenements but it was possible for those with rather more spacious abodes. In Amozoque, don Mariano de León y Vargas had the luxury of a large house with many rooms. He called his wife, Micaela Zerrano, into the *sala de asistencia*—one of the receiving rooms present in the houses of the rich—and then he closed the door and snuffed out all the lights. He grabbed her by the hair and, dragging her around the room, called for his sword to kill her.[60] Clearly there were other people present—why else call for a sword—but don Mariano de León y Vargas was able to isolate his wife and also had enough authority in his household to be able to keep her in a closed room without interference. Doña María Andrea Ascárraga suffered a similar fate in Chalco: her husband made one room in their house a virtual prison. He shut her in with no contact with anyone other than her spouse, with very little food and none of the medicines she needed. Finally, she got word out and a lawyer was able to present a complaint in her name.[61] In Mexico City, doña Mariana Manzano accused her husband of shutting her in a room.[62] Also in the same city, doña Josefa Monroy related how her husband shut her into the last room of the house, tied her to a ladder, and hit her.[63] These were events that happened in cities but doña Rafaela Rodrígues suffered a similar fate in the rancho de Piedra Grande when her husband dragged her into a room in their home, locked the door, and beat her.[64]

In all these instances the people involved had the honorifics of don or doña and thus they were of the upper class and usually had larger, more spacious residences to match their status. Their entourage was composed of family and servants rather than the closeness of neighbors that characterized the poorer quarters. The fate of women who were enclosed in such circumstances contrasts with one plebeian example uncovered. In the small town of Atotonilco el Grande, María Ramona Badillo told the officials that her husband had the practice of enclosing her in her own house (note that she does not say a room but rather

her house which was probably not much more than a room) and would only open the door every twenty-four hours to give her some food. Unlike the previous examples, María Ramona Badillo's neighbors intervened and saved her.[65] The closeness of living arrangements of the poor was actually to her advantage in this case. Taken as a whole, these examples, however, provide us with an alternative reading of the closed door for women. For these women, the shutting of the door must have seemed very ominous rather than giving them a feeling of safety. Recogimiento was, for them, a place of peril.

This pattern also held true for sexual violence — it occurred when men were able to close the door and enclose women. The individuals in question ranged in age and race, although none of them had the honorific doña. In one instance, the victim reported a pattern of abuse, but in the others it was a lone incident. In Chalco, for example, Victoriana María (eighteen years of age) described how her father would wait until her mother had left the house and then close all the doors. He threatened to hit her and then had sex with her.[66] María Clara Mota does not provide her age but she was a widow so she had presumably has some sexual experience and had dealt with men. She was suspicious when Isidro Guarneros began to lock all the doors after she had agreed to enter his house in Amecameca. She protested but was not able to resist him and was also the victim of sexual assault. (He later went to her house and broke down her door to sully her reputation even further after she complained that he had raped her.)[67] When María de la Cruz Mendical (seventeen years of age) came back from an errand in Puebla she found José María Cordoval in the room she shared with her mother. He closed the door, told her that now that they were alone he had to enjoy her, and proceeded to rape her.[68] These women were all of an age at which they might have been able to predict the danger of being enclosed. But at ten years of age María

Candelaria was probably still quite innocent. In the middle of the afternoon she was standing in the doorway of her sister's room in Mexico City when her brother-in-law sent her sisters to buy bread. He then closed the door and raped her.[69] Francisco Martín enticed Juana Pasquala (nine years old) into his house in Ecatepec; he then closed the door and raped her. He kept her locked in the room until after the orations of the night, when he finally freed her.[70] In all these instances it is clear that the purpose of enclosure worked against women when they could not control it. The theory behind recogimiento was that the women thus enclosed would be safe and chaste, but the reality was that enclosure, when controlled by men, could be much more sinister and dangerous for women. It also highlights the tension between the sexes over controlling and limiting women's movements and hemming them into particular spaces.

Refusing Enclosure

The moralist Francisco de Osuna wrote about a pattern that occurred among plebeian or middle-ranking couples when a wife ceased to be submissive. She wanted to sleep apart, and would not eat with her spouse, obey him, sweep the floors, nor prepare meals on time. This conduct on the wife's part was part of a pattern of misbehavior, but these were only symptoms of the larger problem that she had become *callejera*—that is, she was in the streets too much. She had rejected the enclosure of the house in favor of the freedom of the immoral streets. Osuna advised that if a few punches did not work to resolve the problem, then the husband should take her into a room, close the door, and give her a dozen lashes.[71] Osuna hits upon one of the major strains that arose for women—especially plebeian women—from the concept of recogimiento. It was all very well to want to keep women safe and chaste in their homes, but most individuals needed to leave the house simply to make the household function. The desirability of interiority clashed with the realities of daily life and the needs of a household. Spouses clashed over whether wives could or should be absent from the house because daily realities did not correspond to the idea of recogimiento.

Nancy Van Deusen writes that "[i]n colonial gender relations, couples 'played' with spatio-temporal moral codes in determining the right of enclosure or recogimiento."[72] In all probability, most wives were able to negotiate this contradiction—those who did not do so successfully found their way into the documents because of their spouse's reaction and violence. But these cases provide us with a glimpse of the way that men reacted when they felt control over their wives slipping, when they believed that their spouses no longer respected their authority, and the desired interiority for women's lives. It was a frequent refrain that wives were too often absent from the home; many Mexican husbands repeated these ideas to ecclesiastical judges.[73] This tension over women leaving the house was deep-seated. In his 1990s study of Mexico City men, anthropologist Matthew C. Gutmann reported some husbands refused to allow their wives to leave their homes without first asking permission.[74] Manuela Quintero, a twenty-four-year-old wife in Puebla, was explicit in her understanding of her rights. She stated that she only went into the streets "with the permission of her said husband."[75] Manuela Quintero's testimony is interesting because she does not dispute her husband's right to limit her movements; she simply insisted that he had given it to her. Other women resisted the right of their spouses to control their mobility and sometimes they also had to contend with other relatives. In Calimaya, Potenciana Torivia, for example, not only had a husband who wanted her to stay in the house but also a mother-in-law with the same agenda. Joseph Mariano, her husband, was so suspicious and jealous that when she went outside to pee and a horse went by, he beat her suspecting that she was meeting a lover. His mother

supported his behavior saying that her daughter-in-law was simply rebellious: she had been told not to go into the streets except to go to mass and to refrain from visiting her own mother.
Joseph Mariano's mother painted a picture of her son as a reasonable man who was only desirous of protecting his own hon-
or—to do so he had to enclose his wife. The portrait sketched
out by Potenciana Torivia was different—she knew a man who
called her a "whore" and took away all her clothes, beating her
and kicking her out of his house.[76]

In the small town of Tenango del Valle, María Tomasa faced
a similar alliance between her husband and her mother-in-law.
Her husband came home to an empty house one day. He went
to find her but could not. According to her husband, when she
finally came home she could not satisfactorily explain her absence. María Tomasa recounts that her husband and mother-
in-law then stripped her of all her clothes, tied her to a column,
and beat her all over terribly, even in her pubic area.[77] In both
these cases the underlying theme was that wives who were absent from the home were up to no good. After all, the choice
to be in the street was one that signaled dishonesty and immorality. A servant's description of his master's wife shows this
connection: he portrayed María Josefa Ramos as "pretty libertine and a friend of being in the streets."[78] The husband, and,
in some instances, the husbands' mothers had to protect their
honor by disciplining their wives and daughters-in-law even if
the husband's jealousy might have been unfounded.

The distress that men felt at the absence of women from the
enclosure of the home was not always so sexually charged. The
rejection of the enclosure of home could be construed as a denial of husbandly authority, as expressed by Mexico City resident don Joseph Mayorga, who testified that his wife had complained about him because "she did not want to be in my house
or company" but rather wanted to live a sus anchas (freely, in

a free space).[79] At times men expressed their displeasure more in terms of women simply not conforming to the model set out for them. Also in Mexico City, José Eugenio reported that he came home early from his work three times in the previous week only to find an empty house. His wife only returned home after the orations of the night. His conclusion was that his wife did as she pleased when he was working.[80] Don Martín Daniel, an *indio cacique* (indigenous leader) in Tetepango, reported the same of his niece; he punished her because she was not home when she was supposed to be there.[81]

The case for a husband's rights to find his wife at home was made forcefully by Rosa María Espinosa in Pachuca when she pleaded for her husband's freedom. He had killed his first wife and then finally been imprisoned for the murder but, according to Rosa María Espinosa, it was a justified homicide. Not only did the first wife not bring a meal out to the fields, when her husband returned home, starving, he found the house empty. Completing the picture, the first wife eventually returned sheepishly—clearly her absence was suspicious and she was rebellious.[82] In Puebla, Julian Torija hit his wife when she finally came home after leaving her children alone in the house.[83] José Trinidad Sánchez cut his *amasia's* wrist because she went out to do an errand and he did not find her at home.[84] In Mexico City Vicente Velásquez, a soldier, was suspected of having killed his wife because he reported that many times he would go to their room and she was absent.[85] There is less sexual tension in these cases—the men in question framed their objections more in terms of the lack of obedience—but the underlying question was, nevertheless, what were the women doing when they left home? Female enclosure was not as easily enforced nor as effortlessly accepted by women. The idea that women were supposed to be at home almost constantly highlighted the contradiction between the concept of recogimiento and the reality of daily life.

Conclusion

When going beyond the ideals presented by moral authorities and the prevailing norms for women in relation to their housing, it becomes clear that there were many contradictions between theory and reality. Although closed or open doors were vital to the message of morality and honorable behavior that women tried to convey to their neighbors, being inside and recogidas did not save them from sexual or other types of attacks. The interiority of Mexican housing was supposed to provide a safe haven — a feminine moral space — that was in opposition to the masculine, sexualized, and dangerous space of the street and the countryside. Yet, it was within the walls of residences that women found themselves beaten and raped, imprisoned by husbands and mothers-in-law, and harassed when they came home late. Even doors, which stood as moral signifiers with clear-cut rules that should have guaranteed safety and honor, could be broken down and disrespected.

The prevailing interiority of Mexican architecture and city planning meant that the notion of what was inside as opposed to what was outside was central to the negotiation of space. The division between in and out or public and private differed according to time and place and in fact it was ambiguous even for middle-period Mexicans. Because Mexicans tended to spill out from their residences working, socializing, and cooking outside their residences, the boundary between interior and exterior was diffuse. Yet it was an important notion because of its moral connotations. It was perhaps for this reason that the threshold became such an important liminal space; it became a "no-man's land" for women who observed life on the streets or in the tenement's courtyard from the relative safety of the doorway. At the same time, insults and invectives hurled at residents from the area around the threshold would be attached to the house, so the threshold could work in both directions: from the inside out and from the outside in. It was a place from which women passed judgment on those who walked by but also a place from which those on the street could pronounce upon the morality of those within. Because life was messy and did not always conform to the rules set out in manuals or simply by cultural convention, Mexican women had to negotiate their way through the pitfalls of open doors, and leaving the house to do errands. What should have been simple was made complicated by the contradictions between what was apparently the rule for women and their day-to-day realities.

4. Beyond the Door

Mexicans did not just react to their built environment. They also moved about within their homes, in and out of buildings, within their urban cores, and out into the countryside. As they went from one place to another they had to be conscious of the implications of different spaces—whether they were permeated with morality or otherwise, whether they conferred honor or not, and, especially for women, whether a space was safe or not. Just as individuals had to be aware of what spaces they crossed into, their hosts also needed to take care not to allow rowdy or disreputable people sullying their home's reputation. Living spaces were not impermeable fortresses—even the wealthy with their spacious apartments composed of many rooms had visitors and multiple comings and goings of servants and trades people. As a result, in both elite and plebeian homes the internal activities of couples were often observed or heard. The audiences of neighbors, family members, and caretakers intervened or reported on violence within couples. But some men and women also sought out audiences; they used this proximity of residents in order to mete out exemplary justice and to humiliate. They sought out places where their actions would be observed by even more people such as at the end of mass or in the market. Husbands often borrowed the language of official punishments as well as a partially public humiliation for their wives when they very obviously took them out to the countryside to whip them. As neighbors saw women being dragged outside of city limits they would know the sequel and decide to intervene or not. Audiences had to choose complicity with the acts of violence that they observed or refuse collusion by intervening to stop these punishments.

If the city core was also the core of morality and honor, then the inner sanctum of homes was also associated with these values. But Mexicans did not just stay at home in the safety of this shelter. Men and women not only circulated the city streets but they went outside of the urban limits when they traveled, when they gathered foodstuff or herded livestock, when they fetched water, and any number of other tasks. But apart from the morality-honor associations with space, there were also gender connections to inner and outer areas. While the home was a privileged female space, the streets and the countryside were linked to men. When women entered into these male spaces they were more at risk because they were sexualized but also because they were isolated and vulnerable. Husbands at times brought their wives specifically into male spaces such as the monte or the barranca when they wanted to humiliate and punish them. In doing so, they were forcing their spouses out of the moral center, but more specifically, into a male preserve. Moving out of center was always risky, but more so at night when spaces that might have been considered harmless in the daytime became perilous.

Gender and the Street

The threshold was so important in the spatial conception of Mexicans because it was the dividing line between the moral interior and the raucous street. For women it was doubly significant because their status as chaste and honest women was central to their identity, and leaving the house—going outside—meant sacrificing that protection. The interiority of Hispanic housing meant that it became "a female space shielded from the gaze of outsiders."[1]

But life was not so simple that women could just remain indoors—their household tasks took them outside, as did a number of obligations such as attending mass. In order to brave the moral perils of the street, proper women needed to defend themselves whenever they left the enclosure of their residence. The moralist Juan Luis Vives likened it to a battle; he warned women to prepare their hearts whenever they put a foot out of doors. The nineteenth-century manners writer Diez de Bonilla continued on this vein by recommending that women use either a chaperone or clothes that concealed their bodies when they left the house.[2] By seven years old, young girls needed to understand that their place was in the home; a moralist recommended that they should not even go to mass often but rather hear the inspiration of God away from the noise of the street.[3] For parents whose girls did not meet this high standard of solitude, it was imperative that they never leave the walls of the house without proper accompaniment.[4] In a sense, the various moralists recommended that women either stayed at home or only left the house if they covered themselves either with clothes or human protection that were equivalent to the enclosure of the house. They went out of their homes but moved around in a type of bubble of protection that projected to all they met that they were not "that" kind of woman. They were still protected by the association with their homes.

This sense of taking the walls of the house with them was harder for plebeian women who did not have chaperones or necessarily sufficient clothing that projected the aura of protection that wealthier women did so easily. Van Deusen describes how plebeian women could have "negotiated recogimiento according to moral principles of self-identification (a private internalized space) that transcended the spatial limits of the home."[5] In a way, they had to bring the protection of the home's walls with them by projecting a picture of enclosure using these elements. The meaning of the street and its associations with men and sexuality played an important role in the spatial conceptions of middle-period Mexicans for both men and women.

From Inside to Outside

To push someone from one space to another was a potent message for Mexicans in this period. Such actions could take place within a building (from one interior area to another) but more often they occurred from the inside to the outside. In Xochimilco, Gertrudis Martina, in her general complaints about her husband, Matheo Salcedo, told court officials that he had thrown her daughter into the streets; consequently she worried for her daughter's honor.[6] Gertrudis Martina leaves us with a puzzle: was she worried about her daughter's honor because her daughter was then literally in the streets or was she concerned because of the message her husband conveyed by his action? Did Matheo Salcedo simply kick out a recalcitrant child or was he sending a message to their neighbors that the daughter was unworthy and dishonorable? Don José Antonio Sotomayor appears to have been sending a similar message when he expelled his wife, doña Inés Matamoros, from his Mexico City house.[7] Also in the same city, don Francisco Molina seems to have intended a similar insult when he dragged his cook by the hair to the zaguán. When asked about this incident, Molina stated that he was simply disciplining a servant. He noted that he also threw her down the stairs.[8] Both actions had similar overtones: one was an ejection along the horizontal grid (from moral interior to immoral exterior) and the other was along the vertical axis (from the honorable upper floors to the less honorable lower floors.)

Mexicans often ejected individuals from their homes when their conduct was inappropriate—if they were being unruly and riotous rather than showing the proper respect for the interior of a house. Recall the caretaker who expelled children who were playing in the patio of the large house where she worked because they were not displaying "interior" or nonrowdy behavior. Such expulsions could also be practical—the householder could be simply protecting themselves and their property. Moreover, they were safeguarding the reputation of their household by not allowing disorderly behavior in their four walls. Yet, it was also an act that conveyed an insulting message and many of those driven out from households reacted with anger and violence. In Chietla, Guadalupe Salazar went to Barbara Hernández's house to find out why Barbara Hernández had fought with Guadalupe Salazar's wife. Barbara Hernández objected to his presence in her residence and to his questions that seemed to be recriminations. She told him that neither he nor his wife "had authority in her house." She tried to throw him out using a broom and then a *metlapil* (pestle used for *metate*) but Salazar broke the metlapil and then took the *otate* (stick used to stir tortilla dough) and hit her on the head.[9] In a similar incident in Mexico City María Cerna wanted to avoid trouble when her husband and nephew came into her house and engaged in an argument. She pushed her nephew into the street. Later, in the street, he came up behind her and wounded her in the back.[10] The nephew's anger had been transferred from the husband (with whom he was, after all, arguing) to the person who had pushed him from inside to outside. Perhaps that action was the greater insult.

Pushing another person out of a home was offensive even

if that person had brought about the slur with his or her own conduct. Tulancingo resident Tomás Morales felt betrayed and affronted when he went to visit a former lover, María Josefa Uribe, along with her daughter, she kicked him out of the house. The fact that he was in a state of inebriation and was insulting them by his raucous behavior inside their home did not register in his mind. Their reaction bothered him so much that he pushed María Josefa Uribe and stabbed both her and her daughter.[11] Boyer recounts a similar outcome in an incident when a woman, Paula María, tried to eject an obstreperous and disrespectful young man from her house. She stated that she would not allow fighting in her house, whereupon the young man stabbed her in the stomach.[12] In his analysis of the fight, and to underline why a mature woman might take on a drunken young man instead of relying on the other men present, Boyer writes: "In fact she was defending her honor and the reputation of her person and family. It was her space, not Marco's."[13] Like the previous examples, the woman Boyer describes understood the necessity of protecting the sanctity of the moral interior. The people ejected from homes followed a similar logic to that used by the women (in chapter 3) whose doors were broken down by men and who then tried to reclaim their recogimiento. People who were turned out from houses understood the slur against their masculinity and at times they reacted in anger and with violence.

Ejection from a home could also have a larger symbolism when that home was one of the multistoried buildings characteristic of Mexican architecture. In these cases the stairs, which held so much symbolism within the etiquette of the wealthy and powerful, could be turned into a powerful weapon of humiliation. When Juan Francisco sent his wife to complain to the alcalde mayor of Otumba that the official's pigs were in his field, Graciana María (the wife) had to go to the Casas Reales (official

residence of the alcalde mayor) that was located in the upper
floors of the official residence at the village's central square. According to official accounts, Graciana María was, in general, an
"extremely insolent and bold" woman, and she had acted disrespectfully to the priest and her own mother-in-law to the point
that she laid hands on her. But the alcalde mayor's wife was not
intimidated by this audacious woman. She not only beat her
severely but made her roll down the Casas Reales' stairs.[14] The
scope for insult here was greater since there was a vertical division of spaces—it was an ejection from the vertical grid. Although it is not clear from the document how Graciana María
approached the alcalde mayor's wife and whether she used the
proper etiquette for ascending stairs and entering the reception rooms on the upper floors, it is possible that it was her improper and therefore insulting behavior that precipitated this
violent rebuke. Certainly, this usage of stairs as part of an insult and a spatial strategy of humiliation seems to be limited to
the upper classes; it was not a behavior present in the incidents
reported from tenements.[15] The expulsion from home, in this
case, was doubly humiliating because it included a removal from
the noble floors at the top of the residence—it was both a vertical and horizontal removal.

In larger houses or buildings, the action between spouses or
between different members of the community did not always
take place statically in one room. In fact, at times a victim was
either taken or dragged from one space to another or escaped
from one spot to another. Occasionally these provided routes
of escape from violence, but sometimes they provided the privacy for sexual or other types of attacks. Doña Susana Soriano
testified that when her husband turned violent she ran to the
interior of the house seeking out servants, but generally she
went to the kitchen because the cook would interpose herself
between doña Susana Soriano and her husband.[16] Within the

flat roof

typical Mexican residence the roof was a flat area much like most Mexican houses presently—it was very much a place that was accessible and used for various purposes. This area, known as the *azotea* could be used as a place to escape to or as a place of privacy. Barbara Martínez complained to Puebla civic officials that she regularly had to run to the azotea to escape her husband's violent attacks.[17] María Gertrudis Martínez told Cuernavaca town authorities that when her husband tried to kill her she escaped to the azotea.[18] On the other hand, in Mexico City, after deflowering an eleven-year-old girl, Marcos José Allala [*sic*], a man of more than fifty years of age, continued to have sexual relations with her in the azotea.[19]

Admission into the Home

While it was important to eject unruly individuals from homes in order to ensure that the domestic space remained honorable and respected, there was also the question of who to let into the house. Control over who had the right to enter was fundamental to paternal and husbandly authority—it was the essence of keeping a household on the straight and narrow path of morality and only men who did not inspire respect could not control the space of their homes. Both men and women claimed this authority, but it was not always respected, leading to tensions. In San Juan del Río, José María Resendis believed that he had the authority to disallow a visitor to his house. He ordered his wife not to talk to an old family friend, Quintana, nor to allow him to enter their home. Quintana, on the other hand, reported that he had known the wife since she was seven years old and saw no reason to stop seeing her.[20] Essentially he chose to disregard the husband's authority to govern his household and to control who entered his home. This disdain for the husband's authority caused tension within the marriage because it undermined the accepted pattern of power.

Sometimes it was a woman from the home who chose to disregard the authority of the head of household. María Justa Bravo had been separated from her husband, don Juan Francisco Méndez de la Granda, for nine years; essentially she was the head of her own household. She lived in spacious apartments in Puebla, where she had various rooms, including reception rooms. When don Juan Francisco Méndez de la Granda tried to reconcile with her and effect a reunion of their marriage, he went to her residence and, in the manner of proper etiquette, knocked at the reception room's door asking to be admitted. His wife, however, was not impressed and she told him to go away and to leave her house. How humiliating that must have been for don Juan Francisco Méndez de la Granda, to be summarily refused entrance to his wife's inner rooms. But it got worse. He waited around in the corridor and shortly saw a monk arrive, knock at the door, and be admitted. It was then that he decided that his wife was immoral and asked the civic authorities to place her in a house of deposit.[21] Don Juan Francisco Méndez de la Granda was trying to exert some spatial control over his wife. If he could not maintain this power over her when she lived in her own home—independently—then he would have her placed in a space that she did not control. Essentially respect for a head of household meant respect for the space that they controlled; that is why Sergeant Miguel Ortiz was specific about never taking his inamorata out of her house, because that would imply "lacking respect for her parents."[22]

Control over who entered the house extended beyond wives and daughters to the entire household, including, in the case of Miguel de Alcozer, his mother-in-law. In Puebla, Miguel de Alcozer objected to the relationship that his mother-in-law had with a priest with whom, he believed, she was engaged in a sexual affair. But after the death of the priest in question, Miguel de Alcozer's mother-in-law continued to defy his authority over his household by keeping a portrait of her alleged dead lover in the estrado.[23] These rooms, which existed only in larger houses or apartments, were reserved usually for women and often isolated behind screens. They were probably remnants of the Islamic culture that had been adopted in Mexican houses. Miguel de Alcozer objected to his mother-in-law's conduct for many reasons, but for him the absolute acme of her immoral and disrespectful behavior was the placement of the priest's painting in a place that was so interior, so intimate, and deserving of a great deal more respect. Her action in placing the painting in the moral core of the house sullied this space. The crux of his mother-in-law's disrespect was her contempt for his right to control who and what entered the space of his household.

Showing deference to the sanctity of the home was central to the way Mexicans understood the role of the head of household. They could either work within the boundaries of this respect or make a statement by breaching this line. When Miguel Antonio decided to attack Juan Mariano de la Cruz because he suspected him of adulterous relations with his wife, he did not enter Juan Mariano de la Cruz's house in Pachuca. He waited outside, knowing that Juan Mariano de la Cruz would eventually come outside to urinate. When Juan Mariano de la Cruz did so, Miguel Antonio confronted him saying, "[S]o you know how to make married women fall in love," and then he stabbed Juan Mariano de la Cruz.[24] Miguel Antonio also attacked Juan Antonio's wife and mother-in-law, as well as one brother who lived nearby. He was clearly in a jealous rage, yet he did not enter Juan Mariano de la Cruz's house. Perhaps it was more practical to wait outside when attacking someone, but yet, when in a jealous rage, why delay? The spatial structures that governed people's conduct daily in Mexico overrode the rage that beat in Miguel Antonio's heart. Despite his anger, he still respected the boundaries of the home and allowed Juan Mariano de la

Cruz the respect as head of household that Juan Mariano de la Cruz did not afford him. There was an inherent honor afforded to male heads of household.

The same deference was not owed to women who were heads of household, as seen when men simply broke down the doors of women living alone. This identical attitude and lack of respect for women within a residence can be seen in another example. When doña María Ignacia Santillan left her husband, fleeing their marital home in Mexico City, she took refuge with some friends. She recounted that her husband burst into this home, infuriated that she had left his side. He closed the door to the street and began to beat all the women present. Only an armed guard was able to stop him.[25] He was incensed that she had left the space that he controlled—thus showing him disrespect—but he also demonstrated a total lack of deference for the space where his wife had taken refuge. Evidently when people entered a home governed by a male head of household, they assumed that they needed to act with deference and respect. In contrast, households where only women were present did not inspire this same kind of esteem. This pattern can be seen over and over: as women struggled to protect their households the men in their lives simply breached the walls of their homes. Historian Gerardo González Reyes expresses this lack of respect by conceiving of rape as an insult or an aggression against the "propriety of one's house."[26] In short, men not only attacked women sexually but they also showed contempt for the sanctity of their homes. Clearly, homes were not a space in which women could expect to be safe.

Although single women living on their own did not inspire much respect in terms of their right to control the space of their residence, a wife was supposed to have more status even if it was simply derived from that of her spouse. Married women had an inherent right to honor because they fulfilled the notion of a chaste person satisfying her given societal role. A number of authors have documented the way that women claimed this right to honor because of their status as married women.[27] This right to honor, however, could be inverted into an insult. In particular, some husbands attacked the dignity of their wives by an affront to the space associated with their wives. If the moral interior was the space occupied preferentially by women and especially by the wife, then what bigger insult than to bring a mistress-lover into that space. Doña María Josefa Mijares reported that her husband was not only violent and unfaithful to her but lately he had brought his mistress, doña Regina Gauna, into the marital home in Mexico City. Doña Regina Gauna clearly was a participant in this campaign of humiliation because she left notes to doña María Josefa Mijares in a corridor of the house. These notes were placed in a shared part of the residence where the servants and other members of the household could potentially see and read them. The missives contained insults and abusive language, but most especially doña Regina Gauna boasted that she was engaged in a sexual relationship with doña María Mijares's husband. Doña Regina Gauna went as far as to say to her rival that if she wanted to have sex with her own husband, she should come and wait at the foot of doña Regina Gauna's bed to see if he had any energy left over at the end of the lovers' sexual activities.[28] Without a doubt, husband and mistress took delight in debasing doña María Josefa Mijares. They displaced her as the rightful occupant of the moral interior of her home and made her into a supplicant; they also displaced her from her rightful place by her husband's side. Again, it was a question of who was let into a space; in this case, the choice was made in such a way as to supplant the rightful resident, and humiliate and insult her in the meantime.

Other men also followed this pattern but not to the same extreme. Doña Ylaria Hernández reported that her husband brought his mistress into her room in Mexico City and obliged her to serve the mistress like a servant. Again there is a pattern of inversion, with the mistress occupying the space and the position that the wife should. In this instance, doña Ylaria Hernández also reported that her husband hit her if she did not serve his mistress quickly. [29] Doña Petra Guadalupe de la Cal described the way that her husband brought his mistress to live in their Puebla house and that the situation had deteriorated to such a degree that she continually would encounter them in the throes of sexual congress.[30] Perhaps it was difficult to find a place for illicit amorous trysts if you were part of the upper classes of Mexican society—note that all the participants in these examples used the honorific don or doña. Yet, plebeians had no problems conducting extramarital sexual relationships even without the large residences that most of the elite enjoyed. The choice of bringing a mistress into the house was a clear strategy of humiliation for the wife. It was an inversion of the spatial conventions in which the head of household protected the morality and sanctity of the home and instead deliberately brought into the residence a person who defiled the moral interior.

Intervention: Caretakers and Neighbors

People moved in and out of buildings and within the residences, and they had close neighbors who were present in different parts of the edifices. So Mexican houses were dynamic places with different areas in which to escape or hide and various people who could be witnesses. The people who shared accommodation—whether as family members, servants, slaves, or neighbors—at times intervened in the events in another part of the building or house. In the tenements, privacy was hard to achieve as the households within rooms and apartments were extended and large, and, in addition, the living accommodations meant that a lot could be heard from one area to another. Thus, Mexicans living in such arrangements often intervened if they heard evidence of quarrels and domestic violence. María Trinidad Delgado only agreed to a marital reunion with an abusive husband if he found lodgings in a tenement "where she could count on the help of female neighbors whenever it was necessary to contain her husband."[31]

Historical studies of domestic violence show that neighborly intercession depended somewhat on the local culture: in New York City tenements, neighbors intervened regularly, whereas in London these interventions were less common.[32] In large Mexican cities it was often the caretaker who got involved. Ana Rodríguez, the caretaker of the Casa de las Piñas in Mexico City, burst into one of the rooms when she heard shouting.[33] Another caretaker in Puebla saved María Josefa Galicia when she yelled for help as her husband was hitting her on the head with a brick.[34] A Puebla caretaker rescued María de la Luz Rizo, a doncella of ten years of age and servant in one of the households of his building, when her mistress was beating her with steel pincers.[35] When Pedro Vásquez attacked his wife, she escaped to the caretaker, who called the Puebla guards.[36] Building residents often went to the caretaker when there was a disturbance—they asked them to take charge, which they regularly did. Caretakers either intervened directly or sometimes called the guards.

In other instances it was neighbors who interceded directly. In Mexico City, doña María Inés de Araus recounted how her husband would take her into a room, lock the door, and try to suffocate her by blocking her nose and mouth. She gave a key to her female neighbors, who came in and released her.[37] There seems to be some premeditation in this scenario. Why give the neighbors a key if not to enter into the house in order to rescue her? In Atotonilco el Grande, María Ramona Badillo also suffered imprisonment by her husband, who would only open the door every twenty-four hours to give her food. Again, it was her neighbors who took it into their hands to liberate her.[38] When the soldier Roque Molina was lurking about in the corridor outside the room occupied by Guadalupe del Real and her family in Mexico City, it was the neighbors who alerted the family.[39]

Because village residents did not live as tightly packed as in the tenements, neighborly intervention was not identical in the communities of the countryside. But family and neighbors did maintain vigilance when they believed that fighting could lead to bloodshed. María Magdalena was returning from fetching water when she passed by Nicolás Francisco's corral in Cuernavaca. She could see into the house and she observed Nicolás Francisco fighting with his wife — he hit her and killed her. María Magdalena called out for help and alerted other residents to intervene, although in this case it was too late to save the wife.[40] In the village of Tetelpa, María Apolonia went to the governor when, after hearing a small child crying and then peeking into her neighbor's house, she saw Calletana [*sic*] Justa hanging from the rafters.[41] In the villages and towns of central Mexico it was both sound and sight that alerted neighboring residents of something amiss, but the closeness of residences did allow for intervention and reporting.

The importance of neighbors and reliance upon them for rescue is highlighted even further when they were absent. Teresa María's mother recognized the danger of empty houses when her son-in-law's conduct seemed questionable; because the neighbors were absent and Teresa María consequently was all alone with her husband, her mother took her back to her own house in Cuernavaca.[42] When her amasio Doroteo attacked María Dolores de la Luz on a Sunday in Cuernavaca, she ran out screaming, but because her neighbors were gone to the market there was no one around to prevent him from stabbing her.[43] In Tulancingo, Juana María Ximénez had to defend herself when

charged with killing Sirilo Bentura. The court officials asked
her why she did not just scream when Sirilo Bentura tried to
rape her. She stated that her husband was in prison, her neighbors were too far away to hear her screams, and since Sirilo Bentura was standing in the door (blocking her exit) with a knife,
she decided that she needed to defend herself.[44] The closeness
of habitation was a characteristic of the Mexican built environment that colored daily life; it meant sociability and tensions
over shared amenities but it provided the protection of community. Living with so many others and in close proximity also
meant that there was an audience for most acts of violence—one
which men and women often tried to use to make their point.

The Power of an Audience

With the closeness of living arrangements, it seems logical that
the majority of Mexicans had a built-in audience for most of
their activities. Sometimes it was the permanent audience of
neighbors that caused the problem. For example, in Puebla, José
de la Cruz Campos beat his wife because he found her drinking and rather tipsy in the presence of neighbors whom he did
not know.[45] In this case it was the audience that provoked the
violence. But often Mexicans used external spaces when there
were potential observers in order to make their acts of violence
or insult more widely known.

Revenge was sweeter, it seems, when widely disseminated
and witnessed. José Victoriano Millán felt the sting of such a
campaign when María Cayetana Saldíbar passed by his house
in Xalatlaco and said in a very loud voice, "Here is the black
executioner." One witness, who happened to be sitting in his
door, recounted how María Cayetana Saldíbar spoke loudly to
her companion, an indigenous girl, saying, "[L]et's go quickly
here because there are black executioners here who might kill
us."[46] Whatever María Cayetana Saldíbar's problems with José

Victoriano Millán, she chose the place and the time to avenge herself by this insult. According to the witness, José Victoriano Millán was in front of his house talking to some young ladies. The choice of place is notable because, as seen in the previous chapter, it was the area around the threshold, in front of the house; it would have been associated with José Victoriano Millán even had he not been present. In addition, she chose to pass by and casually insult José Victoriano Millán on Sunday at 4:00 p.m., when many residents of Xalatlaco, a small Mexican village, were relaxing after mass, enjoying the break of a Sunday afternoon. María Cayetana Saldíbar's insult was designed for maximum effect with a built-in audience of Sunday afternoon loafers.

The choice of Sunday as a day to make an impression upon a crowd was no coincidence, since mass provided an automatic public for any such actions. The people gathered to attend church were probably the largest group anyone could assemble on a regular basis in Mexican towns and villages. The end of mass was a most common time for insults and acts of revenge violence among women, but any religious event could provide the right setting. Punishment and church were associated in the minds of some; Shoemaker writes that most penances in eighteenth-century England took place in front of the culprit's local church.[47] The Mexican Catholic Church also punished wrongdoers in exemplary processions or other forms of penalty. More informally, people chose the area around their local church and its events to attack another person. The advantage to this strategy was that generally there were other people nearby who could witness the assault and their presence had a multiplying effect on the insult's impact.

These attacks on the edge of Catholic Church events and property were quite numerous. Doña María Manuela Moreno y José was stabbed in the back when coming out of mass in Mexico

City.[48] When Juana Cabrera wanted to avenge the fact that her comadre had a sexual relation with Juana Cabrera's husband four years previously, she caught up with Sebastiana Torres at a burial in the church of Belén in Puebla and bit her in the hand.[49] The widow Juana María left mass at 10:00 a.m. in the village of Almoloya, but rather than having a peaceful morning, Agustín Manuel and his wife, Sebastiana María, followed her upon her exit from church trying to provoke her with insulting words and brandishing weapons.[50] Thomasa Gertrudis Lópes's troubles with another couple followed her when she went to mass in the village of Tecomate. As she left church, Petrona insulted and hit her. Injured in one eye, Thomasa Gertrudis Lópes went back into the church and asked for help from Marcelino, a respectable man, who was talking to the priest. Petrona intervened again, saying, in front of the priest, "[W]hat does this *meca* (common racial slur), this wild whore want?"[51] Rita Trinidad also was set upon by a group of women at the end of mass in Xochimilco; in this case, they cut off her braids to symbolize her supposed licentiousness.[52] Don Pedro de Rivera took his wife to the plaza in front of the church of San Hipólito in Mexico City on a Friday, where he ordered her onto the ground, lifted her skirts, and beat her.[53] His strategy of place and time was clearly to have an audience for her humiliation, but he also used the language of bodily humiliation in order to further deepen the degradation.

The end of mass seems to have been a place to jostle for position in the hierarchy. In the small village of Teotihuacán, Josefa Cadena apparently brushed against doña Teresa Fernández, the wife of a local official. Accounts differed on what actually transpired, but doña Teresa called Josefa Cadena a black whore, whereas Josefa Cadena was said to have murmured some disparaging comments about doña Teresa Fernández's chastity and fidelity to her husband. The incident ended in blows as doña

Teresa Fernández, her daughter, and friends, all beat Josefa Cadena.[54] Hierarchy was also the issue on the day that the archbishop visited Tulancingo to confirm the village children. The local church was extremely crowded that day, and doña María Blasa y Velasco objected when she believed that the mayor was jumping the queue, trying to get his family into the church ahead of others, so she hit him. The alcalde did not take this lightly; he returned her blow and later charged her and engineered a campaign to denigrate her status and position within the town.[55]

There were also places that women were likely to meet, such as the fountain or a stream, where, if they did not have access to water within their residence, they would go to fetch it or to wash clothes. In 1846 in Huauchinango, María Juliana got into trouble when she provoked a fight at a water fountain because of jealousy.[56] Marcos Paz complained to the judicial authorities that his former lover, Juana Hernández, told lies about him at the water fountain in Puebla.[57] There was a similar incident in a Puebla *muladar*—a place where residents deposited their garbage—when two women encountered each other then insulted and fought each other.[58] But the market was an even more frequent place for women to run into each other—they needed to buy daily necessities, and many had stalls there and thus went there on a regular basis buying and selling. Yet, the violence that erupted in the market between women seems to have been spontaneous, arising out of misunderstandings rather than geared to an audience. Men at times used the market or plazas to avenge themselves against a woman using the naturally occurring audience. Tomás Morales, for example, would come by María Josefa Uribe's market stall in Tulancingo and make loud threats because she refused to continue her relationship with him.[59] The market was a natural place to spread gossip and it provided an automatic audience of customers and vendors. Using such a space to widen the reach of insults was very effective.

A Partial Audience

Men also used a combination of isolation along with an audience to impose exemplary violence on their wives. There was an audience only for part of these acts of violence, but their tacit compliance with what husbands were doing was also humiliating for the women involved. When husbands decided to not only punish their wives but also make this reprimand public and humiliating, they followed a pattern understood by the community. The husbands started with a very public dragging out of the woman so that all could see what was happening, and then would take her to the monte or the barranca. The space outside the town limits was considered a male preserve and for women it was akin to the street—a highly sexualized place.[60] The man forced his wife into an alien region and there he usually stripped her, tied her up, and whipped her. This pattern, as Stern notes, is an imitation of the three-step process that officials used to punish criminals: first, the very public transporting of the prisoner to the place where punishment was exacted; second, tying up the captive, sometimes to formal apparatus such as a stock or post, at times to a tree; finally, the whipping and humiliation. As Stern notes, these "rites of familial power and authority" took their cue from the official ways of asserting power and the rituals of power that were routinely undertaken within their communities.[61]

Women in the sample talked about the experience of being dragged away from their home and community. Gertrudis Guadalupe Quevedo noted that her husband had twice taken her out to the countryside outside Xonacatepec—she worried that he wanted to kill her.[62] When Anastacio Magos heard some nasty rumors about his wife's behavior in Huichapan, he threatened to "take his wife to the monte."[63] When Lazaro left jail in Teotihuacan, he dragged his wife Josefa María to the monte and "he hanged her from a tree and beat her with a stick until she was deformed."[64] Visencio Antonio Rubio took his wife out to the countryside near Metepec, where he insulted her honor and threatened to kill her.[65] Tlalpan resident Pablo Doroteo took his wife to the monte where he stripped off her clothes, tied her hands, and beat her, trying to make her confess that she had taken a lover.[66]

In some cases the husbands who undertook these exemplary punishments went too far. In the Cuernavaca area, Juan de la Cruz reported to a local official that he had found the dead body of a woman called Sebastiana María hanging from a tree near a field.[67] In another incident, when the authorities interrogated José Bernardino Islas Antonio about his wife's cadaver, he said that he had to take her to the monte because he was jealous and angry; later her body was found with many bruises from whipping and her wrists clearly had been tied. He tried to conceal his actions by throwing her into the barranca.[68] Although at times the documents only reveal the end portion of this process, it was frequently a semipublic course of action. When neighbors saw a man drag his wife or lover to the edge of town and into the monte, undoubtedly they knew the sequel. That they did not always intervene shows that it was an accepted form of discipline that husbands could impose on wives. In addition, the fact that men did not hide their intentions nor the act of taking the woman out of the urban limits was a means to not only exact punishment physically but also emotionally through the humiliation of having part of the penalty be witnessed. Bystanders easily recognized this scenario of dragging a woman out of the home and out of the urban core. Those who witnessed such actions knew the outcome and also understood the message being delivered by the husband—that his wife was unworthy of the moral center and had to be punished in the appropriate place: the unruly periphery.

Outside of Center

The areas outside the city limits were masculine and sexualized—a place in which men felt powerful and in which the
normal rules of the polity did not govern. The idea that the areas outside the town limits were places of immorality came primarily from indigenous culture in which the center is equated with morality and the periphery is chaotic and immoral.[69]
Spanish beliefs also integrated the Islamic notion of center as
orderly and connected to Heaven; each concentric layer beyond this center is further from the core of order and morality.[70] Europeans also held notions that associated places with
immorality. For example, Europeans believed that crossroads
were the place where witches and sorcerers met with the devil, and therefore the meeting of roads was connected to sexual
danger. The ancient Nahuas also sexualized crossroads, calling
them the "the crotch of the road."[71] An eight-year-old girl, Seve-
rina María Josefa, seems to have unwittingly suffered because
of this association. Her mother sent her to the edge of town to
await her brother. She went to the Royal Road and at the place
where there was a cross she saw a boy coming along on a mule.
She did not know this boy nor was she able to identify him later but the boy jumped off the mule, took her to a nearby cave,
and raped her.[72] The cross and the road seem to have acted to
provide a sexually charged atmosphere that was certainly not
obvious to the eight-year-old girl, but the boy clearly felt it. The
edge of town was, for the boy, a territory that was outside moral influences.

The fact that sexual attacks occurred in the countryside is
not so mysterious—they happened in dark corners of the city
and behind the closed doors of homes as well—but the attitudes of the men who committed these acts was slightly different, and, in addition, these sexual attacks were more often
opportunistic acts between relative strangers. Accused rapists

who committed their crimes in the countryside also recounted their actions and motivations differently; in particular, they
referred to the influence of the devil.[73] José María Balderrama
recounted how he was on the road between Acaxochitlan and
Tulancingo crossing through the monte when he met a young
child. But the "devil entered him" and he raped her.[74] The reference to the devil was in part a metaphor for lust, a socially
acceptable manner of expressing a strong sexual urge, but the
place where these urges were felt was also important.[75] No de-
fendant spoke of the devil's intervention within city limits; the
devil's place was outside the moral center.

Whether the devil entered into the equation or not, men often took advantage of the periphery in order to rape young girls.
María Martina, who the authorities thought looked to be about
eight years old, was on her way back from an errand to the Hacienda de Colón in Izúcar when a boy caught up with her on
the road. According to her account, he said what she assumed
to be many bad words — she stated that she could not repeat
them. Possibly he was trying to evoke a sexual response or he
thought this was the appropriate sexual foreplay when meeting a young girl out in the periphery. Yet, despite her lack of response, he threw her on the ground and used his finger in her
vagina, hurting her "in her hidden parts."[76] Amado Díaz, accused of rape, declared that he was passing by a rancho of Teacalco on the way back to the Hacienda de Tonaca when he saw
a young girl walking with a boy. This young girl was María Francisca, a doncella of eight years of age. Amado Díaz "proposed
a carnal act to her." In his account, she accepted and took his
hand when he dismounted from his horse. Why would a young
man expect a prepubescent girl accompanied by a male pro-
tector to willingly engage in sex with a stranger? This scenario
would not have occurred so easily to him had the same circumstances been reproduced in the city center. That he was lying

or embellishing the truth is not hard to conceive, but most accused did provide a rationale for their acts that they believed was acceptable—and often it was accepted. Therefore, true or not, Amado Díaz's account did contain a relatively socially acceptable rendering of the events. María Francisca reported a different version: she saw a rider who threatened to kill her, and when he dismounted, a witness and bystander, Eusebio, stabbed him.[77] All these examples provide an image of the area outside of town—particularly the monte and the roads—as the devil's territory where women were sexualized. In addition, it was a masculine terrain just like the street was within city limits. It was also a place where opportunistic rapes between men and girls or women that they knew could easily be accomplished.[78]

The Barranca

For middle-period Mexican women, the barranca also must have been a much-feared place. Not only was the barranca situated in male territory outside of the moral center, it also was an opening in the earth. It evoked mystery but also violence and male power. In a study of dreams among the residents of twentieth-century Tzintzuntzán, George Foster found that his informants described nightmares as slipping off a path or falling into a barranca.[79] These ravines, which dot the Mexican countryside and sometimes intersect villages, clearly suggested a dark place of violence. Husbands often beat their wives at or near the barranca and frequently deposited their dead or nearly dead bodies in these ravines. When José Mariano wanted to demonstrate that his wife's character truly was incorrigible, he reported that she not only slept with a man at night in a barranca but also slept another time, with the same man, in a cart used to transport feces.[80] The juxtaposition of the two examples is interesting because, at least in contemporary Mexico, barrancas are sometimes used as informal garbage dumps.

Women did have to go to certain barrancas—often it was in the ravines that water was available for the community, and so women or young girls went there to wash clothes or fetch the household supply of water. It is not clear whether the ravines used for violence against women were the same ones used for these daily chores. There was a definite association between the barranca and violence against women, but more specifically it was a place where husbands attacked wives rather than mistresses.

Although the barranca was a place to dump bodies, it did not necessarily mean death for women. In fact, it was also used, much like the monte, as a place to beat wives. When Victoriana Thomasa asked to be granted an ecclesiastical divorce from her husband, the witnesses that she presented catalogued various attempts on her life by her husband. Miguel Antonio, a former indigenous governor of Xalostoc, recounted how Victoriana Thomasa's husband took her to the barranca where he tied her to a tree, stripped her of her clothes, and beat her. He also cut off her braids in the barranca. His conduct is the equivalent of the pattern that was associated with the monte, he simply chose a different locale. Another witness confirmed Miguel Antonio's account but also added that Victoriana Thomasa's husband tried to throw her into the barranca but that passersby prevented him from doing so and saved her life.[81]

A barranca near Malinalco was the setting for some exemplary justice meted out on the body of Juliana. Although Juliana was never willing to identify her attackers, a witness came forward to give at least an incomplete account. Apparently some men dragged her to the area of the barranca, where they beat her viciously but especially in the area of her vagina. According to this witness, she was engaged in an illicit relationship with one of the men who were party to the beating. Juliana was pregnant at the time of the assault; she subsequently miscarried and died without ever revealing the details.[82] This attack is singular in that attacks on the vagina were usually carried out by women — it was a type of sexual policing. The men who attacked Juliana followed one part of the male pattern (the location in the barranca) but not the other (tying to the tree and whipping). It is possible that the variation was because Juliana was not their wife and thus such violence was not permissible; but by attacking her in the vagina, they brought a female pattern of violence into a male space.

The more common pattern was to leave a woman's cadaver or the nearly dead body in the ravine. Angel Blas tried to kill his wife several times, and once he threw her into the barranca and left her there because he thought she was dead.[83] Manuel José Barragán fought violently with his wife. She then left to tell her woes to the authorities in the next community. He followed her, knowing that her actions spelled trouble for him, and he caught up with her and killed her in the barranca.[84] In other cases, people from the village found bodies in the barranca; some might have been killed in situ and others simply deposited there.[85]

The Night

Although it may not seem to be spatially related, the night was also considered outside of center. The setting of the sun acted to modify spaces that might have been relatively safe in the daytime but became dangerous in the dark. It also carried a charge of the erotic, and sexualized women who left their homes in the dark. It was important for middle-period Mexicans to close their doors at night and for women, in particular, to maintain a version of recogimiento. Other societies as varied as Canada, England, France, Brazil, and Colombia also imbue the night with significance — Alan Hunt writes that "'space' not only has a spatial but a temporal dimension." In the city, he argues, a street corner after sunset becomes a much "more charged heterosocial site."[86]

Hurl-Eamon reports that when London women were caught out
of their homes at night they were assumed to be immoral. She
adds, however, that men also suffered to some degree from this
tarnishing of reputations.[87] Muchembled writes about the danger associated with darkness and night: people were more aggressive and only the young wanted to be out of home.[88] Maria
Odila Silva Dias writes that Brazilian poor women who did not
have slaves or servants to do their errands tried to slip out under
the cover of night to buy food or to do other tasks and were unjustly labeled as dissipated simply because they left their houses after dark.[89] In her study of middle-period Popayán, María
Teresa Pérez finds that the night was associated with men, with
an inversion of social regulations: it was a space for lawlessness
and masculinity.[90] Carmen Castañeda, in a study on rape in colonial Jalisco, writes that such acts occurred preferentially after
dark.[91] The ancient Nahuas assigned moral values to time, thus
being more explicit and formal about the meaning that darkness imparted to space. They divided the night into periods of
greater or lesser danger according to the closeness in time to
the rising or setting sun.[92]

Early modern Europeans associated the night with the devil
and satanic rituals and according to Muchembled perhaps used
this connection to limit raucous festivities at night on the part
of the peasantry.[93] The link between the devil and the night was
introduced into Mexico with the conquest and was still being
expressed by Catholic Church authorities in the eighteenth century despite a lessening of emphasis on the devil in that period.
The eighteenth-century archbishop of Puebla, Francisco Fabian
y Fuero, stated in one of his edicts that the night was "when the
Prince of Darkness exerts his maximum power."[94] Brother don
Nicolás Simeón de Salazar advised eighteenth-century priests
that they should not provide the sacrament of confession to any
woman between sunset and sunrise unless it was in the case of

an extreme urgency.[95] The association between the night and the devil continued into the twentieth century among Nahuats of Puebla.[96] Whether caused by the devil or not, middle-period Mexicans believed that the setting of the sun altered spaces and made them more dangerous.

The night was a time when bad acts were supposed to occur. In contrast, these events were not meant to happen in the daytime. Don Francisco Grez, who acted as legal defender for a man who raped and murdered two young sisters, tried to show that the alleged crime was not proved when he stated that "a man, in his right mind, as bad as he might be, is unlikely to undertake such horrendous evil under the sun of 3:00 in the afternoon."[97] The legal defender implied that evil was committed at night. María Ignacia Samudio echoed this naïveté when she explained that she went to meet licenciado don Pascual Cardenas to receive a piece of cloth because it was in the daytime; he dragged her into an empty house and raped her despite the time.[98] As seen previously in this chapter, it was vital to close doors and maintain recogimiento at night. The moral core of every household — the home — remained safe if it was closed off from the night. But those who ventured out into the night were certainly asking for trouble because the night amplified the danger of already perilous places. Men also often took advantage of the dark and empty streets or countryside to have their way with women.

The countryside and the street were always dangerous places for women because they were male territories. But, at least in the daytime, men had to exert a certain kind of restraint; they were limited by the expectations of morality and the gaze of other people. At night such restraints seem to have been less strong or effective. María Vicenta Sánchez recounted to the authorities how José Talavera took advantage of the night and the absence of people when he met her in the streets of Mexico City on a Sunday sometime after the orations of the night. He grabbed her by the arm and took her to a room, where he violated her virginity.[99] Joseph de Leiba also took advantage of the night when he met the seven-year-old Luisa Francisca, whose mother had sent her out to buy candles, again on a Sunday night, after the orations in the small town of Taxco. Perhaps because Taxco is much smaller than Mexico City, Joseph de Leiba did not take Luiza to a room but rather dragged her into "the darkness of the small barranca" and there he raped her.[100]

Juan Bonifacio was more explicit in the way that he believed the night amplified the effect of male spaces. He and his friend were roaming around the countryside in the area of Tulancingo. They met doña María Dolores Xímenes, whose reason for being out at night outside of town was that she was going to church. The moon was full and very bright and it fooled her into thinking that it was sunrise rather than the middle of the night. Therefore, although she was in a dangerous male space, doña María believed that her errand was a pious one and that she should not be in danger. But when Juan Bonifacio met her, he insisted to her "that at these hours you are going out whoring." This avowal was hardly the statement associated with a woman on her way to mass. But the hour and the space meant that, despite her piety and the urgency with which she wanted to get to mass, doña María had put herself into a dangerous spot. The legal defender of Juan Bonifacio's co-accused and friend summed it up in the terms of the time, "that ultimately this woman was incautious and she sought out the danger."[101] The effect of nighttime should not be too highly exaggerated since men attacked women during the day, but it worked by amplifying the danger already associated with being in male spaces, such as the street and the countryside. It was the realm of the devil and the temptations were stronger in the darkness, or perhaps it was just easier to rape and abduct without an audience.

Conclusion

By defining the interior of houses and cities as a moral core, Mexicans classified other peripheral spaces such as the street, the edge of town, or areas outside town (the barranca or the monte) as immoral. This dichotomy did not necessarily make sense, because neither the city center nor the interior of homes were always places of morality. In fact, women were often in danger inside these supposed spaces of morality and sanctity. Yet, the designations were powerful images that dominated middle-period Mexicans' ways of thinking and provided them with a means to express their opinions of those around them. When they kicked a person out of their house, their act was not just a practical one but also an action that pronounced judgment on the person's morality and honor. Who was allowed to stay in a home was as important as who was permitted to enter; Mexicans could invert the model of interior-moral by inviting their lovers into their households. When Mexican husbands scolded their wives for being out in the streets too often and for too long, they evoked a powerful image that was not challenged either by the accused women or the court officials who heard their cases. The spatial configuration of Mexican towns, cities, and their surrounding areas was one that dominated the thinking of people even as they negotiated its contradictions — the reality of attacks within the home and danger everywhere did not mean that Mexicans gave up their conceptions of core as moral and periphery as dangerous and erotic.

The division between public and private was not clear-cut because the life within Mexican homes was often visible outside its walls, and certainly often could be heard by neighbors and passersby. The space directly outside the home and the threshold was symbolically still part of the house — it formed a type of liminal space that was identified with the people inside. Because of this spilling out of the house's identity and that of the household, insults proffered in front of the house were as effective as those said within its walls. In addition, because of the permeability of the Mexican home's walls, neighbors prevented this interior space from becoming a prison or beating ground for women, intervening when they believed that male violence went too far. The audience of neighbors or other residents was a safety measure for many women, but these audiences also served as witnesses to humiliation. The importance of this task of witnessing was heightened when husbands dragged their wives off to the monte or the barranca because it was clear to all involved what the ensuing punishment would be. By choosing to not intervene, neighbors were tacitly condoning the husband's actions. Clearly the fluidity of homes meant that private spots were not so secluded, unless neighbors and others colluded with the actions happening within the walls of a room or home. The way that Mexicans of the middle period lived half in and half out of their households made the separation between public and private, and inner and outer, an unstable division—one that every man and woman had to negotiate in order to maintain status within a given social set as well as a sense of honor and self-worth.

5. The Body in Daily Life

Unlike the built environment, bodies are inescapable. Even so, it can be easy to lose sight of our bodies' significance in relation to the way that the world is constructed around us. Because of our fundamental connection to our own bodies, they become a way of categorizing and understanding our reality. Middle-period Mexicans used their bodies and those of their neighbors to place themselves within their social order; bodies conveyed many messages about rank and hierarchy. But the body also conveyed much more: it was an indicator of morality and birth; it could indicate sexual history; it could express enmity or love; and more. Mexicans had to read the bodies of those people they met in everyday situations.[1] They needed to use their bodies to communicate either their superiority or their acceptance of inferior rank: men could do so by doffing their hat and bowing slightly; women would avert their gaze. Within the upper reaches of Mexican society, a whole etiquette existed about when to dismount a horse and when and where to greet an honored guest. No one escaped from this bodily dance of messages and gestures, whether they were part of the elite or the poorest of poor.

This was not a one-way communication, but rather a dialogue that was ongoing and dynamic. It erupted into violence when an individual did not conform or did not accept his or her social position. Mexicans acted upon those who refused the proper deference, misbehaved, or were aggressive in their body language. Control over one's own body was essential to proper conduct, whether that meant containing appetites or avoiding staring or spitting. In the struggle for power and status that was often rife within middle-period Mexican society, challenging that control over body was at the root of much of the conflict that appeared in the documentary record. Just as Mexicans used their bodies to convey either respect or disrespect, others acted upon bodies to enforce subservience and to exact humiliating deference. They pulled hair to force the body into a position of obsequiousness; they took away control of self by pulling a wife or a lover by her hair; they yanked at clothes and grabbed genitals. At the core of this bodily communication was the fact that the body served as a metaphor for social order and honor. Because the body was the vehicle for people to mentally map and organize their world, it was a symbol upon which it was worth acting.

Since Bryan Turner's landmark study in 1984 in which he pointed out both the absence of the body in sociological studies and its importance from an analytical viewpoint, there has been a deluge of works that delve into every aspect of the body from the most basic to the most abstruse.[2] Not all of this work is of use for the examination of middle-period Mexico, so only those concepts that help flesh out the kinds of incidents encountered in the archives will be mentioned. Following an exploration of how the body can be theorized and how middle-period Mexicans understood the body from both symbolic and practical points of view, an assessment will be made of how these ideas operated on a daily basis in Mexican cities, villages, and the countryside.

Ideas about the Body

Unlike the built environment, which has multiple variations and components, the human body has one basic model, so no description is needed. A body is a body, is it not?[3] Yet what the body meant in middle-period Mexico might not be an exact copy of the way a twenty-first-century person would understand it. Because our understanding of bodies is socially and culturally constructed, the way bodies are understood changes over time. There are different approaches to studying the body but one of sociology's contributions is to advance that a body is not merely a biological entity but rather "a thing of culture."[4] By approaching this problem from the viewpoint of social construction rather than as a given natural phenomenon, we can make sense of the diverse ways that people have understood their bodies over time and across cultures. Body image, in particular, is part and parcel of the way that a specific society constructs expectations and ideas about the body. So while in the twenty-first century an extremely thin girl might be a model or an anorexic, in middle-period Mexico she might be considered devoutly spiritual but she certainly would not be judged attractive or sensual. Body language is also very much specific to local culture—something that travelers encounter when they move through societies with mores and ways of life that are alien to them. The ways that people interacted both with their own bodies and those of others occurs within a framework of ideas—the way that people used their bodies to convey messages had to be understood by others—but the manner that they presented themselves was also part of their specific bodily culture.

While there is a considerable amount of literature on the connection between spatial concepts and violence, strangely not much work exists that directly discusses a link between bodies and violence. There is, of course, a huge literature on the body within sociology, anthropology, philosophy, and, to some extent, history. But these authors do not all make connections between the symbolism of the body and violence. The new school of history of violence, described in chapter 1, provides a way to make sense of the symbolism of violence, and a lot of this material is relevant to bodily perceptions and violence. These authors suggest a direct correlation between the symbolism of the body and the acts of violence that were perpetrated on bodies.

Historians can detect the conceptions and self-perceptions of bodies of past peoples by examining the documentation created because of violence and criminal acts. It is also important to look at other writings, such as manuals on decorum or morality, which elaborate some of these codes. Criminal trials allow us to reconstruct what some historians have called the mise-en-scène, the scenario, or the script of violence — basically the patterns that can be detected within the seemingly random violence. There is a direct association between these prototypes and conceptions of the body.

The "inner logic" of plebeian violence came not from a codification but rather because it had become part of rituals and part of a local culture. Instead of having manuals that dictated the correct approach to a confrontation, plebeians simply "knew" what to do and they "knew" what various acts, such as picking up a rock or dragging a woman into the countryside, meant. Just as the act of entering into certain spaces was rife with social expectations and cultural symbolism, bodily acts also carried messages that were very clear to the middle-period Mexicans. The way that violent men and women acted upon the bodies of those around them had quite simply become part of their culture.[5] Although many of the actions that people engaged in seem to be either the product of passion or simply practical things to do when engaged in a conflict, they take on a ritual quality and therefore also have a symbolic content. Because these confrontations became what Farr calls "ritualized altercations," they can be read.[6] Conduct that is governed by symbols does not have as its sole objective the action itself. Rather, the objective includes what the action communicates. As a result, such "symbolic behaviour [*sic*] not only 'says' something, it also arouses emotion and consequently 'does' something." In order for this process to work, however, the actors and the audience have to share "a common language, a symbolic language."[7]

Because these practical actions within the fight became imbued with symbolism they can be connected with the larger local culture. They take on a value with systems of honor but also within understandings of the body. In his study of Artois, Muchembled connects the violent acts that he studies to a French, or, more precisely, an Artois understanding of the body. The men he studied would read their opponents' bodies; Muchembled links the body to spatial notions by stating that the human body was a type of territory to be protected but also interpreted.[8] In this way a person's body is like a little island floating among similar islands: it was up to the individual to shield him- or herself with defenses such as posture and clothing. Each person had to be able to decipher the bodies of others in order to survive. Kenneth Greenberg connects this reading of male bodies more explicitly to systems of honor. Southern men, according to this historian, "read the character of other men through the external physical features of their faces and bodies."[9] For Greenberg, it was the nose that held the most symbolic content, whereas for Muchembled the hat was central and even had its own "semiological code."[10] Farr and Hurl-Eamon extend this form of analysis to female violence.[11] Farr goes furthest in explaining how French women applied the prevailing norms about chastity, religiosity, and rank as they pertained to symbolic elements such as their hair and their headdresses, and reinterpreted them in ways that allowed them to preserve their honor and character.[12] The larger cultural context in premodern societies was, according to Turner, mostly concerned with the control of female sexuality. Male authority but also legitimacy and honor were part and parcel of this bodily control.[13] By turning away from solely male violence to include conflicts between women and between men and women, a larger societal view that encompasses love, marriage, relationships, and all the tensions and troubles that were part and parcel of these aspects of daily life is engaged.

All these symbols and the language derived from them might have been utterly confusing had they not been organized within generally recognized and understood metaphors. A type of grammar or syntax made the body symbolism comprehensible and practical for the negotiation of daily life. Middle-period Mexicans derived their ideas about the body from a couple of sources. One of the most important was the notion that the body was an organizing principle for social relations. Different parts of the body were related to social positioning. This metaphor allowed Mexicans to easily understand the social relations that governed their lives but also imbued specific body parts with symbolic content. Gallant found that metaphors allowed Greek peasants to decipher and make sense of their world—in their case they used the metaphor of the household rather than the body.[14] A later discussion will show how the body became a very potent framework metaphor for power relations within the couple. In addition, the language of honor also helped to organize beliefs regarding different parts of the body. As a result, therefore, the head, which had the primary role in systems of honor, was also the most important center of honor for the body. It took on a central role within the grammar of violence.

Apart from the technique of close reading of documents, how can we approximate what this framework of symbols and violence was? Hurl-Eamon describes violence "as a sort of physical language."[15] Each act has to be considered as a part of the whole and as having some kind of symbolic content. This author recognizes patterns in eighteenth-century London violence that mimic the practices of judicial officials. For example, Londoners threw garbage in a parody of the custom of bombarding prisoners at the gallows with refuse.[16] Many other historians have detected this kind of trickle-down effect of the imitation of official practices by the lower classes. But the procedures of local officials were not the only source for the symbolic content of violence. The belief systems of both the Spanish and the Nahuas (in the case of central Mexico) were vital in shaping the way that people thought about their bodies as well as how they acted out when they were angry.

Apart from the practicalities of aggression, people tend to attack in ways that are governed by cultural norms. For example, in his studies of eighteenth-century Amsterdam, Spierenburg finds that Dutch knife fighters did not hit the head, whereas in France the head was a principal target for humiliation and attacks.[17] It is possible to read these patterns and connect them to the local culture. The methods that people used to humiliate were a type of inversion of the system of honor: what was considered most important in the belief system was the most likely place on the body to be hurt. It is possible to work backward to find the logic or the syntax of these violent acts. For example, as Farr explains, "If stripping a headdress was a ritual of degradation, a palpable allegation of moral impurity, then its inverse, publicly donning the article, could symbolize affirmation of honor."[18] People took cultural elements that affirmed honor and status and turned them upside down in order to debase another person—they inverted the grammar of honor in order to make it a language of humiliation. The mutual understanding between the aggressor and the victim made the ritualized altercation a more potent humiliation. It is only possible to read this language of violence within a context of knowledge about the symbolic content of the body.

Body Symbolism

Because of its capacity to take on so many assorted connotations, the body was an important political tool. As a result, there was often a top-down direction to the messages about the body. As Anthony Synnott writes: "The body is not a 'given,' but a social category with different meanings imposed and developed by every age, and by different sectors of the population. As such it is therefore sponge-like in its ability to absorb meanings, but also highly political."[19] Use of the body as a metaphor for political messages was an ancient practice dating back to as late as early antiquity.[20] In colonial Mexico the culture of the body was at least in part derived from religious teachings. Church and state worked very much hand-in-hand to develop and reinforce the kind of hierarchical message that was imposed upon the colony and its subjects. In most hierarchical societies, "both the body and the signs surrounding it were bound directly to status."[21] Both Hispanic and Nahua culture used the body as a way to express rank and privilege. Bodily attitudes as well as adornment such as jewelry and clothes denoted status in both traditions. Thus the body and its decoration served as a way to show one's place; it was also used as a way to represent the larger sociopolitical system. The body became a metaphor for social organization because it is from the body that our form of classification is derived. As Donald MacRae points out, our ideas are derived from the human body, an erect biped with a bilateral symmetry. Because of the human form, up and down, right and left are predominant aspects of our spatial organization, and these are transposed onto our conception of social organization and values. Therefore, "[W]hat is superior is up or high and what is inferior is down or low. (Low is often dirty, but high is not necessarily clean.) Right is law, morals, the holy and the strong; left is sinister, profane, weak, and (often) feminine. Backward and behind are slow, hence stupid. Forward and in front are active, oriented, and intelligent."[22] It is easy to see how the ideas that middle-period Mexicans had about their built environment were influenced or derived from the inferior-superior axis of the body. Because their houses and cities served as reinforcement for the messages about status and position, the bodily metaphors of middle-period Mexico were all the more strong.

In Western European culture the body was used as a metaphor for social order and thus hierarchy followed naturally out of this image. This representation had its roots in religious doctrine. According to Spanish moral writers, the body served as a trope for the structure of power and authority within the Catholic Church. Christ, they stated, was the head of the church and therefore the faithful had to obey and work for the church because they represented the limbs.[23] This representation was also used to justify the king's authority within the political sphere: he was the head of the body politic and thus his subjects owed him natural respect.[24] Human anatomy thus provided a model and a justification for the division of labor: "The sovereign head, the noble heart, the base gut, the labouring [sic] hands."[25] These different parts of society were interdependent just as it was for a human body.

Spanish moralists also used this metaphor to represent gender relations, particularly in marriage. The husband took the role of the head—here literally the head of the family—while the wife and other household members were the limbs, who owed submission and their work to the paterfamilias. Osuna wrote: "Women, subject yourselves to your husbands like to a lord because the husband is the head of the wife like Christ is in the Church." He states further that wives are like limbs in relation to the head.[26] Taking this metaphor further, Fray Alonso de Herrera wrote that in marriage, men and women became "one flesh" that could only be divided by death.[27] Osuna also used this image linking it to the biblical story of Adam and Eve: because Eve's body was formed from a piece of Adam's body, this became the model for the union of flesh in marriage. At the same time, Osuna reminded men, "your wife is a big piece of yourself: now you are not two but rather one flesh." As a result of the union of marriage, "just as you are obligated to maintain your own body you must maintain your wife, work for her, give her food and drink, as well as clothes, and all that you would normally provide to your body."[28]

The use of the bodily image was not just the theoretical musings of intellectuals, politicians, and religious leaders; it crept into the attitudes of average people and thus appears in the documentary record in rather fragmentary ways. The reciprocity that is implied in the bodily metaphor for marriage was accepted as the norm by middle-period Mexicans — the expectation was that men would provide and women would then subject themselves to husbandly authority.[29] The image and the logic behind it also stole into the arguments that husbands and wives presented to the judicial authorities. Pedro Domínguez, for example, reasoned that his wife's petition for an administrator to manage their Mexico City business while they were separated was frivolous because "in effect husband and wife are legally the one same person."[30] He hoped to stave off outside interference by using the bodily image of oneness — one flesh — in order to maintain control over the restaurant. It was a strong image and one that persisted in the minds of Mexicans well into the twentieth century. In the testimony of two women from the village of San Miguel Acuexcomac in the state of Puebla, the words of the moralists regarding body and marriage return almost verbatim. Doña Esperanza told anthropologist María Eugenia D'Aubeterre Buznego that "man is the head of the house, head of the woman, for this reason we have to obey the man, our husband, because they are like the head of the woman, the head of the house." Doña Lucía recounted: "Marriage is to make a life together. . . . [T]hey have to live in union, the two together, because they are made into one flesh."[31] Clearly the image of men and women's bodies being joined in marriage and made one as well as the implicit power structure that this bodily transformation entailed was a lasting and influential metaphor.

The Head

The use of the body to make more tangible the abstract relations of power of the state, the church, and marriages also gave the different parts of the body a particular significance. Because in all the images that described the seat of power being associated with the head, this area of the body took on more importance. Perhaps because the head was associated with kings both secular and godly, it became the core of honor for the body. In European culture, honor was centered in the head.[32] Nahua culture also imbued the head with particular import and symbolism: breath carried both emotions and moral value; faces reflected their character; and through signs, such as a nod, the head expressed emotions and communicated symbolically.[33] The idea of the head's inherent dignity continued on well into nineteenth-century Mexico.[34] In a legal commentary on the sentencing of a man convicted of murdering his wife, J. Mariano de Salas wrote that many elements of the crime merited a severe punishment. But he singled out the fact that the convict had wounded "a part of the body as noble as the head."[35]

As a result of these connections and beliefs, the corporeal attitudes of the head and actions surrounding it took on greater symbolic consequence. Bodily language reflected this notion in all sorts of manners. The way that individuals held their heads was indicative of their status and rank within society, but also of their honor. Men and women conveyed their respect for others by bowing their heads in the presence of persons of higher stature and their superiority by holding their heads high.[36] Escoiquiz goes into somewhat more detail about bodily attitudes; it is clear from his manual that individuals constantly had to gauge their relative inferiority or superiority in regards to whomever they encountered and adjust the way that they held their bodies.[37] In the middle period, writers advised young men of the upper classes to keep their heads straight, not bending forward or leaning to one side; rather, they were to keep their heads slightly bent although with a straight back.[38] Diez de Bonilla includes a guide to decode the head's messages: "A bent head means underhandedness; leaning to the left meant hypocrisy; moving unnecessarily represented a lack of moral fiber; too high along with a slow pace and grim stare meant arrogance and pride."[39] The emphasis on heads as the seat of honor was not solely a facet of European or, more particularly, Spanish thought. The ancient Nahuas also believed that the head had special qualities and was indicative of rank and privilege. According to López Austin, the "hierarchy of superiority was correlated to the most noble part of the human body, and by their faces the highest-ranking men were patently recognized."[40] Because both Spanish and Nahua cultures identified the head as the marker for rank and honor, it is not surprising that it played such a key role in the conception of the body in middle-period Mexico.

The head, therefore, was a particular locus for adornment that indicated the individual's status. The connection between adornment and hierarchy is most obvious at the higher levels of society. For example, a king, as Quentin Bell so eloquently expresses, could only act out his role in public with maximum finery, "and for that purpose could hardly wear too many jewels, too much fur or precious metals."[41] The Aztec rulers who preceded Spanish colonial rule also used embellishments to the head, such as jewelry, lip and ear plugs, and headdresses of rare and valuable feathers.[42] Both societies had traditions of sumptuary laws that limited plebeians from imitating or even, at times, acquiring the kinds of decoration that would allow the common folk to imitate or resemble their social superiors and thus demean and make worthless the bodily gestures that separated the social ranks.[43] It was both clothing and adornment that gave the bodies of monarchs or commoners a social meaning and identity; anthropologists have concluded that all human societies share this urge to embellish our bodies in all manners.[44] Other parts of the body will take on particular symbolism—for status, morality, eroticism—but the head remained the most important part of the body in terms of the representation of hierarchy. Thus, those things that covered the head were highly emblematic.

For the vast majority of people in middle-period Mexico, the kinds of decoration that they placed on their head could not have such associations with elevated rank. Hats, scarves, or veils are the most obvious adornments for the heads of people who were not part of the upper social ranks. Yet, within the documents, it is rare to find any reference to hats for plebeian women, and only rarely for men.[45] Men indicated deference to others of higher rank by doffing their hats, and manners guides instructed them to assess the relative rank of those they met knowing that they should always uncover their head to a person of superior rank.[46] Women did not have an equivalent except in the bodily attitude of their heads. Spanish moralists recommended the use of a veil as a head covering but this was related to morality rather than rank.[47] Casta paintings, which show racial designations for late eighteenth-century Mexico, often depict men with hats and women with some kind of head covering reminiscent of a scarf. The women loitering around a threshold in figure 9 have covered their hair with a shawl or serape, but the woman in the street has her head uncovered. Such choices do not seem to have been extraordinary for plebeian women. The clearly more

9. *Poblanas.* Carl Nebel, *Voyage pittoresque et archéologique dans la partie la plus intéressante du Mexique par C. Nebel, Architecte. 50 Planches Lithographiées avec texte explicatif,* Paris: Chez M. Moench, imprimé chez Paul Renouard, 1836. Lithography by Emile Lasalle, from a drawing by Carl Nebel. This scene shows women either covering their heads with their serapes or going bare-headed. Note that their hair is tightly pulled back. The two women in the center show the conduct described in chapter 3 of standing in the threshold.

elite women in figure 10 have covered their heads to be in the
street; their choice of covering—a mantilla or lace scarf—shows
a connection with Spain and also demonstrates their wealth.
These coverings, however, did not play a role in the kinds of
incidents that were recorded in the sample. The head was vital
to the kinds of minute calculations of relative rank that middle-
period Mexicans made on a daily basis. Perhaps because they
did not have such evident markers of status, plebeian Mexicans
had to use more subtle means to assert their social position,
such as their bodily attitude—particularly the way they held
their heads and their gaze. But before moving on to the ways
that Mexicans used body language both to communicate with
others and to act upon the bodies of others, one more aspect
of the head's embellishment needs to be addressed.

Hair

Although it may seem a mundane element of the human body
since generally everyone has it, historically hair has held an incredible hold over the imagination. It is a dominant symbol that
prevails in all cultures: it tells the world about both who you are
and to which group you belong; it is a deeply personal attribute
that is most commonly shown or not in public; it can be changed
in a myriad of ways but it is also governed by rules.[48] Hair can be
used to demonstrate public inclusion as well as social rank. But
it also has some mystical qualities to it, making it an even more
important bodily element. In many cultures people consider
hair to be liminal—it is both an integral part of the body yet
it sits outside the body.[49] Because of this strange inside-outside
state, some cultures believe that hair contains the essence of
the body from which it comes.[50] Body hair was attributed with
qualities that made it more powerful and mysterious than one
might imagine from a contemporary point of view. For example,
eighteenth-century Europeans believed that men's beards were

10. *La Mantilla.* Carl Nebel, *Voyage pittoresque et archéologique dans la partie la plus intéressante du Mexique par C. Nebel, Architecte. 50 Planches Lithographiées avec texte explicatif,* Paris: Chez M. Moench, imprimé chez Paul Renouard 1836. Lithography by Emile Lasalle, from a drawing by Carl Nebel. The elite women in the foreground have covered their hair with lace mantillas and are appropriately clad in black. Look to the back of the picture and note the poverty-stricken couple at the curb whose clothing is ragged. The woman has her hair loose and she provides a stark contrast from the women who are the main subject of the illustration. Above the poor couple, there is also a woman leaning out of the balcony on the second floor; she is clearly not well behaved and is not well covered either.

composed of "resorbed semen" and thus a full and bushy beard was a sign of masculinity.[51] Diez de Bonilla warned that proper women should not shave men, thus perhaps implying a sexual and therefore moral association.[52]

The ancient Nahuas also thought that hair had magical qualities. In their case, this idea was rooted in the fact that hair covered the head and thus protected and was infused by the *tonalli*—an animistic force located within the skull. As a result of the associations among the hair, the tonalli, and the head, hair was linked with honor for the Nahuas.[53] Because of its connection with protection of the tonalli, the Nahuas steered clear of washing or cutting hair, especially among individuals in dangerous or demanding work such as priests or long-distance merchants.[54] Perhaps because of its magical, symbolic attributes, hair also served to define people in many other ways.

One of the most basic ways that hair was a label of people was through the gendered ways that it was cut, dressed, or covered. Length was probably the most basic way the men's hair was differentiated from women's within European culture. Moral authorities considered longer hair a feminizing trait; the Spanish moralist Fray Thomas de Trujillo denounced men whose desire for fashion and beauty led them to allow their hair to grow longer. He stated that this style emasculated these men and asked, in a rhetorical fashion, "[H]ow many women would like to be a man like you and have your liberty?" He noted that men's shorter hair was a sign of their superiority over women and called men who indulged in these "effeminate" fashions "naked of honor and clothed with shamelessness."[55]

Among the ancient Nahuas, hair could denote gender as well, although it was not so much length as styling that separated men's from women's hair. Among the Aztecs, haircuts for young men symbolized the fact that they had captured a prisoner at war and were thus a full-fledged man. In addition, the elite soldier corps had particular hairstyles. Failure at war — and, it would seem, as a man — also was made tangible through hair. Those who did not make the grade in battle were punished by having their heads shaved.[56] Gender was not dependent on length of hair, clearly, but length was just one way to show the difference between masculine and feminine. However, it was important in both cultures to show gender, whether this was done by the length or the styling.

Beliefs surrounding hair and what it meant varied across societies. Because of the diverse cultures surrounding hair, its styling often also denoted ethnic difference, though in a colonial situation these differences were frequently interpreted as part of a relation of superiority-inferiority. On a more generalized scale, western Europeans contrasted what they perceived as their "controlled hair," which they deemed to be superior, to the "beardless" indigenous men of the Americas and the "unkempt" hairiness of the African.[57] It must not have been difficult for the conquering Spaniards to assume that beardless men (remember the connection between facial hair and semen) as well as those with long hair were effeminate and therefore inferior. Europeans believed that hair could be read; it was a clue to character, but more important, it could also indicate resistance.[58]

Beyond the relation between hairstyle and the colonial sense of superiority, hair continued to signify ethnic difference well into the colonial period. Both indigenous men and women persisted in wearing their hair in ways that were related to, but not identical to, pre-Hispanic hairstyles.[59] According to Osvaldo Pardo, by the seventeenth century most indigenous men had begun to wear their hair shorter, probably to accommodate the newer fashion of wearing hats.[60] Nevertheless one reference was found of a man who still sported the traditional *balcarrotas* hairstyle in 1790.[61] Men who used this fashion let their hair grow longer at the sides of their faces; in the colonial period the style seems to have become associated with the preservation of indigenous ethnic identity.

Hair also was intimately associated with morality, but this connection was strongest for women. In men, the moral overtones of hair mostly were breached when they flouted gender conventions. Both Hispanic and Nahua moral authorities believed that the way that women either dressed their hair or covered it showed their propriety and honesty. There were ways of adorning or styling hair that were associated with prostitutes, and others ways that society considered respectable. Within European culture, by the late medieval period it began to be considered immodest for women to show their hair — therefore hair coverings became more common, although the rule about hiding hair was often flouted in spirit by using jeweled nets and transparent veils.[62] Nevertheless, Spanish moral authorities reiterated that women with a claim to moral purity covered their heads when they left the enclosure of their houses, and more properly used a plain veil.[63] Moral authorities such as Astete and Trujillo also denounced the use of pearls, gold bangles, and the practice of curling that beautified the wearer but put the soul in danger not only because the woman sinned but also because she attracted men into sin as well.[64]

The Nahuas were less concerned with head coverings than the actual manner of hairstyle. Nahua prostitutes wore their hair loose, half-combed, or made horns in their locks.[65] Unruly hair seems to have been a physical indication that a woman had been adulterous, and more generally the Nahuas seem to have made disheveled hair into a metaphor for sexual misbehavior.[66] Hairstyling or covering helped to define a woman — it placed her within certain categories of women. Probably because of the predominance of indigenous women, the most commonly cited hairstyle in the sample was a braid or braids. This form of hairdressing seems to have been the norm for middle-period indigenous women, but apart from being an ethnic marker, it bears remembering that braids would have controlled loose and unkempt hair. Braids might be said to be the direct opposite of the prostitute's hair: rather than free and untidy they were tightly bound and very neat.

The moral overtones that were integral to hair also made it an ideal locus for punishment. Cutting off hair or shaving the head was a sentence used by Aztec judges for some miscreants. For example, individuals caught drunk apparently had their heads shaved publicly in the market.[67] Early in the colonial period, Spanish officials initiated the practice of combining head shaving with flogging as a standard penalty for those indigenous people who broke laws. Missionaries adopted the practice of head shaving as a consequence for those who infringed the newly imposed Christian rules, particularly rules of morality. The Spanish crown found this practice worrisome, however, because it was particularly insulting to the indigenous population, and therefore denounced it in a 1560 decree.[68] Throughout the colonial period, however, secular authorities continued to shave off indigenous men's heads when they broke the law.[69] Spanish royal officials also were concerned about another missionary practice — haircuts for indigenous men who converted to Catholicism — as this ritual, they believed, could scare off potential converts.[70]

Shaving the head or cutting hair has been a penalty for sexually transgressive women in many cultures. The idea of shaving the heads of women seems to have originated in the early modern period. Farr notes that this particular penalty began to replace flogging, banishment, or even hanging in France at around the mid-seventeenth century. Jurists incorporated the symbolism of the hair as impure and representing immorality into their thinking — thus shaving restored chastity, piety, and the hierarchical order.[71] This practice continued in colonial

Latin America.[72] Mexican women often acted as a group to
punish adulterous or sexually promiscuous women by cutting
off their braids. Some Mexican husbands, however, inverted the
logic of haircutting in response to female sexuality and instead
lopped off their wives' braids when these women denounced
their spouses for their adultery.[73]

The cutting of hair was fairly extreme. It was much more
common for colonial officials to pull a miscreant by the hair as
they were either subdued or taken into custody.[74] Pulling hair
was understood as a response to incivility. For example, when
Juan Velásquez was rude to a Mexico City official, the latter
retaliated by pulling Juan Veláquez's braid.[75] It was generally
accepted that officials had the right to pull hair in the line of
duty. An incident that occurred in Coatepec in 1771 confirms
this tolerance. When Salvador de Ayala pulled Juana de Dios's
hair, she complained. Witnesses who came to her defense cor-
roborated that although Salvador de Ayala had been a town
official at one time, he had not been reelected and thus had
no right to pull anyone's hair.[76] Yet, pulling hair was extremely
common. Undoubtedly it was a practical way to subdue another
person, but in addition, because of the symbolism that hair held
in Mexican culture as well as the judicial connotations of hair-
pulling, it was also a practice rife with moral overtones. To be on
the receiving end was supremely humiliating. Also pulling hair
was linked to the kinds of body language associated with honor.

Body Language
The symbolism of the head only functioned while it was held high.
In effect the head's impact as a signifier of status and honor was
dependent upon body position. According to a period etiquette
manual, men had to gauge the relative rank of those they met
and adjusted their bodily language with a deep, medium, or slight
bow when they approached them.[77] As a result, the language

of the body was integral to a person's presentation, but also the inverse: their humiliation. Escoiquiz did not hesitate in his advice to young men of this period regarding their posture. He wrote: "Whether you are standing, sitting, or walking you must always keep your body straight and above all, your head must be upright."[78] Advice to women was not as forthright, mostly because keeping their heads vertical meant looking directly in the eyes of those around them—an act that was socially unacceptable at all social ranks. Cerda warned women to lower their eyes and not look directly at other people.[79] Gender determined the straightness of the body and therefore the head's position, but the embarrassment that pulling the head down meant was equally felt by men and women.[80] Attacks in this period usually meant pulling the hair (and therefore the head) into a lower position. Such an action forced the opponent into a submissive position and also replicated the way that judicial officials subdued criminals.

Pulling hair and wrenching the head downward was considered justification for return violence because it was highly offensive.[81] The reason why pulling hair and bringing the head down was insulting is complex and interrelated with many factors. Pulling someone's hair causes pain, and that, on its own, might be an affront. But in middle-period Mexico, pulling hair in this way was part of a scenario of violence. It was an action used by officials when they subdued and arrested people. In a manner similar to the practice of husbands taking their wives to the monte, individuals replicated a script taken from observing others being arrested. Pulling hair made the victim into the submissive, dishonored person. It was a debasing act not just because it replicated the actions of officials and criminals but because it forced the head and the body into a bowed position. It was a forced deference. All these elements were intertwined and, of course, happened very quickly. The responses of aggressor and

victim were instinctive because they were following a scenario
that was familiar to them.

Middle-period Mexicans understood how to humiliate using
the head and hair but also how to maintain their dignity. The way
that men and women looked at each other was very much related
to the way they held their heads. Just as today's parents, in some
cultures at least, tell their children to avoid staring, the moral
authorities who governed civility said the same. In middle-period
Mexico, young men learned to discipline their eyes, neither moving them around nor looking fixedly and arrogantly at others.
An anonymous author stated, "[W]hen you talk to someone do
not fix your gaze on their face but keep it a bit lower especially
if the other person is of superior rank or a different sex."[82] The
sexual nature of staring was hinted at in a manual for priests
taking confession—the author advised these men to make sure
that the woman confessing sat to his right with her eyes lowered
and to avoid looking directly into her face.[83] Cerda repeated
over and over his stricture that women should lower their eyes,
that they should not look directly at men, that they should not
look around them nor look back at those who observed them,
and that widows should cover their eyes. Diez de Bonilla added
that men should not stare at women.[84] For women, the direct
stare was often associated with a sexual message that probably
transcends boundaries of time and culture. Stansell writes about
the "open searching gaze" of the prostitute in nineteenth-century
New York City.[85] The gaze is important—it was not just a way
to see and collect information but also a manner of signaling
interest, possibly sexual, to another person.[86] The Nahuas also
understood that staring could have a sexual connotation and
warned men that it was immoral to stare at a woman but also that
wives should avoid being the object of male gaze, again because
it had a sexual, immoral nature.[87] Spanish moralists echoed this
message. Moles states that "when a man looks at a woman with

lust he has already committed adultery in his soul." He believed
that the eyes were the soul's doors, a sentiment echoed by the
nineteenth-century moralist Diez de Bonilla, who wrote that the
eyes were the soul's mirror.[88] Trujillo, Galindo, and Astete made
women responsible for avoiding the male gaze by moderating
their clothing.[89] No doubt a lot of sexual longing went into the
looks that middle-period Mexican men and women gave each
other. But a direct stare, particularly between two people of the
same gender, also meant something that the moralists did not
capture: defiance and aggression. Women who looked intently at
each other often ended in blows. Their aggression was perhaps
not rooted in sexuality but rather arose because of the flouting
of conventions regarding body language.

The very ways that people moved their bodies when they
walked down the streets were prescribed by moral strictures.
Moral teachings imposed very restrained movements on both
sexes, but this emphasis on quiet, demure bodies was stronger
for women. Young men, according to Escoiquiz, "when walking, should not jump or run, go at a moderate pace without
lifting feet too high, nor stomping, nor dragging feet on the
ground."[90] Diez de Bonilla had similar advice for both young
men and women who showed their seriousness by the quality of
their walk—neither too fast nor too slow. He went as far as to
connect the walk's pace with the soul's condition.[91] According to
Doctor Don Juan Elías Gómez de Terán, it was possible to judge
a woman's morality by her walk: if her character was straight
and clean, her bodily movements at the walk would reflect her
moral character.[92] Moles was more direct and wrote that some
women walked in a dissolute manner.[93] In their counsels to young
women, this containment of movement was equated with morality. Cerda instructed women to "go in the street with a measured
pace and honesty."[94] Córdoba had more precise instructions. He
told women to avoid hand gestures, to walk without haste nor

slowly, and to avoid loitering, which indicates a lack of seriousness of character. Finally, he urged women to behave with modesty and careful gestures in all their actions and movements.[95] The ancient Nahuas had very similar recommendations for their young women. The antithesis of a good woman, in the view of the Nahuas, was a person who moved a lot, lifting up the earth and using her body voluptuously.[96] These messages were very much associated with sexuality—they were a means to prevent the transmission of erotic communication between the sexes. It was understood that when women went into the streets or the countryside, they were entering into a male space and therefore their bodies were sexualized. The type of body movement—not only in their walk but also their gaze—was designed to lessen the effect of this sexualization.

In addition to the reduced erotic charge of a contained and repressed walk, clothes also provided a kind of protection against the sexual nature of the street. Women's dress could act as a kind of barrier to stares—it was akin to taking the walls of the house with them. The psychologist John Carl Fluegel notes a parallelism between the house and clothes, writing, "Clothes, like the house, are protective."[97] Women chose to prevent the eroticization of their bodies by their body language and their fashion choices or they chose to emphasize their sexual charge. This notion of clothes as protection was not a particularly Mexican one—it is found in many cultures and across many different time periods. Clothes perform a dual and interrelated function: they serve as a shield against moral danger. In addition, dress itself had a moral function.[98] These two aspects of clothing were intertwined because in order to perform as a protective buffer the clothes had to conform to certain standards. What constitutes modest garb is very much determined by culture and community standards. Garments can come to be symbolic of character—they project out what the wearer wishes to communicate about their moral standards.[99] Dress is also "a symbol of social control as it controls the external body."[100] In middle-period Mexico (as in many other places), that meant that respectable women wore clothes that were designed to screen the wearer, to hide the figure, and to obscure the face.[101] Vives, in fact, recommended using a cloak that would cover all but one eye; Diez de Bonilla praised Lima's women known for never going out in public without covering everything but one eye.[102]

The Hidden Parts

Within the metaphor of the body in middle-period Mexico there was a large blank regarding the area from the waist to about the ankles—none of the philosophers or the moralists mentioned either the vagina or the penis when they constructed images of the body politic or marriage as a body. In the Mexican documents these organs are usually referred to indirectly with allegorical qualities. Vaginas were described in several ways: *partes pudendas* (genital parts), *parte natura* (nature's part), *partes inferiores* (lower parts), and, most frequently, *partes ocultas* (hidden parts).[103] But all of these names obscured rather than specified. In the same vein, the penis was usually simply referred to as *sus partes* (his parts).[104] These were areas that were unmentioned but yet everyone was very much aware of their presence; they were also slightly mysterious, especially the vagina.

There were, of course, associations between the vagina and morality, although these remained unsaid in the civility manuals and the morality treatises. Middle-period Mexicans, however, did make a connection between the vagina's size or capacity to receive a penis and the woman's, or more appropriately in this case, the girl's morality. When parents reported the rapes of young girls usually everyone accepted that the victim had not consented to sex and that she had been violated.

At times, however, this sympathy was overturned by the

accusation that the girl was not harmed sufficiently to consider that she was really sexually immature. The most egregious example of this link between size of vagina and morality occurred to a young rape victim called Luisa Francisca. Neither her mother nor the authorities in Taxco were certain of her age but she was still losing her baby teeth, so she was probably prepubescent. The *curador* (defender) of the accused asserted that because Luisa Francisca was a mulatta (race equaled lack of morality), her illegitimacy (a defect of birth and lack of good parental models) and her class (natural perversity of the plebeians) rendered her not deserving of consideration as a victim. Rather, he argued that she had not only consented to sexual relations but also used them to extract a promise of marriage. But the crowning proof of her perversity was that the midwives reported that "she was able to receive the Man [penis] without endangering her life and was only hurt in the way that all women are in their first carnal act." He connected all the social elements of race and status to her vagina size and argued that despite her age, she had a "natural perversity that was an incentive to sensuality and accelerated her natural development."[105] In another similar case, the defender, Pedro Montes de Oca, argued that the nine-year-old girl Juana had *malicia*—that is, that her sexual maturity was more advanced than her age. He claimed that her vagina was large enough to have sexual relations without terrible consequences.[106] Although these connections were neither formal legal principles nor were these ideas written down in the manuals published in the period, they did make their way into the thinking of middle-period Mexicans. They allow us to understand why people attacked the vagina or the penis in order to make a statement about an individual's morality.

Legs were another aspect of the body that were to be hidden, especially for women. Of course, legs have little or nothing to do with vaginas, but there is a connection both because they were concealed under skirts and because they had a similar sexual-moral association. At least one man admitted that his lust for a young girl was aroused by a fleeting glimpse of her legs.[107] When casting doubt upon Rafaela Gómez's morality the witness stated that she "lived with loose legs"—a clear indication that legs could be associated with moral principles.[108] Middle-period Mexicans also found it amusing—probably because it was humiliating—when women's legs were inadvertently seen by all. In Puebla, María Abila Ortega recounted how she told her husband about how a woman fell and her naguas came up. She and her mother had found this incident exceedingly amusing and they had laughed heartily.[109] A man also was in the habit of lifting naguas—exposing women's legs.[110] Legs were a private, sensual part of women's bodies, and so exposing them to view was not only a form of mockery and a violation but also a sexual statement. The exposure of body parts that were normally hidden and considered private was always a way to humiliate and punish. Shoemaker writes of similar reactions in England when "men and women had their private parts exposed or attacked, perhaps as a punishment for their sexual immorality."[111] Doña Josefa Monroy complained that her husband took her to the arches in front of the church of San Hipólito and hit her with a saber—he ordered her to lie down on the ground, and he lifted her skirts and hit her.[112] Her husband's actions were rather more dramatic than the usual scenario of domestic violence—it was showy and meant to attract the attention of neighbors and onlookers. But the crux of his actions was that he revealed his wife's "hidden parts"—her legs and buttocks—and exposed her shame. It was a calculated form of humiliation.

Clothes and Self
Spanish moralists had plenty to say on clothes. In fact, their tracts read almost as a how-to for sexy dressing. Women who

dressed in luxurious fabrics such as silk, brocade, or gold cloth, or in colors such as red or purple, could not, according to the moral authorities, claim purity of heart.[113] Astete and Galindo recommended wearing black clothes made of coarse fabric that demonstrated that the women who dressed this way did not want light conversations or visits. By their form of dress, the women who followed these prescriptions showed by their body's exterior what their interior or soul resembled.[114] The admonitions for restraint in female dress were part and parcel of an attempt to impose a kind of spirituality on women that contained and repressed all their passions. Apart from the appetite for fashion, moralists also advised restraint in eating and other pleasures such as sleeping, laughing, dancing, or going to the theater.[115] These writers saw women's bodies as the battleground between good and evil—in essence they were advocating using the body as "a location for the exercise of will over desire" and they hoped to recruit young women and their parents into the project of purity of soul "by subordinating the flesh."[116] The connection between self-control in all things of the body then filtered into the language of women and men. When women petitioned or complained, they referred to their recogimiento but also their behavior in regard to these rules. When men criticized their wives or other women, they pointed to their lack of control over the bodies—most often they accused the women of being drunks, which was the ultimate loss of control.

Despite the constant admonitions to cover up, Mexican women of the middle period adopted the most evil fashion of the time: the décolleté. Their plunging necklines that emphasized the bust—those "two soft cushions of carnality," in the words of Moles—were symbols of lechery and the cause of much sin.[117] In 1668 the Archbishop of Zaragoza, as well as several other bishops, threatened that no woman should enter a church with her chest, shoulders, or back uncovered or only slightly hidden by transparent clothes on pain of excommunication. In 1656 Pope Alexander VII, along with other prelates, exhorted his fellow clerics to condemn the use of décolleté in Italy.[118] In 1685 Pope Innocent XI ordered excommunication for women going in public without thick clothes and ordered confessors to not give absolution to those dressed with flimsy coverings.[119] The décolleté concerned Puebla archbishop Francisco Fabian y Fuero enough that in 1767 he issued an edict prohibiting its use in churches.[120] In 1808 the Mexican archbishop Lizana y Beaumont reiterated this condemnation.[121] Fashionable women tried to circumvent this ban by using lace scarves and gauzy material to cover their busts. But at times women got into trouble for their fashion choices. Don José Manuel García was incensed when a priest at the Cathedral scolded his wife for her form of dressing—a décolleté—and threatened to expel her from the sanctuary.[122] While it was sinful to uncover body parts, it was also immoral to add volume or height, to paint, to pierce, or to in any other way alter the body and to overdo the wearing of jewelry.[123] The ecclesiastical calls for modesty were grounded in a long tradition which, although it called for covering the human body to control lust, wished to avoid the resurgence of this passion through the very covering of the body.

Fashions preoccupied people so much—because they were so intimately associated with the body—that they exemplified identity more than any other bodily element. Individuals chose how to present themselves to the world, but at times states have also tried to control identity through clothes, notably with sumptuary laws that aimed to preserve the divisions between classes but also to promote morality and frugality.[124] Moralists insisted that women and men should wear clothes appropriate to their station in life: middle-class women should not dress sumptuously nor should aristocrats dress down.[125] For Mexicans, the eighteenth century was marked by an anxiety to categorize racial difference. These categories often implied the choice of clothing as an essential racial-ethnic quality, but race was also associated with character attributes and defects. The famous casta paintings epitomize this trend. In each individual scene, couples and their offspring show the results of racial mixing. The clothes worn by a Spaniard are totally different from those worn by an Indio or a Mulato, for example, but in addition, and more important, the clothes as well as the setting give an indication as to professions and economic standing. In certain paintings the actions of those portrayed, fighting or falling down drunk, provide the viewer with information that associates race and dress with morality and conduct.[126] The individuals portrayed lack self-control, which places them on the periphery of social respectability; but even without the message of conduct, "nudity" in these paintings has the same effect. The paintings' message is that race equals morality and honor but an adjunct of this message is that clothes do define the person.

On a day-to-day basis this connection between dress and social identity meant that people reacted to one another based on their external appearance, and much of this judgment was based on attire. The kinds of calculations as to body language mentioned earlier were only possible when people dressed according to their rank. But, to take this logic further, people reacted to each other based on their assessments of morality—and this evaluation was also true for their moral appearance.[127] The external shell that women presented to the world was vital; it probably determined how they were treated in life and after death. This link between clothes and morality helped excuse José Silverio Moctesuma after he killed his lover, Ana Gertrudis Cardoso. Instead of concentrating on his act, the judges inquired about her character, which was subsumed by her unfortunate fashion choices. One witness stated that "the said Ana Gertrudis Cardoso had a boisterous and unruly nature; she was known publicly for her exterior conduct and her provocative dress." The defense attorney for José Silverio Moctesuma explained away his client's conduct by referring to the victim's conduct, notably "the stimulus of a provocative woman who, with the liberty she enjoyed and her scandalous dress, invited the unsuspecting youth to unleash the animal passions which dominate men."[128] The connection between appearance and morality that Mexicans of the middle period made was not always so explicit but was below the surface of many conflicts. At times, however, witnesses were unambiguous in their judgments. When describing the scandalous boy Diego Fernández to the authorities, licenciado don Albaro Josef de Osio y Ocampo noted that he was illegitimate and originally from Guatemala, but most of all his clothes were those of "a mongrel hanging around the Plaza."[129]

Women were perhaps more conscious of the need to present themselves as moral through their appearance. Doña María Guadalupe de Castro, despite complaining that a soldier had seduced and deserted her, emphasized in her petition for reparations that she lived according to Christian rules and "subjected herself in her dress and food to her spiritual director's maxims."[130] From a male point of view, Ramón Huertas argued that when he saw a young woman out at night in the plaza with only a girl servant accompanying her, he assumed that she was a woman of the world—in other words, she was at the very least dissolute and perhaps even a prostitute.[131] Mexicans made assumptions about the people that they met based on the way they dressed, but they also chose to present themselves to the world through their fashion statements.

Because as a species humans choose to wear clothes, dress forms a kind of skin or margin for the body: clothes are a boundary, but one that can outline, emphasize, hide, or extend the body.[132] Choice of fashion becomes a way for people to mediate their way through social situations, but it also becomes highly symbolic of the self.[133] It was for this reason that Mexican officials who appeared in the processions so richly analyzed by Curcio-Nagy chose to list magnificent materials and garments to be worn—their attire was symbolic of their power and stature.[134] Therefore, just as form of dress indicates a person's interior as well as rank, ethnicity, and sometimes profession, an attack on clothes was almost synonymous with an assault on the body. Clothes are "an extension of the bodily self."[135]

Because clothes can lend a person more dignity than he or she otherwise possesses and also "add importance to the body of the wearer," an attack on them does the inverse.[136] One anonymous moralist counseled young men that it was rude to pull on the clothes of another person.[137] Because clothes were so intimately associated with the body, pulling a dress or jacket was an invasion of personal space, and ripping it or removing it was symbolic of bodily assaults. Taylor lists several such incidents that were considered highly insulting in golden age Castile, including removing another man's hat, touching another man's cape, or spilling water on a woman's skirt.[138] When Mexicans attacked each other, they often also tore at shawls, shirts, and other items. Their actions were not only practical—these things were at hand—but also symbolic. The assault on clothes was an extension of a strike against an individual—it hit people hard since clothes were of great value for middle-period Mexicans, but essentially it allowed the aggressor to strike at the person without causing the kind of bodily harm that would carry with it serious repercussions. In addition, pulling clothes was somewhat similar to pulling hair since the action dragged the body out of line, displacing the posture that indicated morality and hierarchy.

Conclusion
The patterns that violence followed lead to a perception of the outlines of a grammar not only of violent acts but also of the body. This syntax intersects with the codes of honor that prevailed in

middle-period Mexico and situated a framework within which Mexicans operated, guiding daily decisions regarding body language and behavior. It is by connecting the symbolic culture of the body to the metaphors that governed social relations that it is possible to uncover the way that Mexicans understood the body and why they followed certain scenarios when they erupted into violence. In a sense it is a circular logic: violence shows us the points of importance in the body, but these were the locus of attacks because they were important.

From the central metaphor of the body—with the head as core—the messages imparted by the body become more complex, with coverings, alterations, and movements all conveying their own series of implications. The symbolic apparatus that revolved around the head, that is, hair, but also body coverings and movements, was put into operation every day by Mexicans of the middle period. Men and women had to make multiple microdecisions regarding their deportment, their bodily attitudes, and their choices of clothes. Many of these decisions were probably unconscious—the product of social conditioning and the prevailing culture. But other choices became more salient when people reacted to them. Body language, like the ideas governing honor, did not work in a social vacuum, but rather had to be confirmed and reinforced by audiences. The language of body and honor was part of a conversation, a dance of messages that most middle-period Mexicans must have navigated relatively effortlessly. It is the breakdowns in this system that come to attention and allow an understanding of its workings with an inverse logic.

6. The Head, Honor, and Aggression

How many people in middle-period Mexico read civility manuals? The simple answer is that it is not possible to know, but certainly the vast majority of the population was neither literate nor had access to books. So how did they become familiar with the rules governing politeness, and, more important, all the tenets governing the body? There is an intangible way that a common language of body symbolism developed in Mexico, as in other places and times described by historians. The theorists of the body have not been able to determine how exactly the ideas surrounding the body (or other matters) filtered down into a more generalized culture, but historians have detected this process in many instances. The language of symbolism was not something that was taught formally, except perhaps at the very highest levels of society, but it became universal because the plebeians were not isolated from the elites. They learned from the body language of their peers and were educated by example when judicial authorities acted upon their bodies. Lower-class men and women noted that those in the highest ranks used their heads to indicate their rank, for example, but also that they imposed a lowering of the head upon those that they considered inferior. In this manner a commonly understood vocabulary and grammar of the body was established without being written down through the daily interactions and the acts of violence that cemented it into the culture.

The bodily metaphors that prevailed in Mexican culture can be detected not just in the literature surrounding civility and morality but also within people's actions. There was an intersection between symbolism and clashes that can be seen in patterns of violence. Some of these patterns seem mundane (husbands attacked wives); others might seem more exotic (groups of women patrolling female sexuality) but they were really not so extraordinary. Mexicans of the middle period recognized and understood these patterns—they knew how to behave, regardless of whether they were participants or spectators. The scenarios of violence were part and parcel of their culture. Even elite members of society were aware of these frameworks, although they believed themselves above such violence. There was an unwritten code that people learned by living rather than by reading a manual, but it was not less real when fighting words were uttered, stones were raised, or knives were unsheathed, and a crowd gathered to see the action. Middle-period Mexicans assaulted particular places in another's body because of the symbolism associated with that distinct part, and as such they created a grammar of violence that associated blows with messages. Scenarios of violence that encompass hitting different parts of the body, in particular the head (and its constituent parts: the face, eyes, mouth) and genital areas must be understood. What ties all these various forms of hitting together, however, is that all the blows were designed to restore honor and dignity.

The Head
Because of the centrality of the head in the symbolic language of Mexico, a very large portion of the reported aggressions were

aimed at this part of the body. Thus heads dominate much of
the criminal documents and consequently play a starring role
in the scenarios of violence. Heads are actually constituted of
different parts, each with its own symbolism. Although the head
as a whole was the central symbol of honor, faces, mouths, eyes,
and hair all had their own separate symbolic capital. Because
the different sections of the head meant something distinctive
in the culture, the scenarios of violence that played out with respect to each area was different and often implied particular
weapons. For example, it was common to use sticks or stones to
hit the head in general, but if aiming at the face, most people
used a knife. The reasons for trying to cut a face were not the
same as those for hitting the head. At the same time, the eyes
and the mouth were not so much an objective as weapons of aggression. Thus the head was a complex area with many different target areas and scenarios of violence.

The starting point is an examination of generalized aggression
against the head. Because of the choices made in selecting documents for this study, and because only violence in which wom-
en were involved (either as victim or aggressor) was included,
the sample is skewed to certain patterns. Therefore, the vast majority of attacks on the head were between husbands and wives.
This is not to say that such aggressions could not take place between a man and his mistress, or between two women, or even
between two men. Rather, it is just that this pattern is reflected in the sample. There were also situations in which a man attacked his mistress according to the pattern most common for
husbands, but a careful examination of the circumstances usually reveals that these two had been living as man and wife for
a while. In our society, this relationship is called a common-
law marriage, but such a category did not exist in middle-period Mexico; here it is called a quasi-marriage. The people surrounding such couples recognized the validity of the connection,

sometimes calling it living in *estado.* Judges also acknowledged that if a man supported a woman he began to have equivalent rights to a husband even without a formal or legal marriage.

Middle-period Mexicans had no trouble recognizing the scenario for violence between spouses. They did not always elaborate it in their testimony, undoubtedly because they believed it was self-evident. But looking at the evidence, it is clear that spouses picked up what was at hand and hit the head. The weapon of choice in this scenario was commonly a stick or a stone of some sort. These were things that were at hand—most Mexican streets apparently had many loose rocks just waiting to be used as projectiles or to bludgeon.[1] At times, however, the rocks were more specialized, particularly when the attack occurred in the home or kitchen, where men picked up stone implements used normally for grinding corn. It would seem rather casual and certainly unscripted—a man or a woman simply picks up whatever is at hand because of uncontrollable anger.

Could this pattern be ascribed simply to serendipity and common sense? Perhaps so, if it were not for some witnesses who revealed how much this scenario was a pattern—a way to deal with certain situations that was expected and scripted. In Izúcar, María Crecencia, whose husband beat her head with a rock, reveals that picking up a stone was not a casual event but rather an action that conveyed a particular message and set into motion a scenario of violence. When she got up early to cook, her husband was irritable and they began to fight. She picked up a rock. Later she testified that she did not pick up the rock to hit him but clearly she understood that her action was a provocation. Why? Because she had engaged in the scenario of violence that they both understood and she aggravated the situation. Mexicans, like the golden age Spaniards described by Taylor, recognized the body language of violence—in Castile, when a man reached for his sword, put his hand to his side, or took off his cape, it was an act equivalent to lifting a rock.[2] Her husband then picked up a stick and hit her on the head and arms. The judicial authorities understood his reaction, writing: "María Crecencia provoked her husband's anger by lifting a rock."[3] What is particularly interesting about María Crecencia's words is that she recognized the mistake she made in lifting the rock; she did not attempt to explain away what her action meant but rather tried to make it seem like a misunderstanding. Yet, what else was her husband to understand? They were fighting, exchanging heated words, and then she picked up a rock. Clearly, in his eyes, she defied his authority and went from words to actions.

Spectators also recognized the scenario of lifting a rock. Bernardina Gerónima, who ran a pulquería in Actopan, recounted an incident that demonstrates how Mexicans were familiar with the significance of certain acts. She told officials that Bernardino Oropesa came into her pulquería one day and, having bought some pulque, was passing the time. His wife entered the establishment and he said to her, "What are you doing here? Do you have to come in because I am here?" His wife answered that she had come in to beg for a tortilla because she was dying of hunger. Her words must have been humiliating because she was in effect telling the assembled drinkers that he was not supporting his family and that he was an ineffectual head of household who did not provide for his wife. Bernardino responded by picking up a stone. But the spectators, knowing the sequel, grabbed him and prevented him from hitting his wife. She escaped a blow to the head on that occasion but he killed her later.[4] Kathryn Sloan also finds that witnesses recognized the import of picking up a rock and intervened when one party to a fight did so.[5]

This scenario, like so many others (such as taking a wife to the monte), was rooted in the kinds of experiences and sights that middle-period Mexicans witnessed in their practices of daily life. Most especially they mimicked the kinds of actions that officials took in order to restore the peace but also to affirm their authority. Since the kind of scenario examined here was centered on power and status, it is not surprising to find its model within the actions of officials. This tug-of-war between various levels of authority was an archetype for the scenario between husband and wife. The model is shown in the conflict between Phelipa Ramona, an India cacique and principal, with the *alguacil mayor* (constable) in Tlalmanalco, don José Piña. The alguacil mayor passed by Phelipa Ramona's house one day and told her to cut some branches from one of her trees. Phelipa Ramona did not jump up to obey but simply stated that she would get her sons to cut the tree later. Don José Piña got mad and used his staff of office to hit her in the head so hard that the blow loosened some of her teeth.[6] In this instance the official used what was at hand but the object happened to have official connotations—it was the very symbol of his office and his authority. Yet, the rest of the scenario is remarkably similar, since he attacked Phelipa Ramona's head in order to reassert his power and status.

The Head and Power Relations

The scenario that led husbands to hit their wives' heads was rooted in defiance of the directionality of deference. Returning for a moment to the bodily metaphor that was the foundation of marriage—the husband was the head and thus was to be obeyed, and the wife represented the limbs that had to submit to and work for the head—it is possible to see how wives' rebellion upset the balance of the marriage and the direction in which submission and deference were supposed to flow. When wives talked back, refusing to accept their spouse's authority, they engaged in a power struggle that challenged the man's authority and, essentially, his headship. These were domestic fights that went beyond the customary spats and expanded into hurtful words and actions that could not be ignored. When in Puebla, María Pascuala and her husband, Abram Hugarte, for instance, were angry with each other one day, the disagreement escalated when María Pascuala answered back badly—in what he described as "indecent terms." Undoubtedly, she used some of the rich language of insult that Mexicans had developed. When provoked, wives often called their husbands cuckolds (*cornudo* or *cabrón*), insulting them to the core of their masculinity. In this case Abram Hugarte could not consent to his wife's conduct because to do so would be to acquiesce to a loss of stature in the marriage. He picked up a *tepalcate* (a piece from a pot) and hit her in the head.[7]

Some women were explicit about the power relations but also the expectations set up because of the bodily metaphor of marriage. Puebla wife Ana Ortega, when challenged by her husband to be obedient, answered back "that it would be better if he maintained her." Her husband had criticized her choice of items to pawn—a strategy that most poor Mexicans used to survive—and she turned this around to indicate that husbands were supposed to support wives before asking for submission. Ana Ortega extended her rebellion by refusing to prepare food for her spouse, and then when he returned home at about 9:00 p.m. she began to insult him, calling him a *chivato* (a stool pigeon). Pedro Vásquez had had enough, and he picked up a spindle—an item that would have been lying around, since he was a weaver by trade—and hit her in the head, behind the ear.[8] In Tehuacán, Mariana Lucas refused to prepare a meal for her husband, José Ventura Camacho, apparently because he had prevented her from continuing an affair with Antonio Leon. She countered that she was not unfaithful but simply could not cook if her husband did not support the household financially.

He picked up a stick and hit her head.[9] By hitting their wives in the head, Abram Hugarte, Pedro Vásquez, and José Ventura Camacho were reasserting their right to the role of head of the household. They were also attacking the body's most noble part and thus knocking down their wives' honor a peg and re-claiming their own rightful place as head.

These were not premeditated actions but ones that sprung out of anger and frustration. They followed a pattern but were not long and drawn out, like a duel, for example. It is clear from the choices of weapons that the men grabbed what was at hand—in two cases simply using the ground to bludgeon their wives' heads, perhaps because of the unavailability of objects. The use of ac-tual weapons was rare—limited to four cases—and perhaps somewhat class related. In both cases in which husbands used swords to hit their wives, the men used the honorific "don."[10] Many men picked up the tools of their trade (spindle, measur-ing stick, machetes, or pincers), but also those of their wives' kitchen (such as the stone used to grind corn, the metlapil). But sticks and stones were still the most frequent objects that men used. Most men seem to have carried knives despite numerous prohibitions against the practice, so it was not for lack of a more effective weapon that husbands chose what was at hand. The choice of these objects was meant to make these attacks non-lethal. Hitting the women in the head was a way to reassert au-thority without killing or marking them, but because skulls are delicate, the women sometimes died as a result of their wounds. The scenario of hitting a wife's head was designed to remind the woman that she was not the head of the household and that she was supposed to defer to the paterfamilias.

There were men who did not follow this strategy, although according to the documentary record they were a minority. It is very probable that quite a few Mexican men accepted rebel-lious behavior on their wives' part simply to keep the peace. In addition, many wives simply left the marital home and tried their luck elsewhere if their situation was too harsh.[11] But there were some women who stayed in the marriage but refused to accept their husband's authority, although most still framed their mutiny within the framework of accepted ideas regarding marriage. Twenty-five petitions for ecclesiastical divorce were found in which the supplicant was a man—women filed the vast majority of these requests. Of these twenty-five, six husbands presented as grounds for separation that their wives had ceased to perform their wifely duties; essentially they had rebelled against the marriage and the husband's authority. These men were extraordinary for the period because they chose to complain to the Church rather than simply use what was considered to be their right to discipline their wives with violence. Spanish moralists were clear on this topic: men had the right "to correct and punish" their wives, whereas women did not have the corresponding right to strike their husbands except, perhaps, in self-defense.[12] The idea that women owed their husbands respect was pervasive and often used as a rationale for male violence. In the words of a defense counsel, don Miguel de Vaena, these rights became a type of *fueros*—the equivalent of a special jurisdiction.[13] In Mexico City, don Augustín Mesa complained that his wife had hit him in the head; he added as an explanation that she was a libertine.[14] These men protested that their spouses absented themselves and therefore the women did not look after the house, including cooking and maintenance of clothes. The men, therefore, had to pay to eat and even hire someone to wash and mend their clothes.[15] Mexico City resident María Josefa Martínez would not even prepare her husband a cup of chocolate and asked him to pay her for the kinds of services usually performed by wives.[16] There was a kind of equation at work based on the bodily metaphor of marriage—men who provided for their wives expected in return both obedience and the kinds of duties that women usually carried out in the household. What some Mexican women expressed at times was that this equation was not one-sided; in fact, if the man wanted submission and work he had to supply the money to support the household. Many wives complained about their husbands' fecklessness and the general lack of food and clothing for the family, but Ixtacalco resident doña Luisa Ayala went one step further. She used the equation of support equals obedience to justify her resistance by stating, "What is the authority of a husband who does not maintain his wife? Where there is no food there is no obedience."[17] Another woman, Leonarda Galindo, who lived in San Juan de los Llanos, stated that "any man who does not discharge his marital obligations should not have a wife."[18]

These vignettes provide a glimpse of the reasons why Mexican husbands often felt that they needed to reassert their authority. It is clear from the complaints emerging from ecclesiastical divorce and mistreatment petitions that the reciprocal duties set out by the bodily metaphor of marriage did not always work. Wives often declined to submit to the head of their household but generally it was because their husband did not provide for the family—essentially he did not act like a head.

Of course, successful peaceful couples rarely entered into the documentary record to celebrate their wonderful life together, but nevertheless the records provide a hint that most Mexicans accepted their mutual duties. Calimaya resident Leonardo Rafael stated of his wife, "I give her all that is expected in food and clothing, without failing my obligation." Juan Antonio de Zepeda echoed this sentiment in Mexico City by stating, "As a decent man I sought to provide and assist her with all that I have been able to acquire from my own work."[19] The tension provoked by the failure of the arrangement can be seen in the confrontation between Juana Pérez and her husband in Puebla. She was out in the street collecting money when she met her husband, who proceeded to grab her head and hit it on the side-walk—perhaps because there was no rock available. A few days later the authorities brought them together in a *careo* (a face-to-face confrontation), and while her husband accused Juana of being drunk, she countered by saying that he did not assist with the household finances.[20] It is always possible that Juana was tipsy, but it is more likely that the husband did not want to be reminded of his failure as a provider and thus reasserted his authority by degrading hers.

Authority and the Head

Women expected their husbands to provide a daily sum of money in order to support the household. This money was various-ly called the *diario, los alimentos,* or sometimes *lo preciso,* and the actual sum was usually two *reales* a day. In the idyllic view of marriage, men earned and women ran the household, but just as with the idealized spatial restrictions placed on women, this portrait of the model couple was not always the reality. In fact, many Mexican husbands did not earn very much at all and often spent much of their salaries on alcoholic beverages, gambling, or other women. In addition, apart from the work of running a household (which was considerable), many Mexican women earned money on their own—either within the domestic en-closure or sometimes outside of it. The occupations mentioned in the documents vary, but the list includes weaving; making cheese; running errands; cleaning; working in the cigar factory; doing laundry; employment as a *molendera* (preparing tortillas), an *atolera* (making a corn-based drink called atole), a servant, or a caretaker; selling; running a stall at the market; darning stockings; and running a school for girls.[21] Just as in the case of tensions over wives leaving the house, the mutual obligations and roles assigned to men and women diverged from the ideal and thus caused strains within many marriages.

Women challenged the authority of their spouses or simply
the men who set themselves up as their spouses in various ways.
Although Izúcar resident Rita de la Trinidad Romero was trying to break off relations with Genevevo Robledo, he insisted
that he wanted to marry her. He had actually gone as far as going to the neighboring city of Morelos to start the paperwork in
order to proceed with the wedding. But she changed her mind
because of his drinking. When he tried to reassert the relationship, she responded with insults, calling him a cabrón and telling him "to go and see his whores" and other offensive statements. She challenged his putative authority, and even though
he was not officially her husband, he had been in a relationship with her—something that Mexicans recognized as authority over a woman—and thus he picked up a stick and hit her
head.[22] There was a similar understanding between Francisca
and Manuel Valencia, who had been living together in Puebla
as if married. In fact, Manuel described Francisca as his wife.
They both accused the other of being drunk and apparently
they were mildly irritated with each other, but when Francisca
spoke in a way that Manuel Valencia found insolent, he picked
up a piece of wood and hit her in the head.[23] When wives or
quasi-wives addressed their spouse with words that were defi-
ant or rude, many men lashed out. In Actopan, Juan Nepumu-
ceno Oropesa killed his wife by hitting her in the head just because she had been cheeky.[24] In all these instances it was not so
much the women's actions that provoked violence, but rather
their words—perhaps their aggressive talk was similar in nature to what Taylor called "fighting words." They used words that
their spouses could not ignore because they contested their authority. By articulating a lack of respect for the household head,
these women goaded their partners' insecurities and challenged
their role as paterfamilias.

Some challenges were slightly more tangible, such as when

mothers disagreed with their husbands' decisions regarding their children. By law a father had final authority over their offspring; within the bodily model children also were supposed to obey their father particularly. Yet, this respect was not always apparent or even supported and endorsed by mothers. When, in the Mexico City neighborhood of San Pedro Siguatiocaltitlan, José Thomas Mendoza came home one day and decided to chastise his daughter, his wife disagreed and objected to the punishment. Husband and wife then engaged in a fight that escalated when she hit him in the head with a stone; he countered with a much more deadly assault on her head from which she died.[25] In Actopan, Bernardino Antonio just wanted a bit of peace when he went home, but instead he found a household of crying children. Unlike José Thomas Mendoza, he did not want to deal with this situation and asked his wife to calm the children. She paid no attention to him, which infuriated him. Her inaction was a kind of passive resistance, but her attitude — like that of the previous example — was one that dismissed his patriarchal authority. He reasserted his power by hitting her in the head with a piece of mesquite.[26] When Puebla resident María de Jesús Castillo told José María Ortega that he had acted unjustly when he hit their son for taking too long on an errand, he hit her head with a rock.[27]

These men were acting in ways that were fundamental to the reassertion of their authority. Others followed this scenario when other kinds of rights or powers were challenged. When María Hernández's aunts scolded her, she got mad because she was not young and she was a married woman. They were challenging her new status; in order to reaffirm her standing, she hit one aunt in the head with a rock. On the other hand, the aunts declared their status — they had reproached her "like a parent to a child."[28] More common, however, were wives who attacked women they believed to be involved in sexual relationships with their husbands. Apart from the issue of marital infidelity, such affairs were a threat because men diverted funds to the other woman, sometimes even supporting two families. Wives, then, attacked the heads of mistresses in mimicry of the kinds of violence perpetrated on them by their husbands. Antonia Josefa, for example, found Juana Ramona drinking in a pulquería. She accused her of *mala amistad* (illicit relationship) with Antonia Josefa's husband. Despite the insults and jibes directed at her, Juana tried to humor Antonia. But the wife was not dissuaded and she picked up a rock and hit her in the head.[29] Other women followed this scenario, trying to fend off challenges to their position but also to preserve the integrity of their household.[30] There are other cases in which it seems that one woman attacked another for no reason at all. Yet the scenarios appear almost identical so it appears the logic was the same but unstated.[31]

The Face
While the head, as a whole, had connotations of nobility, the face was its most expressive part, providing multiple ways of communicating using the eyes, the mouth, and various facial expressions. The face was also associated with sexuality, thus moralists warned women to lower their eyes and look away if not able to cover their faces. A person's countenance was the object of complex meanings and, as a result, multifaceted scenarios of violence. The slap to the face was clearly an act that demeaned and it may have been borrowed from the kinds of actions that the local elites used in order to restore the hierarchy. This rationale is apparent in the actions of the governor of Naucalpan who, when confronted with words and demands he felt objectionable, hit doña Petra Cortes in the face, "insulting her honor."[32] There were two main scenarios that involved the face. First, people engaged in a fight or humiliated by hitting the face either with a hand or an object. This formula was

probably more straightforward and crosses many cultural boundaries. The second scenario involved cutting the face, often with the goal of marking or scarring it. This scenario is not as common but is certainly found — for different rationales — among histories of men in Uruguay, Holland, Spain, Greece, and Virginia in the United States. Gallant and Spierenberg write about knife fighters whose aim was not always to kill but rather to cut an opponent's face, a goal which, once achieved, ended combat.[33] Elliott Gorn recounts how Virginia men grew out their thumbnails in order to gouge out the eyes of their adversaries, thus marking them as vanquished.[34] These authors, however, write mostly about men. The scenario changes somewhat with the inclusion of women. In middle-period Mexico the cutting of women's faces had profound sexual overtones.

Assaulting the face, in particular with a slap, is an action that historically has been associated with the duel.[35] As a prelude to such a fight, assaulting the face was a symbolically charged act that had to be answered in order to preserve honor and masculinity. But what did such an act mean when performed by a woman on a man or by a man on a woman? Without a larger group of incidents of this type, it is hard to draw many conclusions, but apparently slaps were an insult that led to more ferocious violence. They might have been the gestural equivalent of fighting words; they were also a way of impugning the honor of another person. In the village of Tenancingo, Fernando Juan attended a fandango in a neighboring house. He was sitting on a bench by himself and enjoying some pulque when Augustina María, a woman who does not seem to have had any formal relationship to him, came up and asked for a coin. He refused, but she did not accept his answer. She was very drunk and began to abuse him verbally. Then she reached out and tried to slap him in the face. Fernando Juan did not hesitate — he punched her so hard that she fell down and died as a result of this blow.[36] In this instance, Fernando Juan did not have any authority over Augustina María that could lead to a reassertion of authority among married or quasi-married couples. Yet, her verbal abuse and the attempted slap were serious enough for him to react strongly.

Apart from a provocation, the slap could also be a prelude. In Cuernavaca, when Francisco Doroteo came home and saw his amasia give some food to another man, his jealousy was inflamed. When confronted, she tried to explain away her actions but he was not convinced. First he slapped her face, and then he stabbed her to death.[37] This incident allows us to make a connection between jealousy and the slap to the face, which seems to mirror the affront caused by the jealousy-inspired conduct. Envy was also at the root of doña Rosa de Figueroa's behavior. She thought that don Josef Delgado should have married her, but he chose another woman. When he first appeared in the street with his new bride, doña Rosa de Figueroa came up to him and demanded to know who this woman was. Then she slapped him in the face.[38]

In two of the three examples, an underlying theme of the slap was jealousy. But in all three the slap was a prelude for more action, either in the form of more deadly violence or, in the case of don Josef Delgado, going to judicial officials. When Manuela Suáres confronted Manuela Chica on a Puebla street over an unpaid debt, Manuela Suáres hit the other Manuela in the face for not paying up.[39] In this instance the slap to the face might have simply been the result of frustration over this money. But within the plebeian classes, credit and honor were very much bound together, so the slap could also have been a way of signifying the loss of reputation of a person who refused to honor her debts. All of these cases have some relation to a perceived lack of honorable or proper conduct.

The preceding examples all involved people who knew each other on some level. But more audacious were instances when women attacked an official's face. While these women might have known the identity of the officials in question, the relationship was much more distant: they were separated by rank. Yet, at times, women did attack such men. When Joseph González was collecting fees from the local market in Tacubaya, he ran into some trouble when an indigenous woman refused to pay. The incident turned into a mini riot and is rife with symbolic violence, but here it should be stressed that one woman took a piece of wood (perhaps mimicking his staff of office) and hit him in the face. He stated that not only was his face injured, but as a result, his honor was also damaged.[40]

Women fought back against officials who they believed were infringing their rights or who were going too far in their imposition of hierarchy. They used the messages conveyed by symbolic violence to make their point and to exact some revenge. In Tenango del Valle, a woman simply called María retaliated against a *ministro de vara* when he took an indigenous man prisoner. She insulted him and then grabbed his handkerchief and threw it in his face.[41] While her action might seem ineffectual and certainly not aggressive by today's standards, it was an action full of symbolism. In this period, handkerchiefs were not only an article associated with the upper classes but also they were a badge of politeness. Only individuals of some wealth could afford to buy handkerchiefs and have them laundered; their use showed that they did not just blow their snot onto the ground or floor.[42] Thus, by throwing his handkerchief into his face, María had taken something of value and used it to show her contempt for his class and its pretensions to politeness.

Apart from the preceding case, few cases were found in which Mexicans showed their contempt for one another by throwing something at another person's face. In other studies, practices such as the throwing of urine or the use of excrement were common features of daily life.[43] This action might have been part

11. *Santam[en]te. irritado contra el Demonio el Bto. Aparizio, le tira su orinal â la cara*, from Mateo Ximénez, Colección de estampas que representan los principales pasos, hechos y prodigios del Bto. Frai Sebastian de Aparizio, Rome, 1789. Source: Courtesy of the John Carter Brown Library at Brown University. Sebastián de Aparicio is shown here throwing urine at the devil and perhaps modeling the conduct that Mexicans might use to demonstrate their contempt.

of a larger model derived from religious teachings. In figure 11, Sebastián de Aparicio, the now-beatified monk from Puebla, is shown throwing urine at the devil. It is a bit of a stretch, but this may be an example of plebeians replicating the actions professed by clerics just as plebeians often mimicked the actions of judicial officials. These were, as Shoemaker terms it, a way that individuals "effectively express[ed] public contempt for those who misbehaved." He writes that men and women were "spat at, drenched with water or urine, had dirt or excrement thrown at them or were thrown into the mud, bodies of water, or the kennel (gutter)."[44] But these patterns were not common in the Mexican documents. There were a few cases, however, where throwing something—at times a rather disgusting substance—was part of a scenario of violence and humiliation. Doña María Ferrete tells one such tale. Her spouse, don Joseph Medina y Guerrero, a professional phlebotomist, was perhaps a good earner but not a good husband. He treated her poorly and so she complained to the court. As a result the authorities imprisoned don Joseph Medina y Guerrero. While in jail, he pleaded for her forgiveness so that he could be freed. Finally she acceded, but when he returned home, he beat her and threw a "glass of urine" in her face.[45]

Domestic violence was certainly not rare in middle-period Mexico, so it is not surprising to read about doña Maria Ferrete's treatment at her husband's hands in Mexico City. But the throwing of excrement in her face was unusual within the sample. Likely it represented a more refined type of degradation. It was, however, a form of humiliation that occurred more among women than between men and women. In two other instances, women threw something at the face of another; a third case is a bit more enigmatic. These examples had jealousy as their underlying cause. After María Refugia Ramírez saw Vicenta Briseño talking to her husband in Mexico City, she reproached them but she threw a pitcher in Vicenta Briseño's face.[46] The circumstances were identical but reversed in another case that occurred in Puebla: Joaquina Rojas saw Dolores Rojas talking to her husband despite her many complaints to the authorities about this illicit relationship. In this example, however, it was the amasia who threw something (not specified) in the wife's face.[47] The more mysterious incident occurred between María Cevallos and her neighbor, María Barrios. The hostility between the two was not caused by jealousy but rather because of their children. Their kids fought and the mothers got involved, insulting each other and defending their offspring. When María Cevallos handed a urinal to María Barrios, the former told the latter that she "was going to break her face."[48] There was a lot of ongoing hostility between these two neighbors, but what is interesting is the connection made between the face and the urinal. Although it is not spelled out clearly, the implication seems to have been that one woman was going to throw urine and thus the other threatened her opponent's face in retaliation.

Face-Cutting

Cutting the face was a scenario that often occurred between men, with several historians having documented this pattern for different parts of the world. It was the object of most knife fights, and when one combatant achieved this goal, usually the struggle ceased.[49] When men or women marked women's faces, however, there was a dimension to the act that was absent from the solely male combats. In both women and men, the result of this face-cutting would have been a facial scar. Such mutilations could be considered either honorable or dishonorable. Fluegel writes that a scar on the front of the body was worthy, with the implication being that it happened while engaging an enemy soldier in hand-to-hand combat; the same mark on the back was a sign of cowardice.[50] Greenberg adds that scars could have variant meanings, depending upon the viewer. For example, the marks on a slave's back—the result of being whipped—were for slave owners, a symbol of the slave's bad character, but for abolitionists (and undoubtedly for the slaves themselves), they were a palpable sign of slavery's evils.[51] In Amsterdam, those convicted of knife-fighting were taken to a scaffold and cut on the face so that they would be scarred.[52] By imposing such scars as a part of a sentence, surely the convicts would become degraded and shameful. Most authors write about men fighting and receiving such facial scars, but Spierenberg does document one woman with a mark on her face, which he suggests was indicative of her association with the knife fighters of Amsterdam.[53] The reason why a scar was shameful or not was bound up in the way the victim received it. So if it was a reminder of a discreditable act or acquired as part of a sentence, it was dishonorable. If it was a reminder of a defeat at the hands of another man, again it would be associated with shame. It is important to know the circumstances of such marks in order to understand their significance.

In the case of middle-period Mexico, a very definite association between cutting a woman's face and sexuality existed. Two scenarios prevail in the sample: men who marked the faces of women who rejected or frustrated them sexually, or women who cut the faces of women who were involved with their husbands or lovers. The connection between cutting a woman's face and rejected relationships was not unique to Mexico and certainly found elsewhere, notably in Holland.[54] There were particular reasons why men cut women's faces. In the case of Mexico City resident Anna de Hijar y Castro, her husband was jealous perhaps simply because of her profession—she was a dancer at the Coliseo Theater. But, when she went out with another man (even though, according to her, he was quite distinguished) and she only came home at 10:30 at night, having lost the accompanying servant, he was angry. He threatened to either kill her or mark her face.[55]

The threat was one that was common between men and women—particularly if there was some sexual relationship between them (not necessarily a marriage) or some sexual tension. Like in the previous example, doña Lorenza Suáres complained to ecclesiastical authorities in Mexico City that her husband was threatening to cut her face. To reinforce her claim, she reported that he had done so to another woman before they married.[56] Men used the threat of face-cutting to try to control either their wives or their amasias. In Puebla, Feliciana Pacheco complained that she wanted to leave the terrible relationship that she had with her amasio, José Trinidad Sánchez, but that he threatened to cut her face.[57] Of course, such intimidation would not have been effective had no one actually done it But many men did either mark or try to mark women's faces.

A common scenario was for a man to cut the face of an amasia when she either tried to end the relationship or did so. Puebla resident María Dominga López fled from her liaison with Sipriano Zenteno, who nevertheless caught up with her and wounded her in the face.[58] Also in Puebla, Ana Gertrudis Cardoso, a married woman, had been involved with the militia soldier José Motesuma (alias el Diablo), but she wanted to end it. At about 8:oo p.m. one evening, when she was out walking with don Francisco, a bakery official, as well as four young girls (including two of her nieces), José Motesuma caught up with her. He called her a *grandíssima puta* (a very big whore) and cut her on the cheek. She ran but he caught up and killed her. Later in his testimony he demurred that his intention was not to kill her but to mark her in "the noble part"—her face.[59] The circumstances were reversed in the case of José Antonio Bonillo and his amasia, Chepita. In this case it was the man who was married. But José Antonio Bonillo nevertheless believed that he had rights over Chepita, not only because they had been lovers but because he had supported her financially. When José Antonio Bonillo saw Chepita at night on a street corner in Puebla with another man, he called out to her. She ran away, but he went to her house and waited for her to return. When she did, rather than asking for forgiveness, she insulted him. He cut her face, and later told the judicial authorities that seeing her with another man made him jealous.[60] Dolores Arroyo had been in a relationship with Mariano Mendiola for two and a half years; they even had a child together. But Dolores Arroyo found out that he was married, and along with his poor treatment this fact was reason enough to try to break off the relationship. When she and her sister were walking in the Plaza de Santo Domingo in Puebla at about 8:00 p.m., Mariano Mendiola came upon them and tried to convince Dolores Arroyo to let him see his child and also to continue their illicit relationship. The sisters insulted him and resisted his advance, and he took out a knife and wounded Dolores Arroyo in the face.[61] The scenarios were much the same for Josefa Escobar, María Bernarda Losada, and Cayetana Juáres, all of whom tried to end their illicit relationships and whose amasios cut their faces.[62] In all of these cases the men assumed rights over the women despite being unmarried, and they acted out their jealousy in the way commonly used by husbands to wives. It is not clear whether the possessiveness expressed by these men was always socially or legally accepted; certainly sometimes a man's right over a woman (not his wife) with whom he had a relationship was recognized if he provided her with the *diario*.

But such facial marking also occurred where a relationship did not exist but rather when the man wanted a relationship and was turned down. In a sense this scenario had a logic similar to that of women who tried to leave a relationship: the jealousy came from rejection and frustration. María del Carmen

García declined Mariano Gómez's marriage proposal. At about the time of the orations, in the evening, he came by her house in Puebla and first asked for some wood and then to drink some water. But these requests were just pretexts to get near her; when he did, he grabbed her and tried to cut her with a knife that he had hidden in his pocket. In her testimony she recounted that she had heard from two different women that he had threatened to cut her face because of their refusal to marry him.[63] Clearly he believed that he had some rights to her merely because he had offered to marry her. His frustration at her rejection gave him, in his opinion, the right to mark her face. Such a feeling of possession also came into play in less benign circumstances. In Calimaya, Matheo de la Cruz tried to rape the wife of the ex-governor, don Nicolás de la Cruz. She fought back and he cut her face.[64] Juan Zarate tried to get Simona Franco to leave a Puebla house with him, and when she resisted his overtures he dragged her by the hair and scratched her face.[65] When Miguel García met Soledad Mellado on a Puebla street corner in the afternoon, he cut her with a penknife. He had been trying to seduce her for a long while but she resisted.[66] Even in the prevailing norms and belief systems of middle-period Mexico, these men did not have rights over the women they tried to mark. Yet their feelings of sexual frustration and envy were just as strong and they believed they were within their rights to act out this scenario.

There was a clear strand of jealousy, sexual tension, and possessiveness that ran through the scenarios in which men marked the face of their wives, mistresses, and potential sexual conquests. This mise-en-scène was replicated by women who attacked other women whom they believed were involved with their husbands or lovers. These women were suspicious of others but they were also protecting their honor and the integrity of their families. They used the same language to make their point: they tried to cut or they did cut the faces of the interloper, marking them in a way associated with sexual shame. Clara Teves interrupted a party at the Mexico City house of Joseph Flores. She was looking for his wife, Brigida Aragón, because she had seen Brigida Aragón gesture to her husband and suspected they were having an affair. She loudly called Joseph Flores a cuckold and Brigida Aragón a whore, and then she threatened to cut Brigida Aragón's face.[67] No doubt she was not able to actually make good on her threat because of the assembled people.

Other women were more successful. Puebla resident Gertrudis cut María Juana Faustina in two places on her face. According to the victim, the reason for the attack was jealousy, although she did not give any details. The assault was the culmination of a long campaign of harassment in which Gertrudis tried using insults to provoke María Juana Faustina into fighting, but the latter always resisted.[68] Similarly, in Puebla, Catarina also tried to provoke María Angela Martínez several times before she actually wounded her in the face with a small knife. The reason for her hostility was that María Angela Martínez had had an illicit relationship with José de Jesús Velis previously.[69] Dolores Pérez, María de la Luz Navarro, and Francisca Romero were all also the victims of jealous women who cut their faces in Puebla.[70]

That these women attacked other women rather than their husbands or lovers was not unusual. As Spierenburg notes, "this habit of women blaming each other was a centuries-old cultural stereotype."[71] In addition, it was much more dangerous for them to attack a man. These women were clearly taking cues from how they saw men act out their jealousy and sexual frustration. They took that language and applied it in a way that suited them, creating a grammar of violence. One case combines the two kinds of relationships but uses the same grammar. A man and a woman acted together to mark a woman's face. María

Gertrudis Fuentes de Lara reported that she was going home in Puebla at about 10:30 p.m. when she met Madalena Cipriana walking with a man she did not know. As they crossed paths, Madalena Cipriana shouted, "There goes that crazy one!" and she grabbed María Gertrudis Fuentes de Lara's hair, taking her scarf. During this melee, the unidentified man used his knife to cut her face. Two things are remarkable about the incident. It is the only case in which a man and a woman cooperated in a scenario of face-cutting. But in this case it was the aggressor who had been caught in adultery with the victim's husband.[72] The aggressors, in this case, inverted the logic of moral retribution, just as when some husbands cut the braids of wives who accused them of being unfaithful.

Very few women attacked men in middle-period Mexico. In fact, wives who killed their husbands most often did so using poison, which allowed them some stealth and was certainly not a direct attack. At times women in a public place would take on an official, but usually they counted on the support of others around them and their attacks were transformed into small riots. Two women attacked men's faces on their own. Doña María Blasa got into a fight with the alcalde on the occasion of the archbishop's visit to the Tulancingo church, when it was so crowded that people could barely move. Responding to his use of his staff of office to hit her, she scratched don José Gonzalez's face.[73] Her actions were in the heat of the moment responding to an insult—doña María Blasa turned the affront around and injured the alcalde's dignity and honor. Antonia de Acosta's actions were apparently premeditated and the result of a greater injury. She accused don Nicolás Domingo López, indio principal and the alcalde, of raping her. Not getting satisfaction otherwise, she caught up to him while he was inspecting a field and came straight at him. She said, "[Y]ou old dog, now you will get it!" and she cut his face in seven places, but she aimed

particularly for the mouth and the nose.[74] Cutting the nose did
have particular symbolism: it was often a sentence for theft but
also the nose was frequently associated with sexuality. In England, noses were taken to be "an emblem of sexual dishonour"
[*sic*] because syphilitic infections could be seen on the nose.[75]
These were extraordinary incidents and rarities within the documentary record. But in a range of female violence that would
go from the most subservient wife who only acted to defend
herself through women who attacked other women, these two
would be at the other end of the spectrum of violence. Yet their
actions built upon those of women who rebelled against their
husbands and those whose behavior in daily life was feisty and
spirited. Undoubtedly, they also derived considerable courage
from just how angry they were.

The scenario of cutting or scratching faces implied using a
weapon rather than an object that was found on the ground
or laying about the house. Mexican officials usually inquired
about the article used to wound, in particular whether it was
a cutting instrument. Using a knife had legal implications because carrying knives and other sharp instruments was strictly
prohibited. Initially, Spanish law was more concerned with preventing indigenous peoples from acquiring weapons, and it was
illegal to sell arms to the indigenous population.[76] In 1809 Vice-
roy don Pedro Garibay emitted a *bando* (decree) dealing with
weapons in which he outlined how many prohibitions had preceded his announcement. He despaired at Mexicans' disrespect
for previous laws and decrees and the disorder caused by the
use of prohibited arms by plebeians.[77] These bans on weapons
meant that when men or women were arrested for attacks on
others they had to justify why they had used a weapon. Therefore, the choice to cut a face meant not only premeditation but
also breaking the interdiction on carrying prohibited weapons.
A comparison of the first scenario—picking up an object—to

this second scenario, in which Mexicans chose to use a prohibited weapon to mark someone's face, shows that this was clearly a more serious kind of violence. The anger at the source of this violence had to be red-hot and the goal of marking or humiliating the victim had to be worth the danger of judicial retribution. The passions that caused one person to cut another's face thus were smoldering — the association with sexuality was very much at the forefront.

Eyes and Mouth

Still there is the question as to why was the face such a target. It attracted a lot of attention, not only in the criminal acts recorded in the documents but also from moral authorities for two reasons. The association of the face with sexuality was one aspect of its vital role, but the other was that it could also be used as a violent weapon. Both the eyes and the mouth were potentially offensive. The eyes and the mouth played similar roles in the eroticization of the face. Certain looks could be so seductive that they caused both the person gazing and those observing to sin. Astete compared such lustful looks to a "poisoned knife."[78] Moralists urged women to avert their faces and even cover it in order to prevent the kind of seduction that was apparent in the streets. Yet it seems that their strictures backfired because the "one-eyed gaze" of the *tapadas* (women who covered everything but one eye with a shawl) became even more attractive and disturbing to the moral tone than before.[79] The looks that women could give were not only lustful; in fact, women were known to stare at each other in an aggressive manner. These looks were not the subject of moral opprobrium in civility treatises but certainly the instruction to avoid directly looking at people does imply *not* staring. It was not polite to look intently, either in Hispanic or Nahua culture. The mouth could also be both erotic and aggressive. The Nahuas had more to say about the mouth than the Spanish moralists. For the ancient Mexicans, the mouth was a highly erotic organ—women in the Aztec sex trade emphasized their mouths both by dyeing their teeth red with cochineal and by chewing gum noisily to further attract attention to this area.[80] Spanish moralists were strangely silent on the erotic appeal of the mouth but the documents reveal it to be an effective weapon used for spitting and biting.

Although the moralists regarded the eyes as a weapon of lust and sex, in daily life it was the stare that caused trouble. It was one of many bodily gestures that, according to Villa-Flores, was not only a reflection of a person's inner being or soul but also allowed others to judge one's morality. In his study of blasphemy, Villa-Flores finds that the seriousness of expressions was heightened by gestures of the eyes such as looking skyward.[81] Nineteenth-century etiquette writer Diez de Bonilla states that those who stare were both rude and immoral.[82] In the sample for this book, people did not exactly spell out what a dangerous look was, but they described an intense stare that was obviously directed at one particular person. Middle-period Mexicans recognized that looking intently at another person might invite danger. They tried to avoid doing so unless they were the aggressors. María Luisa Torres told her daughter to avoid even glancing but certainly not to stare at María Andrea Mesa, whom they encountered in the Plaza in Puebla. Clearly her daughter did not heed her words of caution or they were not enough as María Andrea Mesa insulted them, calling the daughter an *alcahuete* (procuress) and a *chivata* (squealer) and hit her with some pottery.[83] María de la Luz Ortiz was selling atole in Puebla when María de la Luz Ruiz passed by her, looking at her "in a very bad way." The look went on and on and when their eyes locked, María de la Luz Ruiz spat, and then came over. They ended up fighting.[84] Reading these accounts, it seems likely that there was previous bad blood between the two families but unfortunately the officials were not interested in the background nor did the participants elaborate on it. But when Rafaela Pérez complained that Pascuala Martínez "was staring at her" and then they got into a fight, she explained that they had previously fought verbally. The two met up in the Huejotzingo Plaza and both had been drinking pulque with friends. Pascuala Martínez maintained that their hostility arose from groundless jealousy.[85] Pedro Trinidad Lara recounted an incident near his fruit stand in Actopan in which María Eufracia Guzmán commented on how his sister was looking at her; the stare led to a fight.[86] These examples demonstrate how people used their eyes aggressively. The intense look was clearly understood as an insult and could be considered the equivalent to a challenge or "fighting words."

Although probably the most offensive action of mouths was probably speech—the vehement insults and "fighting words" should not be forgotten—the actions of biting and spitting were also important parts of the Mexican lexicon of violence. Usually mouths were only used for offense but in two instances they were the subject of an attack. When Pedro Coronel got angry with his wife because she took too long on an errand out of their Puebla home, instead of demurring and apologizing his wife also got mad and insulted him using very offensive words. Finally he bit her in the mouth.[87] He both silenced her and struck back at the source of her verbal assault. In Tlalpan, Pablo Doroteo showed contempt for his wife by putting dirt in her mouth. The circumstances were the typical scenario where the husband takes the wife to the monte—or in this case the *cerro* (mountain) —and punishes her. Pablo Doroteo ostensibly was trying to make her confess her infidelity but he put dirt in her mouth to silence her.[88] The two objectives were, of course, contradictory, so it seems obvious that the attack on her mouth was more symbolic than practical. There would have been any number of other options to gag and silence her; filling her mouth with refuse was a way of showing his contempt for her and for what she used her mouth for: her words, which he believed to be lies.

Biting

Within the scenarios of biting during attacks, there were two distinct patterns. Biting was at times only an incidental part of the attack, often directed at a hand most likely raised defensively. It also could be a principal part of the attack, which meant that it was a principal objective of the attack. In one instance this pattern of multiple bites occurred during a rape. Don Francisco Paredo, a cleric, raped a doncella of nineteen years of age. He shut her into his room in Mexico City, and then both hit her repeatedly and bit her.[89] In the village of San José Atlan, María Rufina was another rape victim whose rapist also bit her repeatedly.[90] In this case the biting was most likely of a partly sexual nature. Both men and women bit each other—which was also true of the Londoners studied by Hurl-Eamon[91]—but here more instances appeared of women biting repeatedly. In some cases, such as the altercation between María Josefa and María de la Merced in Xochimilco, no explanation for the fight or the accompanying bites was provided.[92] But in Puebla, Petra Briseño bit Anselma Hernández and broke a pitcher over her head because of jealousy.[93]

Another incident of multiple biting between women occurred between two women in the Puebla market. Juana María's daughter brushed against Josefa Barbara, causing her to spill some of the food she was carrying. These circumstances show the importance of the spatial context: the crowded market was conducive to such accidents and could lead to violent protection of spatial rights. Although Juana María told Josefa Barbara that she would pay for the food, Josefa Barbara attacked her using many strategies—grabbing her hair, ripping her clothes, and biting her all over. She also picked up some stones and hit her with them. From Josefa Barbara's point of view, the spilling of the food was only part of the mother and daughter's campaign to humiliate her. Not only did they make her look foolish by dropping her purchase, they laughed when she scolded them.[94] In Puebla, María de la Luz provided evidence of her husband's practice of biting her by showing the marks on both her arms. Pedro Sánchez, her husband, countered that these were playful bites and not proof that he was mistreating her. Both husband and wife accused the other of marital infidelity and mistreatment, so the meaning of the case is somewhat murky.[95] In Huejotzingo, José María Fecundo Hernández believed that he had caught his wife visiting her amasio, but when he confronted her, she grabbed him and along with her mother and sister hit him but also bit him.[96] Men and women, and husbands and wives used their mouths as weapons; only the patterns of biting differed. When only individuals reported just single bites, usually on the fingers or hands, these were not offensive but rather defensive wounds and they were incidental to a larger attack. When the night watchman attacked Brigida Gómez in her Mexico City accessoria and tried to rape her, she undoubtedly put out her arms to push him away but he bit her in the hand.[97] The same scenario repeated itself between fighting women as well as fighting couples.[98]

Spitting

Spitting was another form of aggression associated with the mouth but it was an insulting action rather than a direct act such as a punch or a kick. Nevertheless it carried a substantial emotional charge because the act of spitting in the direction of another person made the target understand that they were being associated with unwanted discharge—in a sense this was the same as dirt or excrement. The civility manuals of the day all agreed that spitting was not polite behavior—Escoiquiz warned young men not to gargle or spit while conversing with another person, and the rules for a school for young boys also prohibited spitting.[99] Diez de Bonilla noted that spitting was rude among polite individuals.[100] Perhaps because it was so clearly an offensive practice that crossed classes and cultures, spitting was a powerful insult and one associated—in this sample, at least—with women. This pattern also holds true for London women.[101]

Spitting was usually part of a larger scenario and was frequently associated with other insults and a response to what was considered to be insulting behavior. When don José Quevedo complained that some Mexico City neighbors were insulting and spitting in the direction of his wife, he neglected to add that his wife had also called these women by some racial epithets and had impugned their honor by showing petticoats in the window as they walked by.[102] Another neighborhood conflict occurred in Puebla because of the tension caused by an eviction order. The tenant, María de Jesús, reported that when she was standing in her doorway, the caretaker, María Simona Ochoa, would come by and insult her, increasing the effect of the slurs by also spitting.[103] When Marcela María went to buy a bit of pulque in Tultitlan, she met one of her neighbors, Theresa María, who spat at her while making gestures. Her actions led to a fight.[104] In several other instances it is clear that the act of spitting in the direction of another was meant either as a stand alone insult or to magnify an offense.[105] Petra de la Luz recounted an incident in Atlixco when her father-in-law's mistress walked by her just as she coughed and spit. The woman was insulted by the conjunction of events, and although Petra de la Luz tried to present this as an innocent coincidence, she convinced no one. Her father-in-law came over and punched her; later her husband wounded her with a machete. [106]

The Hidden Parts

The degradation and embarrassment that was associated with the exposure of legs and buttocks or any of the "unmentionable" body parts could be transformed into much more vindictive violence. The attacks on "hidden parts" were related both to the idea of exposing concealed parts of the body (a humiliation in itself) and an escalation of the situation one step further by hurting the victim physically as well as emotionally. Within these attacks, there were also degrees of violence going from squeezing and pinching to actually battering vaginas with sticks and bones. The kind of scenario seen previously—of husbands replicating the punishment that they saw performed by officials—could be altered to attack the vagina. María Tomasa was the victim of just such an assault in the village of Ocuyoacan. Her husband tied her to a pillar, stripped her, and beat her. On the surface this assault was similar to those previously described but, unlike other examples, Pascual Andrés (the husband in question) beat María Tomása in her partes ocultas. The woman who cared for María Tomása afterward was quite shocked at the severity of the injuries and especially their location.[107] Not all of these occurrences are fully described and elucidated in the documents so the motivations for such attacks are often left unclear. Such is the case with the assault on a married woman of Chalmita called Juliana María. Her husband had left her—ostensibly to work in another part of the country—but she was pregnant and living with three other men. These men and one other beat her in the countryside near a barranca. Up to this point the scenario followed the outlines of others previously described—where husbands took their wives out to the monte—except for the number of men involved. It would seem that despite the number of men, they were taking the role of spouse despite their numbers. Another aspect of this case that is unusual was that a witness to the beating came forward. Thio Benito was going to his work at about 6:00 a.m. when he saw these four men grab Juliana María as she was getting water. They broke her jar and began to beat her *partes inferiores* with a stick. Juliana María refused to explain the reason for the beating, although a former alcalde stated that the motivation was an illicit relationship.[108] Her reluctance to testify was undoubtedly because of her shame — this despite the fact that she miscarried and then died in the process. She was not the only victim of this kind of beating. In Mexico City María Gertudis Albares complained to the authorities that two women and two men had beaten her daughter's *partes pudendas* with a bone.[109] These attacks seem to have had a sexual undertone as did the rape of doña Vicenta with a stick by her stepfather in Tula.[110] The same was true of the rape of María Rufina in San Lorenzo, which was done with sticks and rocks.[111] But many further violent acts committed on the vagina were both of a sexual nature and a punishment for sexual behavior.

Other attacks on the "hidden parts" had more overt connections to punishments, particularly when they were carried out by groups. When Jacinta Islas and a set of her friends attacked Isidora Josefa they wanted to discipline her not only for accusing Jacinta Islas's husband of attempted rape but because of the suspicion that this charge was a cover for an illicit relationship with the accused rapist. The group of women grabbed Isidora Josefa, hit her, and tried to strip her of her clothes, but their goal was to put a suppository of chiles into her vagina.[112] If successful, they would have caused Isidora Josefa untold pain, but one of the women dropped the package. Yet they were candid in their admission that this attack on the "hidden parts" was their objective. The use of chiles to cause pain was a particularly Mexican innovation, no doubt derived from the ancient Nahua practice of punishing children with fumes from chiles.[113] It might also have some connections to official practices: Kanter reports that Toluca area officials ordered that a female culprit be given an enema as a particularly humiliating punishment.[114] But the idea of attacking a woman's vagina because of some sexual transgression was not so extraordinary; it was only the form—a chile suppository—that was a novelty. Inflicting pain in the area of the vagina was at times secondary to the main objective, which was, in one case, to cause a miscarriage. When the Galicia family attacked María Manuela Morales, their goal was to abort her fetus even though she was nearly at the end of her pregnancy. They were outraged that not only had she engaged in an illicit sexual relation with their son but she had also flaunted her pregnancy in a shameless fashion. The Galicias broke into her Xochimilco house, dragged her out of bed, and then after hitting her all over, her lover's sister put her hand into her partes ocultas and tried to pull out the baby. María Manuela Morales had scratches in the pubis area as well as inside her uterus.[115] Although doña Luisa Ayala was not pregnant, she reported that her husband put his hand up her vagina and into her uterus, using his fingernails to scratch her cervix open and reach up into her uterus, causing her to bleed heavily. He does not provide an explanation for his conduct, but doña Luisa Ayala believed that his attack on her "hidden parts" was caused by jealousy.[116] These incidents show an extreme violence that was not particularly characteristic of the vast majority of cases. Yet they fall into a pattern that was more common of group retribution for sexual dalliances or improper behavior. Except for the example of doña Luisa Ayala's husband, the conduct exhibited in these attacks was simply the furthest point in a continuum of types of retributive violence by groups.

Men were not entirely immune to this kind of targeting of the "hidden parts." At times women turned the tables and grabbed the penis. José Francisco reported seeing his stepmother hit his father several times and along with grabbing him by the beard, by his balcarrotas, she also took hold of his "hidden parts."[117] On other occasions the action was part of a larger conflict. When don Pedro Martínez insulted and attacked an indigenous couple, the pair retaliated by taking don Pedro Martínez by the pants and grabbing his "hidden parts."[118] Josef de Roxas undertook divorce proceedings because of his wife's violence and insubordination. When he tried to discipline his daughter, his wife objected. Not only did she call him by insulting names, but when he followed her out of the house to catch her and beat her, she took refuge with a friend who lived in an accesoria. Then she turned the tables on him: she and her friend chased him out of the accesoria, and the two women pulled down his pants and grabbed his "partes."[119] These incidents of women who challenged male authority quite literally by grabbing the man's penis were not common. Spierenburg recounts a similar example when a woman, objecting to the fact that her husband had been drinking with a married woman, pinched his privates several times after a reproach for his conduct led into an argument.[120] Clearly there was not an epidemic of penis grabbing; and yet, these few examples should be considered in light of the other incidents of rebellious wives described earlier. Just as those wives refused to metaphorically submit to the head of household, these women refused to literally, by attacking their spouse's symbol of masculinity.

Conclusion

The metaphors that structured and governed Mexican society in the middle period were not simply ideas written down in manuals of civility and morality, but rather concepts that guided people's conduct. Mexicans acted them out using the models derived from civic authorities. Men mimicked the actions of officials when they pulled down a prisoner's head or dragged the prisoner away. They used stones and sticks to attack their wives' or lovers' heads in order to reassert their authority in the family in the same way that *alguaciles* and other officials reacted to those who disobeyed or defied them. They fashioned scenarios of violence that were easily recognized by all in attendance: the lifting of a stone was the gestural equivalent of "fighting words." These various actions formed a syntax of violence that was particularly Mexican, allowed middle-period Mexicans to apply their bodily metaphors, and operationalized the hierarchy of honor on the bodies of those around them. The chain of mimicry that began with husbands who followed the lead given by officials was picked up by wives and other women whom also imitated their husbands when they attacked women whom they considered a threat to the family order. Wives also copied their spouses when they cut the faces of women who threatened the family order by engaging in relationships with the family breadwinner. Yet, cutting women's faces was more complex for men — it represented jealousy, sexual frustration, and thwarted desire. It was a way to punish a woman, but it also was tied into the sexual dynamics of couples and families.

The syntax of bodily violence included hitting the head, slapping the face, and cutting the face. All these actions were designed primarily to punish but they also had as an adjunct meaning the restoration of authority and balance within the household. Mexicans hit others they believed were challenging their role in the household or their social position. These incidents were examples of putting into action the ranking derived from honor but also ideas about the family and social relations. Hitting, in its various forms, allowed individuals to take action to protect their rights or position. People could also strike out with their eyes and their mouths in ways that were less tangible but no less real for those involved. A direct and intense stare or a well-timed spitting were clear messages to those to whom these actions were aimed, and also a clear message to those in the audience. All these actions provided Mexicans with the tools to act out the metaphors that governed their social order and to keep their place within that structure. Their honor, and at times their survival, depended upon the relationships they cultivated within their neighborhoods and communities, and the positions they held therein. They used the commonly understood language of violence to lash out in defense of their positions.

7. Power, Sex, Hair, and Clothes

Aggression toward the body was the inverse of the respect that model individuals were supposed to display in their daily lives. Middle-period Mexicans, of all classes and ethnicities, were educated in the rules of politeness and conscious of their obligations to the codes of rank and courtesy. When they broke these rules they also knew the implications of their actions. When Mexicans hit at the head and other parts of the body, the attacks were meant to restore honor and authority and to punish recalcitrant wives and sexually promiscuous women. Hitting is an obvious form of aggression—blows are certainly painful and dangerous and make an impact by wounding, sometimes causing death. Pulling at the body was a less clear strategy, but certainly one that was practiced almost as commonly as hitting, and with similar goals: pulling either clothes or hair attacked the recipient's dignity, albeit in a less drastic fashion. Middle-period Mexicans most commonly pulled at hair and clothes but these yankings were really aimed at the body—the clothes and hair were extensions of the body. These assaults were part of a strategy of humiliation: although they might restore the honor of the attacker, the aim was to bring down the victim's honor as his or her body was abased by these actions.

While it may not seem obvious at first blush, hair and clothes have a lot in common, as they are both external extensions of the body and they both epitomize the outer representation of the inner being. An individual's hair and clothes showed who a person was: gender, rank, and ethnicity were all indicated by form of hairstyle and dress. Even more significant, both also had important associations with morality. Because of this association with morality, clothes and hair become an extension of identity. As Bell writes of clothes, "it is as though the fabric were indeed a natural extension of the body, or even of the soul."[1] Pulling at either hair or clothes could be done in a mild fashion just to get the attention of another person. Even this gentle tugging, however, was a breach of decorum.[2] In the course of attacks much more violence was perpetrated on hair and clothes—men often dragged women by the hair and attire was often torn to shreds. These actions can be seen as a natural outcome of a brutal assault or they could be unintentional outcomes of a more generalized attack. As Hurl-Eamon shows for London residents, the ripping of clothes could be accidental, but more often it was a way to cast doubt upon the sexual respectability of another woman.[3] But the statements of victims and the general culture of the times makes clear that although part of a fight strategy, these actions also had symbolic weight. The act of pulling aggressively at either hair or clothes affected a person's posture, pulled them out of line, and affected their capacity to stay erect. It was a way of pulling down the head and the honor of another that mimicked the way that officials took criminals into custody and controlled them. As such, this pulling was part of a strategy to both control and to humiliate another. It represented an action that was rife with symbolic messages.

More than any other aspect of the body, both hair and clothes expressed the inside of a person to the outside world. They showed the soul, the morals, and the ethnicity of a person — they were the outer depictions of the inner self. There was a dialectic relationship between the two — they work on each other by enhancing or diminishing the impact of the body.[4] Both hair and clothes had a high erotic charge and therefore they both communicated morality and were the subject of many rules and conventions to rein in their sexual nature. Clothes could act as a barrier to sexuality, at times replacing the house walls, which protected women from men's prying eyes. Hair could be covered or tightly harnessed in braids, which prevented the kind of curls and loose locks that were eroticized. Both were located at the border between the inside and the outside — they both extended out of the body and thus they were a little like the threshold of the body.[5] The insults to hair and clothes were really insults to the body, but not quite as direct. Few people died as a result of being pulled by the hair or clothes, but their inner dignity suffered a deadly blow.

Clothes and Power
Apart from their significance in terms of body control, clothes were also part of an extended bodily metaphor of marriage. The authority that men possessed as a consequence of occupying the head position did not come without obligations — they had to provide for the rest of the body. In their complaints to either secular or religious authorities, wives often pointed out that their spouses had not provided for them. Some linked this lack of support and clothing to higher values. For example, in Mexico City, Josefa Ayala complained that her husband had not provided for her "as he should as it is ordered by the obligations of the marriage sacrament."[6] Again in Mexico City, María Josefa Peralta asked that her husband, a soldier with the *Provinciales* regiment, be obliged to respect her and provide for her

honor by furnishing her with clothing and monetary support.[7] Wives sometimes turned on its head an obligation of obedience in return for support by refusing submission toward men who failed to provide.

Moral authorities were very clear on the lines of obligation. It was the husband's and father's duty to supply his wife and children with all the goods necessary for them to survive. Beyond food, a husband was also supposed to provide clothes—no less an authority than Saint Peter recommended it—without which not only did the man sin mortally but the woman might also be forced into a sin of betrayal.[8] Clothes, then, were part of the basic equation of power within marriages and quasi-marriages. The bonds of matrimony conveyed certain rights and privileges to men but they had to back up these ephemeral entitlements with concrete material support. This connection between sustenance and authority is all the more clear when men who were not husbands claimed authority by the very fact that they supported a woman. They derived their power from their role as provider.

Supplying clothes (as well as food or money) was one of the most basic underpinnings of household authority. The very clothes people wore could also denote authority. One Mexican paterfamilias put it very succinctly when his daughter challenged his authority, stating, "that in his house it was the pants that gave orders not the naguas (petticoats/skirts)."[9] Even in illicit relationships or quasi-marriages, the provision of clothes set up lines of authority and the outlines of a household. When Ignacio approached María Ciriaca Herrero in Mexico City with the hopes of entering into a sexual relationship, he promised that he would clothe her and give her two reales a day.[10] What he was offering was the equivalent to what a wife could expect from her husband: the diario and clothes. When María Salome Maldonado wanted to return to her husband's side in Mexico

City after having lived in an illicit relationship with Joseph Cerda for five years, Cerda told her that she could return to her husband *en cueros* (nude) as she was when she came to live with him.[11] Joseph Cerda was clearly a very intimidating man—María Salome told the officials that she was so scared of him that she peed standing up and also that her husband was terrified of her lover. Joseph Cerda was no doubt aware that he had this effect on people around him but he chose to emphasize his capacity to provide clothes for María Salome in order to call attention to the difference between him and an ineffectual husband. Another Mexico City husband, José María Camacho, also emphasized the fact that he had given his wife all the clothes that she had; before their marriage, he stated, she was en cueros.[12] Joseph Mariano also emphasized his power and its relation to his wife's clothes when, infuriated with her, he threw his wife out into the Calimaya street vituperating her, calling her a whore, but, more important, he first confiscated her clothes.[13]

The fact of providing for women—whether for a wife or a lover—seems to have been an element of masculine identity. It was a way for men to assert their role as head of household and impose their power within sexual relationships. Husbands understood the connection between the provision of clothes and proper conduct on their wives' part. In the village of Santa Catarina Mártir Ayocingo, don Silverio Ferraz noted that, despite the fact that he had treated his wife well and assisted her with all the material goods that she needed, she still engaged in an affair.[14] He seems to have believed that his fulfillment of his duties automatically meant a corresponding fidelity on her part. Don Teofilo del Pozo expressed similar amazement at his wife's failures in light of the fact that he supplied her with a house in Mexico City, clothes, and even a personal maid. He stressed that he had been a good husband.[15] Wives could turn this equation on its head and refuse to care for the spouse's clothes, in

particular not washing them.[16] The equation of provision of
material goods in return for obedience or submission was supposed to work for husbands (so that they would have peaceful
households) but also for those in the household who, in return
for their submission, would have their material needs supplied.
When representing Mexico City resident doña Michaela Posa-
da in her suit against her husband don José Manuel Rosillo,
Manuel José de Monzón emphasized that despite the fact that
wife and children were well behaved in manners and religion,
he refused to sustain them financially, leaving them destitute
in terms of household finances but especially in clothing.[17] If
men expected certain behaviors in return for their material
support, women also counted on sustenance if they conducted
themselves in the appropriate manner.

The lack of clothes could be a way to control women if it prevented them from leaving the house. Father Matías Sánchez
wrote that some women excused their absence from mass by
saying that they did not have sufficient or respectable enough
clothing.[18] He doubted the veracity of their claims. Yet within
the documents it becomes clear that the pattern of wives who
did not attend church services because of their deficient wardrobe was part of a larger configuration of an assertion of power within the household. Doña Gertrudis Gonsález de Arnaez
was able to present a witness who confirmed that her clothes
were in such bad condition that decency prevented her from
attending mass in Mexico City.[19] Her husband, don Rafael de
Traveria, clearly did not live up to his duties. In Puebla, doña
María Josefa Sambrano was supposed to be transferred to the
Colegio de Casadas but stayed home because she was practically nude—she lacked sufficient clothing.[20]

Other husbands actively destroyed or dissipated their spouses' wardrobe. In some cases this sabotage of a wife's respectability was part of a larger pattern of humiliation. In Mexico

City, Felix Morales was clearly contemptuous of his wife, doña Ylaria Hernández, and therefore apart from beating her and taking her earnings, he took her clothes in order to dress the maid.[21] It must have been particularly galling for doña Ylaria Hernández to suffer the "nudity" imposed by her husband when the servant went about in the clothes that she had secured by her work as a servant in another household. Felix Morales's actions can only be construed as a method of humiliation and assertion of power. In Mextitlan, doña Gertrudis Cardenas complained that whenever her mother gave her some clothes, her husband would burn them.[22] In Mexico City, don Matías Hernández also burned his wife's clothes, whereas Leonardo Romero just ripped up his wife's garments along with breaking the dishes.[23] In only one case a rebellious wife turned the tables on her husband when it came to clothes. Doña Merced Mayoli and her mother broke into her husband's Mexico City house after they had been estranged for eight months; they beat him, broke his furniture, and took his cape right off his back. When her husband demanded the return of his cape, doña Merced Mayoli said that she had thrown it in the water channel, although he did not believe her and petitioned the authorities to force his wife to return his clothes.[24]

Destruction of clothing was rather extraordinary because people's garments were valuable — in fact, they were the equivalent of capital.[25] Apart from the widespread practice of pawning clothes, in the event of nonpayment of a debt, officials often seized clothes as an alternative compensation. Licenciado don Manuel Godoy, for example, asked Mexico City officials to take clothes equivalent in value to the rent owed to the convent of la Encarnación by a tailor.[26] When Teresa Nicolasa failed to pay a *real* that she owed, two Xochimilco alguaciles broke into her house and took a shawl and a *huipil* (a tunic-like dress worn by indigenous women) despite the daughter's pleas.[27] Damage to garments was considered serious enough that the parties involved in a fight sometimes asked for a report on damages to attire.[28] Clothing was considered very expensive in Mexico at the time, so much so that many of the poor could not afford it. They often rented or purchased used clothing from local storeowners, whose source was the items that others pawned or from peddlers who waited around hospitals or recent graves in order to steal what the dead wore to their graves.[29] A more common complaint among the women who filed mistreatment charges or asked for an ecclesiastical divorce was that their husbands simply did not provide attire or that they sold or pawned their wardrobes. Nearly half, or forty-seven of one hundred ecclesiastical divorces, and twenty-nine of sixty-one complaints of mistreatment, broached the topic of clothes. Such conduct seems to make more sense from an economic point of view although it could reach extremes, such as in the case of Ynes Méndez, whose Mexico City husband sold even the clothing that friends lent her to cover her "shameful nudity."[30] Why would men destroy a valuable commodity? In cases such as this one, the husband's actions were an indirect attack on his wife. In some cases, at least, such behavior allowed a man to control the woman's movements because it was harder for a woman to leave the house without covering herself.

Not all wives suffered from a lack of clothes because of a deliberate strategy of control and domination on the part of their husbands. In fact, in most of the documentation wives and those who testified for them emphasized that the lack of support was a result of a number of factors, the most frequent being gambling, alcoholic drink, and a general lack of desire or capability to earn a living on the part of the husbands described. Francisco Ortiz, for example, argued that he pawned clothes only because they needed food or money to run their household in Mexico City. He presented himself as a loving husband whose wife agreed with his strategy to support his family. In sharp contrast, his wife, María Josefa Romera, contradicted this rosy picture and stated that he pawned her clothes in order to support his vices.[31] María Josefa Sisneros and doña Lorenza Suáres, both residents of Mexico City, reported that not only did their spouses not support them materially but these two women had to go into the streets and beg in order to survive.[32] Some husbands seem to have treated their wives or their household's goods as a type of cash reserve. Three days after his wedding, Ignacio de Avila took all of his wife's clothes and jewels and sold them, leaving her without the dowry that she brought to the marriage.[33] María Henriquez reported that not only did her husband leave her without clothes but he would also take the mattress, sheets, and any shirts from their Mexico City house.[34]

The lack of support, particularly either the removal of clothing or its nonprovision, was a common refrain for many other women of different classes, of different races, or from different regions.[35] Most of these examples were fairly generic but in some cases witnesses commented upon the circumstances and the reasons for the dearth of material support. In Mexico City, don Manuel Alvárez complained that his son-in-law not only did not like to work, he also pawned any clothes they owned to support his gambling and other unnamed vices.[36] Doña María Díaz Xímenez complained that her husband would abandon her and her children for a year or more at a time, leaving them without even shoes. He would come and go at will, spending his time drinking and gambling. Her Mexico City neighbors confirmed this account and added that the husband would come home and take doña María Díaz Xímenez's clothes to pawn them, leaving her and the children practically nude.[37] Neighbors were undoubtedly the saviors of many such families. Don José de Castro described how he would take pity on Severa Estrada, who lived nearby in Mexico City. She was a devoted housewife with exemplary conduct but her husband did not work so the family was destitute, leaving Severa Estrada and her children often lacking in garments.[38] Doña Mariana Pérez de Segura testified that she knew don Christoval Gutiérrez de Hermosillo and his wife, doña María Rita Xarillo y Galindo, because they rented rooms nearby in Mexico City. From her own home she could hear the noise of the husband mistreating his wife and she saw the evidence of the penury in which he kept his family: wife and children were practically nude. She noted that don Christoval Gutiérrez de Hermosillo only gave his wife four reales a day to sustain the household[39]—an amount that was twice the normal diario of two reales a day that plebeian wives expected. Thus it would seem that the pity that doña Mariana Pérez de Segura felt for her neighbor and her judgment regarding her attire was no doubt framed within her class: it would have been adequate for a plebeian woman but not one who belonged to those with aspirations of honor and rank. Other women simply chose to support themselves, sometimes in spite of their husbands. Doña Lorenza de Medina provided for herself and her three daughters in Mexico City by working, though she was barely able to "cover their bodies" with the fruits of her labor.[40]

Whether men did not provide for their wives and households because of their vices or because they chose not to do so as a strategy of control or power, their conduct reflected upon their masculinity. When men did not fulfill their role as head of household, others questioned their ability as men or their security. Either they were useless incompetents who drank or gambled away any money they had, or they were bullies who overplayed the masculinity hand that life had given them. When husbands did not discharge their role as providers, others stepped in to feed and clothe their extended family. Texcoco resident María Guadalupe Miranda listed the few garments that her husband had given to her over the five years of their marriage: two pairs of naguas, two half shirts, one pair of stockings, and one paño (cloth). Her husband refused her requests for food or clothes, saying that he had no money, and thus her parents supported her. She stated that if not for her extended family, she would be nude.[41] Luisa Riofrío exclaimed at the "audacious ingratitude" of her spouse, who had brought nothing to the marriage in Mexico City; her mother had supported them with a peso every day, supplanting her husband's role in providing the diario. Luisa Riofrío's mother also paid for their housing and clothes, and in effect she took over the role as paterfamilias and treated her son-in-law as her child.[42] In the village of San Mateo Huiculzingo, María Dolores's father made sure that she was dressed after she married, and if not for him, her husband would not have had pants or a shirt.[43] In all their years of marriage in Mexico City, Joseph Pesqueros only gave Joachina Cardoso an old pair of shoes. Instead, her parents gave her old clothes, which Joseph Pesqueros pawned in order to have money to gamble. One witness described him as constantly drunk and dressed in an old cape.[44] These men did not command any respect from those around them — they had forfeited their role as head of families by failing to provide for their wives and children. Although these men did not burn or rip the clothes provided to them by their extended family, those men who did so might have been acting out their frustrations at being supplanted as head of household and trying to reassert that role albeit in a very illogical manner.

Sex and Clothes

Although clothes had an intimate relationship with sexual morality, they also had more direct connections to sexual intercourse. Clothes were an important commodity for middle-period Mexicans, and therefore they often served as a currency. Because of this role, clothing or articles closely related to clothes, such as rosaries or reliquaries, were part of seduction and marriage proposal rituals.[45] These items became a currency associated with sexuality because they were part of the lead up to marriage and thus licit sexual relations. The normal custom when a man asked a woman to marry him was to give her a token to symbolize their pact—this was called a *prenda*. In middle-period Mexico among plebeians, this item was very often a piece of clothing—therefore objects of clothing or jewelry such as rosaries and reliquaries that were worn close to the body were part of the rituals of seduction, but these practices were distorted when the women were not willing partners. Essentially men were mimicking the more accepted customs of the prelude to marriage and using these elements to try to mitigate what was in fact rape. Thus clothes—in the form of a sort of modified prenda—became a part of the mechanics of certain sexual assaults. This practice was also strengthened by the fact that at times family members asked for compensation for the injury of their daughter's rape in the form of goods such as sheets or other items associated with clothing. These practices borrowed from the more accepted language of seduction in the same way that husbands borrowed from the language of judicial punishment when they dragged their wives to the monte to whip them.

The line between consensual sex and rape was often made rather unclear by the man's offer of clothes. Using the vocabulary surrounding seduction and promises of marriage to mitigate their aggressive actions, these men softened the blow of rape by offering a prenda. At times this kind of scenario happened in rather unlikely circumstances, such as among girls well below the age of puberty who would not normally have been considered eligible for marriage. María Gertrudis Pito was six years old when a Chietla neighbor raped her. Her mother had sent her out to get some chicken broth from Father don José Estevan Santa María in the middle of the day—a time when she should have been safe enough. María Gertrudis Pito was shy about asking for the broth so she sat outside the house waiting for the right moment when another neighbor, Nicolás Castillo, came by. He asked her what she was doing. When she explained, he told her that he would give her some broth since in his house they had a lot. He also added that he would give her a real for some sweets, some *naguas de ensima* (skirts), and *naguas interiores* (petticoats) and a paño. What María Gertrudis undoubtedly failed to understand was that his offer of clothing was part of a strategy to secure sex and in effect he was suggesting an offer of marriage-seduction. She was too naïve to make the connection, so she went to his house and he raped her.[46] María Ignacia Samudio was fifteen years old when she faced a similar situation in Mexico City: she was more wary but still fell into the trap laid by the licenciado don Pascual Cardenas. He came to her house and gave her a Quimon Bretaña to use as white naguas. He told her the gift was out of charity, implying that there was no concealed motive for the present. The next Tuesday he asked her to meet him in Tacuba Street, where he would give her a paño. She agreed because the encounter was arranged for daytime and it seemed safe enough. When they met, however, he pushed her into an empty house, where he lifted up her skirts and raped her. She specified that she had been a virgin and that he never promised her marriage but he did give her the paño and promised to support her.[47] Both these men mitigated their actions by giving prendas to their victims. Cunningly they altered the normal ritual just enough to make themselves seem less like a rapist and more like a baffled suitor.

This pattern was repeated with some alterations and certainly not always with such forethought. For example, when the night watchman forced his way into Brigida Gómez's Mexico City accesoria, he raped her, and then in what seemed to be an afterthought, he left her two reales and a scarf.[48] When

Juana María was gathering wood in the mountain not far from her house in Ixmiquilpan, Alonso Francisco came by and solicited her for sex. She refused but still he raped her. When he was finished he took out a small piece of cloth and threw it at her. He said that it was a *prenda matrimonial* (betrothal gift) and that she should accept it as compensation for the harm he had caused her.[49] After Juan Antonio raped Leonarda Antonia with the help of some friends in her *milpa* (small field) outside the village of Nuestra Señora el Tepepan, she reported that she did not know him nor did she have any prenda of his, implying that the sexual act was rape, pure and simple. But Juan Antonio insisted that he wanted to marry Leonarda Antonia and his friend Mathias Xavier was adamant that Juan Antonio had given her a necklace and a rosary as prendas.[50] These men understood the need to give the appearance of consensual sex or at least to mitigate forcible intercourse with an apparent promise of marriage. They did so using garments, cloth, or jewelry because these items represented a commonly understood vocabulary. The link between clothes and sex leading up to marriage was reinforced when parents demanded cloth as reparations for their daughter's virginity—as in the case of José M. Garcia, who claimed a sheet, food, and medicines from Bachiller don José Reyna, who raped his daughter in Tula.[51] Clothes were part and parcel of the rituals around seduction and marriage but they also had other potent symbolisms.

Because clothes were loaded with symbolic content, the use of garments—their wearing, their laundering, and their use as gifts—was scrutinized by middle-period Mexicans. Sloan notes that men often used their serapes to envelope a woman, thus symbolizing their sexual conquest, whereas women wore their *rebozos* (shawls) tightly around their shoulders, mimicking enclosure and recogimiento and thus symbolizing their sexual modesty.[52] Clothes had symbolic content, both in the way people used them and as independent objects. Often carelessness around actions upon clothes provoked sexual jealousy. Looking after a man's clothes, for example, apparently had sexual overtones. Asking a woman to do so was part of a seduction ritual, perhaps because of its relation to giving prendas as part of the matrimonial ritual. María Manuela recounted how Gabriel and some of his friends approached her when she was fishing in a canoe with her aunt near Iztacalco. They began to flirt with her saying, "did she want to sew his [Gabriel's] sheet." She reported that she resisted these overtures but Gabriel raped her.[53] In Puebla, Abundio Alvárez was enraged when he discovered his amasia, María de la Luz Tlaxcalachi, washing another man's shirt. As a result, he beat her and admitted that he did so out of jealousy. María de la Luz Tlaxcalachi's reaction to this charge is interesting because she did not deny that washing another man's clothes was a provocative act. Instead she argued that she had sought Abundio Alvárez's permission to launder her son-in-law's shirt, which he had given her.[54] She recognized that her actions could be construed as suspicious so she covered her bases. Why was sewing or washing cloth that belonged to a man so imbued with sexuality? Perhaps it was simply because caring for objects was an intimate, loving effort. But, in addition, these actions brought women into contact with objects that had been next to the skin of another man so they were an extension of these men's bodies. Thus, when women agreed to sew or wash such items they were engaging in a preliminary contact with this man's body—it was a buildup to the next stage of seduction.

When women cared for items of clothing they were admitting to a relationship with another person's body. In addition, when they accepted a gift of garments or jewelry, they were tacitly consenting to a relationship. Sometimes these bonds were innocuous such as that between parents and a daughter, but even so, a present of clothing between parents and a daughter could

provoke strong feelings in a son-in-law. When there were no licit reasons for the gift, however, the emotions elicited were even
fiercer. When Vicente Hernández went to Tochimilco to visit
his daughter, María de la Luz, he wanted to give her a rebozo.
Her husband objected vehemently, saying that he would not allow his wife to wear anything that he had not bought himself.[55]
The husband's reaction seems exaggerated especially since the
gift was between father and daughter, but clearly he wanted to
control his wife's wardrobe. In Mexico City, don Joachim García de Torres was less successful in this control, and one day he
looked in his wife's trunk and a bag of hers and found some
blue silk stockings, black gloves, and a mother-of-pearl rosary
with a silver crucifix. He estimated that this last item was probably worth at least five pesos. He knew that he had not given
these items to his wife, and they were not part of her goods at
marriage. He was suspicious that they were a gift from a lover
and he was jealous.[56] His experience made the previously mentioned husband's caution seem a little less outlandish.

Of course, the transfer of goods could go in the other directions: from wife to lover. José Ignacio Flores reported that he discovered his wife's affair in Mexico City when he saw a man — no
doubt her lover — selling his wife's white naguas.[57] These incidents reveal that clothes or jewelry in the wrong place or in
the wrong hands were deeply disturbing because of what they
revealed about the women involved. In addition, sometimes
men tried to keep a lover who was trying to break free from a
relationship by keeping some of their possessions, most notably either their clothes or jewelry. For example, in Mexico City
Pablo Durán refused to return Ysidora's reliquary when she attempted to leave his side.[58] The cleric Vicente Antonio Balcázar tried to seduce Barbara Arellano in Puebla when she was
actually engaged to be married to another man. Mother and
daughter kicked the cleric out of their house in an attempt to

end the problem but Vicente Antonio Balcázar took all of Barbara Arellano's clothes.[59] Clothes and decorative items such as rosaries and reliquaries were much more central to daily life for middle-period Mexicans than they would be today, where most of our wardrobes can be cheap and disposable. Thus they served as currency not just for daily survival but also in the rituals—both official and unofficial—between men and women.

Violence and Clothes

Pulling at clothes or ripping them were common incidents in middle-period Mexico, but they were incidents that hid complex meanings below their surface. Clothes had a monetary value—one that probably was more important for plebeians who tended to have fewer resources and therefore fewer garments—and so any destruction of clothing was also an attack on the financial well-being of a person. From a purely practical economic sense, any destruction of clothing was a very real attack on the finances of another person. But beyond their economic value, clothing was significant in a social sense. The garments that people wore defined them morally, hierarchically, ethnically, in gender, and professionally. Clothes were also an extension of the body—they were imbued with the wearer's essence and they had a mystical connection to their owner. An attack on clothing in middle-period Mexico was not just a practical economic attack but was also one that assaulted the very identity, the very core of that person. Additionally, on a practical level, if clothes positioned an individual in society, when these were destroyed it would be more difficult for them to take this social place once again in their milieu. They might join the majority of plebeians who were described as "practically naked."[60] Thus an attack on clothing was also an assault on the person's honor.

Many of the actions that middle-period Mexicans took place during melees seemed random but as seen throughout this book they usually had an underlying rationale or were part of an established pattern. Men and women often borrowed the language from other rituals, especially from those of judicial authorities. While ripping clothes was not an official part of the arrest procedure of Mexican constables, certainly manhandling prisoners using either their hair or their garments was common. Tearing at clothes did occur, however, when officials were frustrated in their job. María de la Encarnación recounted that she observed officials bringing in an old man to the public jail in Santiago Tianguistengo. A woman in the crowd asked why he was being arrested, and was told it was for a debt of two reales. But the question must have irked the official—perhaps he perceived it as a questioning of his authority—so he began to insult this woman, then he picked up a rock and hit her in the chin, and finally, he ripped her shirt into pieces as he tried to drag her away.[61] Clearly this official was reasserting an authority that had been challenged. His actions were part of a crescendo that started with insults—a kind of fighting words—and continued to lower the woman's status by hitting her head with a rock and finally destroying her identity by ripping her clothes. The direction of attacks such as these was not, however, unidirectional. People also struck back at officials. Domingo Santiago, an official with the Xochimilco municipal government, tried to collect tributes at Manuel Antonio's house, only to have Micaela, the debtor's wife, come out insulting him and grabbing him by the clothes.[62] The common theme running through these incidents, as in so many others, was the buildup from verbal insults to physical insults.

Pulling at garments was a very real affront to middle-period Mexicans; they reacted to it with violence even if it would seem to us—as twenty-first century observers—to be a minor event. Antonio Flores, for example, explained the fact that he hit María Soledad with a stone by stating that first she grabbed his serape and pulled it off as he was leaving the house in Puebla.[63] María Soledad could have been simply trying to get his attention—a rather innocent act—if there had not been an altercation over her refusal to lend some atole previously. In this context, a seemingly innocuous grabbing at a garment took on added significance and was transformed into an insult. María de la Luz Ramírez suffered a similar fate. She was in the patio of the church of Santo Domingo in Puebla after imbibing enough to be drunk. She had the bad luck to step on María Rosa's naguas. María Rosa took offense and attacked her, throwing a plate in her face.[64] There seems to have been tension between the two women before this incident, so what might have been the misstep of a tipsy woman became a grave insult. The context and preceding events were important in determining what a serious affront was and what was not. Nevertheless, pulling at clothes was part of the arsenal of offenses for middle-period Mexicans.

Although most frequently the act of tearing at clothes seems to have been an impromptu part of a larger struggle that included blows to body parts, the use of various weapons, and perhaps the use of other tactics, this attack on clothes was more deliberate. When Guadalupe Salazar intervened in the fight between Barbara Hernández and his wife, María Rafaela, in the hacienda Atencingo near Chietla, Barbara Hernández became even more infuriated. Guadalupe Salazar picked up a stick and hit her in the head. In retaliation, Barbara Hernández got some scissors and cut his shirt.[65] Her actions seem to have been much more deliberate than what more normally happened in the course of a fight. Her target was clear—the destruction of Guadalupe Salazar's shirt—and rather than doing so in a half-hearted manner, she chose scissors in order to accomplish maximum damage. What her actions suggest is that the attacks on clothes that were normally just part of what seemed to be a frenzied attack were actions that had symbolic content. Although the details are not as clear, it seems that Pascual Reyes, a shoemaker in Puebla, might have been almost as deliberate as Barbara Hernández. In a fight over his wife's conduct as she continued to insult him, he took out a sharp tool and he stated that he just wanted to cut her naguas but instead he wounded her in the leg.[66] While in the normal course of frantic attacks it was not possible to pick up some scissors or a tool, the choice of tearing at garments was a scenario that was a conscious one. It provided an additional impact in the attack on a person's body.

Although the focus for this book was not violence that had an impact on men, at times incidents that involved attacking men were part of the sample. Within the small number of attacks that intersected with the violence associated with women, however, one pattern that was distinctive to men did appear: pulling at their pants. This kind of action occurred between relative strangers but also between husband and wife. Don Pedro Martínez, for example, was the subject of such an attack when he refused to accept some small naguas as a pawn in his Mexico City shop. The couple whose clothing he turned down was angered by his rejection. He jumped over his store counter and tried to eject them from the business. They grabbed him, by the hair and by his partes ocultas, hit him on the head, and also grabbed him by the pants.[67] This particular incident had class and racial overtones—don Pedro was a native of Castilla (Spain) as well as a middle-class store owner, whereas the couple who fought with him were indigenous and clearly poor. But the pulling of pants also happened between people within the same hierarchical ranking. When Florentino Gregorio and his wife were coming back from the neighboring village of Ototitlan, they met a couple who were friends, and they decided to drink some pulque in Metepec. Antonio Trinidad came out of the pulquería and insulted him. Florentino Gregorio tried to appease the situation but Antonio Trinidad's wife and daughter joined the brawl, grabbing him by the hair and by various body parts. Antonio Trinidad grabbed at his clothes, even taking off his pants.[68] All those involved were indigenous laborers (*gañanes*); the tension was not a matter of class or race but over whether Florentino Gregorio had informed on Antonio Trinidad.

Pulling at men's pants was also something done within couples—here the tension was a domestic one but nevertheless a struggle over hierarchy, albeit within the home. After Josef de Roxas had a disagreement with his wife she left and took refuge in a neighbor's Mexico City accesoria. He followed her there but then his wife, with her friend's assistance, turned the tables on him. They grabbed him from behind and the three tottered into the street struggling when Josef de Roxas' wife pulled down his pants and grabbed his partes.[69] José Mesa got into a fight with his amasia, Marcelina Mandujano, in Puebla, and instead of backing down she told him to "go to hell." He grabbed her by the hair and threw her on the floor. Although she was hurt she continued to fight and ripped up his pants.[70] Tearing apart or pulling off a man's pants were clearly actions that were associated with fights—they were part of a larger framework of violence but the act itself served to humiliate the man and bring down his status. The common theme within these incidents was a kind of reversal of hierarchy where the victims were usually considered socially superior either by gender or by social class. Pants also might have had a symbolism associated with the bodily metaphor of marriage and family. After all, as a middle-period Mexican husband and father stated, "it was the pants that gave orders, not the naguas."[71] Men's garments took on the aura of authority and were symbols of their superior rank—why not make them victims in a struggle over hierarchy and power.

If there were a female equivalent of pulling down pants or ripping them it would be an attack on a woman's naguas. Yet, apart from two men who admitted to lifting naguas and the one woman who stepped on another woman's naguas by mistake, these overskirts were not much of a target in the neighborhood brawls. Instead the target that was general to both women and men was to rip at women's shirts or clothes in general. When Isabel, an indigenous woman, confronted a servant who was washing clothes in a stream in Tlanepantla, the verbal confrontation soon became physical and Isabel attacked the woman grabbing her hair and ripping her shirt.[72] In a fight over spilled food in Puebla, Josefa Barbara attacked Juana María, grabbing her hair, biting her, and ripping her shirt.[73] At times other items of clothing were also the subject of such rage. When Soledad Suáres and Susana Palacios fought in Mexico City, in the struggle Soledad Suáres's shawl was ripped.[74] When Bernarda Sala and her husband attacked doña Josefa Joaquina Estrada in Coyoacán, they grabbed her by the hair, hitting her, and ripping her clothes.[75] There were similar attacks on men as well. In Mexico City, Lazaro José and his wife grabbed Domingo de Santiago by the hair and ripped his clothes, saying that he was a pimp.[76] In a conflict with his amasia's mother in Mexico City, Pablo Durán reported that María Suáres grabbed his cape, then grasped him by the hair and ripped his clothes.[77] Finally, in one slightly divergent example from Puebla, Madalena Cipriana took María Gertrudis Fuentes de Lara's scarf and then wounded her in the face.[78]

Like many other parts of fights and different conflicts, harm done to clothing might simply have been an offshoot of the larger clash. Yet, as Hurl-Eamon notes for eighteenth-century London, clothing was "a significant piece of property."[79] Attacks on clothes, whether deliberate or not, were important because they harmed a person's financial solvency. Yet, there were incidents in which it is clear that there was a deliberation and thought given to the destruction of garments. At times, these assaults had sexual overtones, but more often they were related—like so much of the violence we have seen—to a power struggle either between couples or individuals. The pattern in middle-period Mexico diverges from that found by Hurl-Eamon in that this type of violence occurred as much to men as to women. In London, tearing clothes was part of female on female violence only. In addition, there was a much stronger sexual element found in the assaults on women's clothing for the London sample.[80]

Hair
Hair's worth was much different than that of clothes. It did not have a set monetary value, but despite this, it was no less important. Although there was no market for hair in middle-period Mexico and it could not be pawned, hair was significant—much like clothes—for what it told the world about its wearer. Much like clothes, when either a mob or judicial officials cut a person's hair, their social position would be tarnished—the message that was conveyed by a shorn head was probably even stronger than that communicated by a lack of garments. Shorn heads were unequivocally an indicator of immorality, whereas "nakedness" could be due to poverty or bad luck. Thus an attack on hair was probably more serious than one on clothes, and hair cutting—although present in the sample—was not as common as that of tearing at clothes. Attacks on hair were therefore less relevant to financial well-being and more significant for social position. Hair in all its stylings and dressings was vital as a social indicator that was gender sensitive—for women it meant being either morally pure or sexually promiscuous, while for men it was an emblem of masculinity and respect. Hair cutting was a much more deliberate act than that of tearing clothes, as it was never simply an accidental outcome of a frenzied attack. Nevertheless, attacks on hair especially in the form of pulling and grabbing were extremely common. Hair was a useful handhold when overcoming an opponent, and husbands and lovers often

pulled women by their hair. When young men abducted women they usually pulled them by the braids or the rebozo.[81] These actions were no less insulting than cutting, just less permanent.

Hair and Insult

Was touching or grabbing hair a meaningless gesture? Touching another's hair or grabbing it was an action that could simply have been practical, but it was too intimate to be dismissed as trivial. Hair was an extension of the body that had magical qualities—it was also highly imbued with gender implications for both women and men. Thus while it might have been just as simple to grab someone by the arm to get their attention or to take them to prison, taking them by the hair was more offensive. Anyone who has had long hair at some point in their life also knows that pulling hair can be more painful than pulling a limb.

It was not only Mexicans who reacted strongly to others touching or pulling their hair. Muchembled recounts how, in 1585, Nicolas Sheyte, a young man from the French region of Artois, became so enraged when a group of men grabbed him by the hair and pulled out some strands that he took out his knife and attacked them.[82] Lyman Johnson also describes an incident in Buenos Aires when Pasqual Duarte nonchalantly pulled a chip of wood out of a neighbor's beard. His reward was a swift explosion of violence in which he was stabbed and ultimately he died. Johnson argues that simply touching another man's beard was insulting enough to be an affront to his honor.[83] The nineteenth-century etiquette writer Diez de Bonilla concurs, writing that it was extremely rude to touch another man's face but even more so if the other man was older.[84]

These two diverse incidents concerned men and primarily secular, informal incidents. But there was a great deal of pulling at hair by officials especially when they arrested miscreants.

There was, no doubt, a practical reason for latching onto hair, since in the days before handcuffs it was an easy way to partially incapacitate an individual. Yet, it also was a way to bring a person's head down—in the bodily language of honor it debased people by making them lower their heads. Thus in the syntax of insults and honor, pulling at hair brought a person down and at the same time it was an invasion of bodily space.

In many cases when one person pulled another's hair, this action was just part of the kind of frenzy of attack in which so many different strategies of violence competed and so it is difficult to know which act was the most telling. In a number of cases, hair-pulling was relatively isolated and therefore the victim's reaction to this particular act is clearer. When doña Francisca Ursula suffered such an assault—Phelipa de Jesús had grabbed her by the braid as she was returning home in Coyoacán from hearing mass—she asked for the restoration of her "reputation." She characterized Phelipa de Jesús as a gossip who saw the worst in everyone.[85] Clearly this public hair-pulling, especially by a person known as a rumormonger, was detrimental to doña Francisca Ursula's honor; if unchecked it could allow others to wonder what was its cause. But women were not the only ones who found hair-pulling annoying and harmful to their dignity. Milpa Alta official Gaspar de la Cruz arrested Francisco Diego and his wife because when he and his alguacil were collecting tributes, Francisco Diego's wife, in the presence of all his officers and the rest of the community, tried to pull his hair and that of his alguacil. He wanted husband and wife punished for disobedience.[86] Luciana María was standing in her doorway in Teotihuacan when she laughed as Marta María walked by, thus provoking a fight. But according to Luciana María, Marta María "gave a big pull to her hair."[87] Rather than being just part of a fight, this hair-pulling was the equivalent of the "fighting words." It precipitated what had been a tense situation into an all-out battle. These examples show us how pulling hair could be an insult in and of itself. It was an action that brought disrepute to the victim and tarnished his or her honor.

In the recollections of some witnesses, hair-pulling was part of a generally insulting and degrading behavior rather than being an isolated act. Clemente Joseph Magos suffered more generally from being a husband whose authority was constantly challenged because he lived within the household of another paterfamilias in San Gerónimo Aculco. He dated the problems in his marriage to the time when he and his wife moved to his father-in-law's rancho. His in-laws, as well as their entourage, behaved as if he did not exist. One person, only described as the *bachiller*, would give presents to his wife in his presence, "thus dishonoring him." In front of the whole household, the bachiller implied criticism of his status by "asking why he did not comb his hair." Shortly after his mother-in-law attacked him and pulled out his hair violently.[88] When doña Petra de Rivera described the way her husband insulted her parents in Mexico City, she included the fact that he took her mother by her hair and pulled it.[89] In the village of Ostepec, José Francisco described a similar general conduct that included some hair-pulling. His stepmother would hit his father and several times she grabbed him by the beard, by his balcarrotas, and even his "hidden parts."[90] His stepmother's conduct was violent toward her husband as well as disrespectful; but the pulling of his beard and hair was part of a generalized attack on his body. In both these examples there was a kind of inversion in which people who were supposed to enjoy respect because of their status as husband were treated with contempt. Similarly, María Cornelia Ortiz turned on her Puebla employer attacking her because of what she considered to be an unjustified scolding. In this case, however, instead of pulling at her employer's hair, she tried to cut it off.[91] Cutting off hair was a form of humiliation, but certainly one that was different from pulling hair. It was an attack on hair that, for women, usually had sexual overtones. As such María Cornelia Ortiz seems to have sent mixed messages regarding her employer, or perhaps she did not reveal all her motivations to the notary who recorded her case. Nevertheless, the messages regarding hair and women were often profoundly sexual.

Sex and Hair

Women's hair imparted many sexual messages by the way that it was dressed — it could be curled, unkempt, covered in jewels, and all these forms of wearing hair attracted men's gaze. The looseness of hair was also connected to the sexual honesty of the woman. These imperatives all derive from the moral teachings of both Spanish and Nahua authorities. But what they don't write about is the sensuality of men's hair. Nineteenth-century etiquette writer Diez de Bonilla does mention that it was improper for women to shave men, nor for men to comb women's hair and implies that such actions revealed a lack of modesty undoubtedly because they brought a member of the opposite sex into such close proximity with a sensual body part.[92] In two cases, the act of a woman touching or combing a man's hair was a profoundly sexually charged act. There was an intimacy that was conveyed by this motion that often either signaled a sexual relationship or preceded it. In Puebla, María de los Dolores described her husband's betrayal with another woman in terms of the intimacy that he shared with her. Not only did his amasia cook for him, but she washed and combed his hair.[93] María de los Dolores did not actually mention sexual intercourse but she paints a picture of familiarity and closeness with the woman touching her husband in a way that should be reserved only for those with a very close connection. A more tragic example of this connection between men's hair and sexual intimacy is found in the story of María Candelaria, a ten-year-old girl. As her Mexico City neighbor, María Nicolasa Parra, narrated, she was living next door with her sister and brother-in-law. One day María Nicolasa Parra found María Candelaria combing her brother-in-law's hair. A few days later, she found the little girl out in the corral weeping; when asked what was wrong; Maria Candelaria related that her brother-in-law had raped her.[94] Clearly, according to the neighbor, the story began with the hair combing—it was an act that crossed a line and allowed an observer to presume that there was a sexual connection with the little girl.

Despite these few examples that were relevant to men's hair, women's hair remained quite central to the connection between sex and hair. One element that the moral authorities harped on was the link between messy hair and sexuality. It might be simply a connection between order and morality—ordered locks meant an ordered psyche thus a sexual life that did not cross the boundaries of decency. In one case a husband made a more direct association between messy hair and illicit sexual activity. Simón Antonio Retama told judicial authorities that he came home from a day working on the cleanup of irrigation canals and his wife was not home. It was five o'clock p.m. and so he expected her to be present in the household and he was suspicious. Such absences from the home often provoked violent reactions from men. But in this case, when his wife came home in Pachuca, she provided additional evidence of her sexual malfeasance in that her hair was messy and there were twigs and other bits of waste in her locks. Simón Antonio Retama assumed that she had betrayed him by lying down on the ground in order to have sex with another man. He stabbed her in the chest and she died shortly afterward.[95]

Although these associations between sex and hair are intriguing, the more familiar relation was actually related to punishment. While indigenous men's hair was shorn for all sorts of lapses, the cutting of women's hair was intimately tied to failures of sexual morality. This action was supposed to punish women for having sexual relations with married men or in any other way that contravened social rules. It was a punishment that was enforced, at times, by groups of women usually composed of the offended party—the wife and several of her friends. When people in Xochimilco suspected Rita Trinidad of an affair with Nicolás Cruz, a group of women that included the wife and two friends grabbed her and cut off both her braids as well as wounding her in two places.[96] Rita Trinidad protested vehemently to the authorities that she was the victim of a misunderstanding and that she was not involved with Nicolás Cruz, which makes me wonder whether women who were guilty of affairs would not report any hair cutting because they could not expect any sympathy or retribution. In a similar vein, Isidora Josefa, whose braids were also cut off by a group of women in Otumba, protested that she was innocent of the affair with Jacinta Islas's husband. She also asked the officials to restore her honor before the public and perhaps as a token of this restoration she wanted her braids returned to her.[97] There is an interesting parallel in this request to return the item whose taking caused dishonor in an example from France cited by Farr. This historian recounts how a father demanded the return of a headdress that some ruffians had grabbed off his daughter's head, thus humiliating her and insulting her chastity.[98] This association with dishonor—especially when undeserved—can also be noted in the examples of the two husbands who themselves were involved in extramarital affairs but who turned the tables on their spouses when these women complained, and they cut off their wives' braids.[99] In another somewhat similar example, in the rancho of Piedra Grande near Texupilco, doña Rafaela Rodríguez related that her husband had dragged her around the house by her hair and had tried to lock her in a room, threatening that he was going to hang her in order to cut off her hair. Doña

Rafaela Rodríguez does not provide an explanation for her husband's conduct. But he did. Julian Pérez countered that he returned from a trip to a very cold reception from his wife—she did not want to prepare him any food and when he hit her with a stick she tried to grab his hair.[100] From his perspective he was restoring the proper lines of authority and punishing a recalcitrant and uncooperative wife. Honor was, of course, very tightly bound up with sexuality, so it is not surprising that hair was the intersection for at least some of the struggles over respectability and maintenance of status as an honorable person. Because of its association with sexual mores, hair was an ideal canvas on which to portray exactly who an individual was.

Pulling Hair

Like many other actions that Mexicans engaged in during the middle period, pulling hair was often simply a practical way to proceed when in a fight. This sense of practicality can be seen in the description of the struggle between María Guadalupe Hernández and María Juliana early in the morning in the village of Huauchinango in Puebla. María Guadalupe Hernández was going to fetch water when María Juliana told her that she needed to talk. This request seems innocent enough but María Guadalupe Hernández knew that there was something hostile about this request because María Juliana had surprised María Guadalupe Hernández kissing José de Jesús, María Juliana's lover. Rather than trying to stake out the high moral ground, María Guadalupe Hernández asked María Juliana, "[W]hat do you want from me, you shameless hussy?" She said that she was going to put down her water jar and went back into her house. But María Juliana would not wait—she entered María Guadalupe Hernández's house, grabbed her by the braid, and threw her onto the floor. María Guadalupe Hernández got up, grabbed María Juliana by the braid and threw her on the floor, bit her,

and punched her.[101] It is easy to imagine how these two wom-
en who were rivals for the same man met, exchanged insults,
and then gave vent to their frustration and rage. The women's
braids seem to have been a convenient handhold when attacking and useful in neutralizing the opponent by pulling them
onto the ground. Of course there were other ways to achieve
the same result: tripping, pulling legs out from under a person,
and pushing really hard.

So what is the significance of pulling hair? It was an action that
was designed to demean and debase another person by bringing them low in the most painful manner. It was also an action
that was partially part of the canon of officials whose practice
was often to pull a prisoner by the hair, but, in the case of these
two women, it was also probably borrowed from the kinds of actions that they observed men performing on women regularly. Pulling a person by the hair or braid was most often execut-
ed between spouses or those in quasi-marriages. With pulling
hair, it is possible to trace a type of trickle-down effect in which
officials pull prisoners, an act that is then mimicked by husbands on their wives, and finally then adopted by other people
who were strangers. Why was this bodily language so common
in Mexico in the middle period? It was an action that not only
was practical and painful but also it was symbolically charged.
Pulling the hair meant pulling the head down; it was the syn-
tactic equivalent of a very sharp insult. It served a dual function:
it showed who was in charge while humiliating the person by
bringing their body into submission and deference.

Mexican officials of the middle period had certain methods—some of these were codified, such as the execution of prisoners or their flogging, but others were informally recognized,
such as the pulling of hair. Nonetheless, the common folk recognized that when they thwarted or challenged the local officials
the next step was swift retribution, starting with being pulled by

the hair. When Joseph González, a minister, was collecting his fee in the Tacubaya market, he encountered resistance on the part of certain of the sellers. Don Joseph Juárez, one of the indigenous leaders and mayor of Tacubaya, recounted the scene, stating that the minister was about to take an indigenous woman by the hair when others came to her rescue.[102] The interesting element here is that the people at the market who were watching events unfold recognized what Joseph González's next action was going to be; they connected his status as an official to the defiance of the market woman and assumed the next step. They recognized the pattern. This prototype was fulfilled in another example. When Xochimilco alguaciles went to collect a debt at the house of the widow Teresa Nicolasa, the widow's daughter pleaded with the official not to take her clothes. They interpreted this begging as resistance and they grabbed her by the hair and then hit her.[103] Don Juan de la Peña, himself an indigenous official in Actopan, was the victim of hair-pulling on the part of officials when he and other friends made too much noise one night when they were roaming the streets. He described how the minister had him by the hair and was dragging him to jail. His wife was given the same treatment.[104] It was this action of dragging another person by the hair that was most evocative of the way that officials controlled and humiliated prisoners. Time and time again middle-period Mexicans mimicked the standard official methodology thus making hair-pulling and dragging by the hair a customary action between spouses as well as strangers.

Mexican wives of the middle period often complained of being pulled, grabbed, and frequently being dragged by their hair. Neither they nor their spouses always explained what the reason for such abuse was; it was simply subsumed under the general category of marital cruelty. What is apparent from when either the men or the women gave details was that the common thread was a perceived disrespect. Wives talked back, said no, refused to comply; their husbands then reacted with violence but a certain kind of violence, one that would debase and lower them. When Ojemio Antonio was coming back from work on the hacienda, he met his wife on the road to Coyoacán. She began to insult him using "ill-mannered words." He grabbed her by the hair and pulled her to the ground.[105] Such events could also occur in quasi-marriages. José Mesa was upset when he arrived home in Puebla and his lover Marcelina Mandujano was not home. When she did arrive, like the previous example, she spoke back to José Mesa and told him to go to hell. He grabbed her by the hair and dragged her into the house.[106] In another situation, in Teotihuacan, María Josepha refused to give her husband more pulque; he then grabbed her hair and dragged her out into the patio.[107] In all these examples, the women refused to comply, showing open disrespect for the man. The men's actions were consistent with reasserting their authority but they also, where possible, pulled the women from one space to another. Perhaps this was another way to reassert their control.

One other example is more subtle: the wife does not seem to have challenged her husband's authority, she simply did not meet his behavioral expectations. The incident described happened in Mexico City when doña Susana Soriano did not go out to greet guests in a timely fashion. Her husband reacted with great anger, humiliating her by demanding that she should kiss his feet. He then took her by the hair and threw her on to the tile floor. He also involved a servant who held her by the feet while he took her by the hair.[108] It is telling that this incident occurred between spouses with honorific titles who clearly led a life that was privileged. Although the husband's violence was ostensibly caused by a breach of etiquette that probably would have signified nothing to the plebeian couples who make up the majority of the sample, the retributive violence that he unleashed was familiar. It was a reassertion of authority that merely used more resources (a servant instead of a family member) but employed the familiar grabbing of hair to debase and humiliate his wife.

The numerous other testimonies about husbands pulling wives by their hair don't provide the context—the professed reasons for the violence—they just describe the violence. One of the themes that emerged nevertheless is the pattern of taking women from one place to another by pulling them by the hair. María de la Luz, for example, recounted how her husband accosted her as she was coming back from hearing mass in Coyoacán and dragged her by the hair into the middle of the street. He apparently also had the habit of pulling her hair when they were in bed.[109] Another witness told the story of how María Josefa Romera took refuge in her husband's Mexico City house but that her husband came in and hauled her out of the house by the hair and beat her.[110] There is a painful similarity in the many similar incidents.[111] Husbands dragging spouses by the hair was not solely a Mexican phenomenon. Spierenburg and Muchembled, in their studies of Amsterdam and Artois, respectively, document a few examples of such conduct, although they do not argue that it was a pattern within the violence that they analyzed.[112] In the French example, the man retaliates by grabbing his wife's hair when she accused him of infidelity.[113] An incident in middle-period Mexico replicates this scenario. In Puebla, José María Ramíres attacked both his wife and her daughter dragging her by the hair when accused of an illicit relationship.[114] The parallels between these examples that were separated in time and place provide an eerie pattern of bodily violence that was aimed at controlling women who challenged male authority.

Although the pattern of pulling hair and dragging women from one place to another seems to have been the strongest between couples, husbands and wives were by no means the only

Mexicans who used hair-pulling as a method of attack. Hair was a regular target between people who were not family members because it was a potent insult, but it was also a practical strategy during fights. As in many other contexts there was a conflation of the physical and verbal insults so that words often were reinforced by actions. Shoemaker also found this intermingling of words and deeds in eighteenth-century London. Commenting on an incident when one woman pulled and dragged another by the hair while insulting her, he writes: "It seems likely that such actions had always accompanied public insults, but as the insult itself became less significant (and its content was not specified) concern shifted to the physical attack."[115] These attacks were quite varied in target, ranging from officials, to widows, to rivals in love, to store owners. In only three instances did men drag women who were not their wives by the hair—an exception to the rule elaborated earlier regarding the association of this action with marital relationships—but in these cases, the man in question was trying to engage in a sexual liaison and the woman was resisting.[116] One example was found of a woman who dragged another by the hair: in Puebla Cornelia Ortiz suffered this fate when she mistreated a servant whose mother came and attacked her daughter's employer.[117] In a variant on the motion of dragging a person by the hair from one place to another, in Mexico City captain don Francisco Molina and his wife grasped their cook's hair and pushed her to the zaguán when they suspected that she had been stealing from them.[118] The rest of these examples of hair-pulling were between relative strangers and mostly seem to have used this grasping at locks to restrain an opponent.[119] There was one disparate use of hair—when Phelipa Ramona and her two sons got mad at the alguacil of Tlalmanalco, they grabbed his braid and wrapped it around his throat to choke him.[120] They demonstrated a truly original use of hair-pulling.

Women were not, however, always the victims of hair-pulling as demonstrated in some of the previous examples. But, in addition, some women used the same tactics that were normally employed on them, turned the tables and used them on men. Witnesses often described these women as rebellious and unnatural because they were taking on attitudes and actions that were associated with male behavior. Nicolás de Guadalupe experienced this kind of treatment from his wife in Mexico City. He illustrated his account by telling of one incident when his wife came into the patio insulting him, grabbed him by the hair, and hit him very hard. This incident was simply indicative of her generally rebellious behavior—she drank a lot, slept where she pleased, and mistreated him.[121] Other wives were similarly insubordinate: María de la Luz Carranza and her mother grabbed her husband by the hair in Puebla.[122] Francisco Gerónimo's wife told him off and grabbed his hair to prevent his departure from their residence in the Hacienda de San Gaspar.[123] In Xochimilco, Gertrudis Martina regularly got drunk and both insulted her husband and grabbed his hair.[124] In the Hacienda San Gaspar near Yautepec, Magdalena Francisca defended another woman (a neighbor) by insulting and grabbing this woman's husband by the hair.[125] María Ilaria not only replicated this conduct but tried to drag her husband by the hair to another house in Tacuba, behaving like a man.[126] In other cases, the women in question seem to have been reacting to a perceived threat. In Mexico City, María Ladrón de Guevara (alias la Quata) attacked a man who scolded her by grabbing him by the hair and hitting him.[127] She might have simply struck first in order to avert an attack. In all these examples, the pattern of hair-pulling filtered down from the practices of Mexican officials through the rituals of husbands into a kind of inversion. These women were not original in their forms of attacks—they simply adopted the syntax of bodily attack that they observed around them.

Conclusion

Both clothes and hair are central to a person's identity, providing us with a quick guide as to where this individual situates him or herself within the various social groupings that prevail. A person in uniform gains either respect or fear just because his or her clothes signify authority and belonging to a group entrusted with enforcement of societal norms. At the same time, more informal attire can imply belonging to any number of social groups within youth culture. In middle-period Mexico these distinctions were less diverse perhaps but no less important. Authority was conveyed by symbols such as a staff of office, whereas the luxury of dress might indicate social position. Conversely clothes associated with indigenous or African roots denoted not only racial belonging but relative social inferiority. Hair in all its stylings also provided clues to social and ethnic belonging. Yet there was much more to clothes and hair — they also were very much connected with power and sexuality. Both had profound associations with morality but also were used to be alluring. Thus they could both provoke sexuality and be used to punish a promiscuous woman. The messages conveyed by hair and clothes meant that they were useful as tools within the various strategies of violence that Mexicans used in the middle period. It would be pointless to attack body elements that were insignificant or meaningless, so instead people took aim at elements that were central to another person's being.

When Mexicans pulled at another person's hair or clothes, they were following a strategy that was not usually as drastic as hitting the head or other parts of the body. Few people died as a result of having their hair or clothes pulled. Yet, the damage to their honor and their feelings might have been severe. Pulling could be innocuous or violent — it has to be placed on a continuum of actions from the most benign to quite violent. If part of a larger attack, pulling could be one element of a vicious attack. For example, when one person pulled another down in order to hit them or to perpetrate a more comprehensive assault, this pulling was part and parcel of a strategy of intense violence. When men pulled their wives or amasias by the hair—usually from one space to another—they were following a scenario to reassert their authority that was derived from the common conduct of officials controlling prisoners. Tugging at a person could also be the prelude—it might accompany or follow "fighting words." It could be either part of an attack or warn of it. Whether pulling at hair or clothes, Mexicans followed strategies that were codified in the populace—this was a grammar of violence. While not always harming the other person physically, they were attacking the very core of their identity—hair and clothes provided the messages that determined gender, ethnicity, rank, and morality. Such attacks were strategic in that they did not attract such penalties as wounds and blows, but they were no less important in the negotiation of daily life in Mexico.

8. Culture, Honor, and Gender in Mexico

How conscious are we of the ways that the buildings around us and the people with whom we interact affect our lives? To a great extent, individuals probably do not give these aspects of their existence much thought unless they live in a culture foreign to their own. It is only when trying to read the messages imparted by unfamiliar architecture and body language that such aspects of daily life are highlighted and become important. When struggling to understand alien surroundings and perplexing behavior, the manners by which culture forms us and provides us with a roadmap for our actions becomes much more apparent. Would middle-period Mexicans be aware of their interactions with their built environment and bodies? It seems that since it was relatively unlikely that they traveled between cultures easily or often or that they encountered many foreigners in their midst, they might not have been as sensitive to these nuances in the way that many people in the twentieth or twenty-first centuries would be. Yet middle-period Mexicans signaled their concern with proper behavior in certain spaces as well as with correct comportment and thus body language in both their reactions to others and their descriptions of incidents that disrupted social norms.

The people who testified in court cases or wrote tracts on proper conduct and morality might not have deliberately set out to record the ways that culture constructed the mental map of their world. But, because these aspects of their lives were important, snippets and details slipped into their testimonies and books. It is only because this culture of bodies and space is so fundamental to the way that individuals organize themselves and their relations with others that it is part of the historical record. It is by understanding the way that culture shapes our behavior that we can recognize the means by which such frameworks affect the larger history of places and people. It is in this fashion that the stories related in this book can inform those scholars interested in the great men and events of traditional political history. Historians have often documented the battles and the duels that elite men controlled. More recently, authors have connected these events to systems of honor and belief; what this book does is relate the actions that dominated the lives of plebeians to concepts of honor in the larger sense, and more precisely, to the ways that these individuals understood the spaces and bodies around them.

How people interacted with and understood their worlds were complex and interconnected. Although in this book space and body have been separated into two distinct sections for the sake of clarity, perceptive readers will have noted how the two categories did not entirely remain isolated. It was difficult not to mention how bodily language or violence was linked to particular spaces. Bodies and spaces are very much intermeshed, acting upon each other. People's bodies take on attitudes depending on the context, but this context includes not just the other people around them but also the built environment. It is in this way that spaces and bodies are interconnected through a language of violence that flows out of and is connected to the grammar of bodies and spaces. At the most basic level there are two axes that provide a framework for this grammar: the horizontal and the vertical. These two directions are clearest for space that is divided into core and periphery as well as high and low. For bodies it is the high versus low axis that prevails, but in addition, people placed themselves within a horizontal axis when they operated within the spaces of core and periphery. They chose to push themselves closer to the interior of a church (the altar) or a room (perhaps the home altar) to make clear their position on this axis. These attitudes were a subset of the conventions derived from honor. The language of honor structured colonial and early national Mexico and provided a general code or rhetoric that all sectors of society understood albeit in manners specific to their rankings. The scholarly literature on honor has blossomed in the past few decades with studies on far-flung regions distant and different from the Mediterranean. The next step in the study of honor is to parse out the ways in which honor shapes the daily life practices not just of elites but also plebeians, and to examine the ways that the symbolic culture of a people intermeshed and connected into this framework. It is in the layering of meanings that we can begin to understand how people worked within a grammar not only of violence but also of elements such as space and body.

The language of space and body, honor and violence, as well the various grammars and syntaxes that have been referred to within this book developed in a number of manners. Principally there seems to have been a top-down movement with ideas about honor, deference, and hierarchy originating with the elite stratum of society. Although the higher ups would not recognize what they considered to be their birthright—honor—within other groups, it was clear that this system operated in all classes and ethnicities. Indeed because both Spanish and

Nahua cultures shared many underlying concepts, this frame-work was all the more resilient as it traveled through the var-ious social layers. The language of body also developed to a great extent by mimicry—it was very often the actions of Mex-ican officials that molded its shape within plebeian society but also women seem to have borrowed from the language of male violence in order to act out against other women. It was a way of imposing deference and submission of asserting status and honor or turning that language upside down in order to humil-iate and deny honor or rank.

The various incidents described in this book might seem triv-ial at times—the product of petty disputes and misunderstand-ings. But they were important enough that middle-period Mex-icans lashed out over them, they hit each other and they risked retaliation. They acted in this manner because their sense of what was right was offended; it was a social contract of sorts that provided for social equilibrium and peace. When another person breached these agreements about social status and po-sition Mexicans acted in order to maintain their place within the framework of honor and social rankings. So when a young person entered a room and needed to choose the appropriate chair in which to sit, he or she was not just sitting down but also taking their (appropriate) place within that social group. The young person accepted the social conventions of honor as they were expressed in the grammar of space and body. This young person was negotiating his or her place in daily life.

Notes

1. Negotiating Daily Life

1. Hardendorft Burr, *Hispanic Furniture*, 10, 25, 54, writes that in earlier periods, hosts offered only the most distinguished guests a chair, and although chairs became more regular after the Renaissance, women still generally sat on cushions. Male guests sat on "chairs or stools, according to the rank they held, since the chair at this time and even previously was offered only to a person whom one wished to honour [*sic*]." Those of lower ranks sat on stools. For a history of the social use and evolution of chairs, see Rybczynski, *Home*, 26. Alejandro Cañeque, *The King's Living Image*, writes, "chairs similarly constituted an essential element in the semiotics of power" (149). Such decisions about the choice of a chair would not have been an issue for plebeians since most families of modest means did not have chairs, according to Gonzalbo Aizpuru, *Vivir en Nueva España*, 233.

2. Escoiquiz, *Tratado de las Obligaciones*, 117–19. Although the author of this manual published it originally for the Spanish court, it was reprinted in 1795, 1803, 1851, and 1884, and many copies found their way into Mexican collections and libraries. Escoiquiz's advice is replicated in a nineteenth-century Mexican manual written by Diez de Bonilla, *Código completo*, 41, 170. See also Galban Ribera, *Catecismo de urbanidad*, 26–29.

3. Cañeque, *The King's Living Image*, 119, writes about some of the quarrels between colonial officials over the right to take cushions of black velvet to mass. He argues that although historians have generally dismissed these

arguments as frivolous and entertaining, the struggles were actually a symbolic extension of the political struggles.

4. Gonzalbo Aizpuru, *Introducción*, 111, explains that these ideas about hierarchy and etiquette also filtered down into the lower classes who, in the situation used to introduce this book, would have remained standing while the people who were socially superior to them would have been allowed to sit down.

5. Cañeque, *The King's Living Image*, 137–38; Gonzalbo Aizpuru, *Introducción*, 19–20, says that it is through the study of symbols and customs that historians can access seemingly inaccessible mentalities. She suggests using moral codes not as dogma but rather as a starting hypothesis.

6. Taylor, *The Archive and the Repertoire*, 26.

7. Macias-González, "Hombres de mundo," 267.

8. Torres Septién, "Notas sobre urbanidad," 90, argues that in order to understand the ideas on manners of nineteenth-century Mexicans it is necessary to look back as far as Erasmus. Macias-González, "Hombres de mundo," 267, argues that such books prolonged the mentality of the ancien régime. See also Beezley, *Mexican National Identity*, 19, who notes that there were considerable continuities despite the proclamations of the new republic.

9. Hurl-Eamon, *Gender and Petty Violence*, 65.

10. There is a large historical literature on duels. I have consulted the following: Shoemaker, "The Taming of the Duel"; Parker, "Law, Honor and Impunity"; Piccato, "Politics and the Technology of Honor"; and Undurraga Schüler, "Cuando las afrentas se lavaban con sangre."

11. Spierenburg, "Knife Fighting," 111, 114; Spierenburg, *Written in Blood*, 18; Gallant, "Honor, Masculinity," 361; Muchembled, *La violence au village*, 7–8; and Shoemaker, *The London Mob*, 153, 164.

12. There is a large literature on this subject. A good place to start is Johnson and Lipsett-Rivera, *The Faces of Honor*.

13. Taylor, *Drinking, Homicide and Rebellion*, 81–82. Muchembled, *La violence au village*, 163–65, describes similar prefight conduct including insults, aggressive gestures such as hand gestures, and hitting the ground with a sword.

14. Bourdieu, *Outline of a Theory of Practice*, 11.

15. García Márquez, *Crónica de una muerte anunciada*. I would like to thank Pablo Rodríguez for this insight.

16. Spierenburg, "Knife Fighting," 104.

17. Spierenburg, "Knife Fighting," 105; Gallant, "Honor, Masculinity," 362; and Shoemaker, *The London Mob*, 164–68.

18. Spierenberg, "Knife-fighting," 109–10. Beezley, *Mexican National Identity*, 106, notes that even among puppets the various personalities chose weapons specific to their class. Don Folias used a pistol whereas El Negro chose a knife.

19. Spierenberg, "Knife Fighting," 115–16.

20. Hurl-Eamon, *Gender and Petty Violence*, particularly, 66–67 and 70–71, corrects this imbalance by making gender a central feature of her analysis of petty crime in early modern London. Spierenberg, "How Violent Were Women? 9–28, also addresses the inclusion of women in these scenarios of violence in this article. Other historians have rejected the notion that there could be any similar formulations for female violence, arguing that female violence lacked rules entirely, and was, in contrast to male violence, out of control. See Shoemaker, *The London Mob*, 169.

21. Peristiany, *Honor and Shame*; Peristiany and Pitt-Rivers, *Honor and Grace*; Pitt-Rivers, *The Fate of Shechem*; and Caro Baroja, *La ciudad y el campo*.

22. Taylor, *Honor and Violence*.

23. Maravall, *Poder, honor y élites*, 44.

24. Twinam, *Public Lives*.

25. A good example of such behavior is the Galicia family of Xochimilco who broke into the home of María Manuela Morales in order to beat her and try to prevent the birth of her child. Her crime was that she had announced her marriage to their son while being very visibly pregnant. They believed that the marriage would be detrimental to their status. AGN, Criminal, vol. 40, exp. 16, Xochimilco, 1809.

26. See for example, Shoemaker, *The London Mob*, 51; Taylor, *Honor and Violence*, 120–21. Sloan, *Runaway Daughters*, 117, emphasizes the importance of reputation for market vendors, for "who in the community would buy meat or fruit from a whore or thief?"

27. AJP, paquete 1, no exp. number, Puebla, 1856, Antonio Flores, heridor de María Soledad Martínez.

28. For a new view of the active defense of honor by women in Latin America see Lipsett-Rivera, "A Slap in the Face of Honor"; Chambers, *From Subjects to Citizens*; and Sloan, *Runaway Daughters*.

29. López Austin, *The Human Body and Ideology*, vol. 1, 393–96. I have written more extensively about the syncretism of body and honor between the Spanish and the Nahua in "Language of Body," 66–82.

30. Hall, *The Hidden Dimension*, 108.

31. Muchembled, *La violence au village*, 144, 150–54. Dogs were the "sentinelles avancées du 'moi,'" where bad treatment of animals owned by a person

could provoke strong reactions because they are part of "moi." Dogs watched and protected the boundaries of the ego's territory, 163–65.

32. Farr, "The Pure and Disciplined Body," 408.

33. Boyer, "Respect and Identity," 492.

34. Maravall, *Poder, honor y élites*, 81, 88.

35. See, for example, Lipsett-Rivera, "Marriage and Family Relations"; Lipsett-Rivera, "Mira Lo Que Hace el Diablo," 201–19. Kanter, *Hijos del Pueblo*, 24, also writes that she found few signs of the big political events such as the independence movement in her documents.

2. Space and Mexican Society

1. Tuan, *Space and Place*, 102, writes: "[T]he built environment clarifies social roles and relations. People know better who they are and how they ought to behave when the arena is humanly designed."

2. Stansell, "Women, Children, and the Uses of the Streets," 311.

3. Wood, "Locating Violence," 20.

4. Stansell, *City of Women*, 184, uses the expression "eroticization of public spaces" to describe what upper-class New Yorkers believed that gangs of girls had perpetrated in the streets. Ross, "Fierce Questions and Taunts," 582, notes that London children perceived different spaces as belonging either to a masculine or feminine realm.

5. Certeau, *The Practice of Everyday Life*, 117.

6. Hernández, "Implicated Spaces, Daily Struggles," 65–88.

7. Hall, *The Hidden Dimension*, 43, 50, 97. Muchembled, *La violence au village*, 30, also argues that people have a sense of space that provokes violence because they have to protect their self-identified boundaries. Tuan, *Space and Place*, 107, compares the built environment to language.

8. Hall, *The Hidden Dimension*, 138, explains how urban grid patterns often reflect the way that people organize themselves in other contexts.

9. Spain, *Gendered Spaces*, 111; Rapoport, *House Form and Culture*, 46, says that "[t]he house is an institution, not just a structure, created for a complex set of purposes." He considers the construction of a house to be a "cultural phenomenon" whose "form and organization are greatly influenced by the cultural milieu to which it belongs." See also Cámara Muñoz, *Arquitectura y sociedad*, 88.

10. Spain, *Gendered Spaces*, 33–103; Sennett, *The Conscience of the Eye*, 18; Mannarelli, *Private Passions and Public Sins*, 31, finds that although they were strongly warned against it, elite Peruvian women went into the streets.

Hurl-Eamon, *Gender and Petty Violence*, 81–83, also assigns gendered qualities to space. The street and the highway were masculine spaces. Within London, certain streets and lanes were associated with prostitution and these were considered dangerous for other reasons.

11. Ross, "Survival Networks," 5, notes: "Gender differences were reproduced in patterns of movement in streets, shops, and pubs. Men and women socialized differently and actually knew different people in their own streets." She adds that men had a wider radius of circulation. See also Taylor, *Honor and Violence*, 176–77.

12. Certeau, *The Practice of Everday Life*, 97–98.

13. AGN, Criminal, vol. 57, exp. 7b, fol. 197–99, Mexico City, 1782. In a similar complaint, doña Lorenza Suáres complained that because her husband did not provide for her, she had to beg, "exposing her to whatever audacious man who might detain her in the street." AGN, Bienes Nacionales, legajo 717, exp. 100, fol. 1–4v, Mexico City, 1853. Kanter, *Hijos del Pueblo*, 47, also states that streets were "the domain of men."

14. AGN, Criminal, vol. 632, exp. 9, fol. 271–90, Mexico City, 1779.

15. AJTS, Penales, vol. 8, exp. 44, Mexico City, 1796.

16. Lauderdale Graham, *House and Street*, 15, writes of Brazilian ideas about house and street: "House represented private and protected spaces that contrasted with the public and unpleasant, possibly dangerous places of the street."

17. Viqueira Albán, *Propriety*, 98–103. Stansell, *City of Women*, 41, states that by 1820 in the United States, the urban bourgeoisie began to see households "as more than just lodgings"—the word "home" began to be used and it was conceived as a place where women stayed and worked whereas men left the home to work. This was very different from the working classes whose lives spread into hallways and streets, and work took women out of their lodgings.

18. Kanter, *Hijos del Pueblo*, 38, highlights this contradiction.

19. Wood, *Violence and Crime*, 98; Hernández, *Implicated Spaces*, 110, notes that there was a connection between settings and actions; the precedent of domestic violence in the home meant that this locale became "safe" or "accepted" as a place where men could be violent. Gonzalbo Aizpuru, *Introducción*, 181, writes that spaces determined forms of conduct.

20. Wood, *Violence and Crime*, 103.

21. Viqueira Albán, *Propriety*, 12; Curcio-Nagy, "Giants and Gypsies," 9; and Cañeque, *The King's Living Image*, chap. 4.

22. Wood, "Locating Violence," 23.

23. Wood, "Locating Violence," 30; Gallant, "Honor, Masculinity," 364, also connects ritual violence with the space where it happened, noting that most confrontations took place in public places because the audience was important. See also Hernández, *Implicated Spaces,* 117–19.

24. Boyer, "Respect and Identity," 494–96.

25. Wood, "Locating Violence," 23, argues that "particular kinds of spaces have an important impact on the production of aggression, due to the ways in which they shape the nature of interpersonal relationships and the potential for conflict." Spierenberg, "Knife Fighting," 118, states that in homicides of women in early modern Amsterdam, wives tended to be killed in the home whereas female acquaintances or recent sweethearts were killed in taverns.

26. Wood, *Violence and Crime,* 98, 102, writes that the public spaces were also important to the working classes because people's conduct was open to scrutiny in these areas.

27. Gonzalbo Aizpuru, *Introducción,* 179.

28. Rybczynski, *Home,* 77; Gonzalbo Aizpuru, *Introducción,* 179. Kanter, *Hijos del Pueblo,* 54, writes that rural houses were cramped and lacked privacy.

29. Bailey "I dye [*sic*] by Inches," 273–94, argues that historians need to discover what these terms meant for the society and the time that they study. In eighteenth-century England private meant hidden and public meant openly witnessed. Shoemaker, *The London Mob,* 5, notes that in eighteenth-century London, boulevards and broad avenues were considered public, whereas alleyways, courts, and dead ends were considered private. See also Van Deusen, *Between the Sacred and the Worldly,* 82; and Wood, "Locating Violence," 31. Hall, *The Hidden Dimension,* 146, makes the point that concept of public and private also vary across cultures.

30. Hurl-Eamon, *Gender and Petty Violence,* 87, writes about the ways that eighteenth-century Londoners used the "clearly understood spatial customs" to heighten the impact of their violence and humiliation.

31. Wood, "Locating Violence," 20; see also Wood, *Violence and Crime,* 105–10.

32. Wood, "Locating Violence," 30, also sees this pattern; he says that even though the home was to a great extent an imagined space, its defense was considered a justifiable reason for violence. Gonzalbo Aizpuru, *Introducción,* 179, writes that the concept of *hogar,* or home-hearth as a site of private family life, appeared in Mexico in the nineteenth century.

33. AJTS Civil, vol. 113, 1756, Coyoacán.

34. AJP, 1775, paquete 2, exp. 13 Puebla.

35. AGN, Criminal, vol. 624, exp. 2, fol. 39v-40, Mexico City, 1756; AJP, 1836, paquete 2, exp. 663, Puebla.

36. Rapoport, *House Form and Culture*, 69.

37. Burkhart, *The Slippery Earth*, 63–64; and Taggart, *Nahuat Myth*, 55. Kanter, *Hijos del Pueblo*, 52, writes of the "powerful symbolic divide between house and street."

38. Kagan, *Urban Images of the Hispanic World*, 27.

39. Lipsett-Rivera, "Mira lo que hace el diablo," 201–19.

40. Lira Vásquez, *Para una historia*, 17, argues that this pattern was also present in pre-Hispanic cities. See also Lombardo de Ruiz, "El desarrollo urbano," 138. Lejeune, "Dreams of Order," 33, notes that as far back as the Reconquest, Christian leaders built cities that were "laid out as on an irregular chessboard and had a central square at the intersection of the axes." See also Morse, "Some Characteristics"; and Tuan, *Space and Place*, 38.

41. Kagan, *Urban Images*, 31–32; Fraser, *The Architecture of Conquest*, 25–42.

42. Fraser, *The Architecture of Conquest*, 6–7. See also Rivera-Ayala, *El Discurso Colonial*, 90.

43. Cámara Muñoz, *Arquitectura y sociedad*, 90; Jeffery, "From Azulejos to Zaguanes," 317; Tuan, *Space and Place*, 41.

44. Holler, "Conquered Spaces," 109.

45. Walker, "The Upper Classes," 58.

46. Rapoport, *House Form and Culture*, 30, states that this pattern of core and periphery was imported indirectly from Muslim cities where the nobler crafts were located next to the mosque and the less honorable trades had their workshops further from the core and the mosque.

47. Morales and Gayón, "Viviendas," 345. See also Gonzalbo Aizpuru, "Familias y viviendas," 82–83, 92, who also notes that people constructed jacales in the more central part of Mexico City in vacant lots and in courtyards, and that they were associated with poverty and discomfort. But this pattern may have deeper roots. Gose, *Invaders as Ancestors*, 161, argues that the notion of ordered, sacred living emanating from the church altar produced a "concentric spatial aesthetic" in colonial Peru. Rapoport, *The Meaning of the Built Environment*, 111, states that in most traditional societies there is an association between centrality—or a central urban location—and higher status.

48. Kagan, *Urban Images*, 34.

49. Fraser, *The Architecture of Conquest*, 40–41.

50. As cited by Van Deusen, *Between the Sacred and the Worldly*, 81.

51. AGN Criminal vol. 203 exp. 9 fols. 366–403, Cuernavaca, 1798.

52. López Austin, *The Human Body and Ideology*, vol. 1, 255, 260; Burkhart, *The Slippery Earth*, 63; and Taggart, *Nahuat Myth*, 55.

53. Jefferey, "From Azulejos to Zaguanes," 313–14; see also Rapoport, *House Form and Culture*, 30. Sennett, *The Conscience*, 18, writes that the dualism between inner and outer parts of the city can be traced back to medieval cities that were organized around either a castle or a church at their core, both of which provided a space of sanctuary.

54. Cruz, "Building Liberal Identities," 401; and Jímenez Muñoz, *La traza del poder*, 8.

55. De la Torre V. et al., "La vivienda," 117–18; and Lira Vásquez, *Para una historia*, 107.

56. Gonzalbo Aizpuru, "Familias y viviendas," 87.

57. Gonzalbo Aizpuru, "Familias y viviendas"; de la Torre V. et al., "La vivienda," 119–20.

58. Gonzalbo Aizpuru, "Familias y viviendas," 87.

59. De la Torre V. et al., "La vivienda," 122–23.

60. Gonzalbo Aizpuru, "Familias y viviendas," 82.

61. Gonzalbo Aizpuru, *Vivir en Nueva España*, 188.

62. Loreto López, "La casa," 156–57; de la Torre V. et al., "La vivienda," 118. Rapoport, *The Meaning*, 111, notes that in Cambodia, nobles had raised houses and slaves were only allowed to use the ground floor.

63. Cope, *The Limits of Racial Domination*, 30–31.

64. Morales and Gayón, "Viviendas," 345.

65. Spain, *Gendered Spaces*, 116–21; and Stansell, *City of Women*, 160.

66. Walker, "The Upper Classes," 71, 75–76; and Cámara Muñoz, *Arquitectura*, 93.

67. De la Torre V. et al., "La vivienda," 120.

68. Haslip-Viera, *Crime and Punishment*, 12.

69. Cope, *The Limits of Racial Domination*, 27.

70. Haslip-Viera, *Crime and Punishment*, 33.

71. Morales and Gayón, "Viviendas," 345.

72. Loreto López, "La casa," 161.

73. Loreto López, "La casa," 158. The word *zaguán* comes from the Arabic *ustawaan*, which means either a porch or breezeway. Jefferey, "From Azulejos to Zaguanes," 320.

74. Lefebvre, *The Production of Space*, 209–10.

75. Rapoport, *House Form and Culture*, 40, 80, goes on to say that it divides the sacred from the profane.

76. Kanter, *Hijos del Pueblo*, 53.

77. Loreto López, "La casa," 161; Nuñez, "The Interaction of Space and Place," 20, writes that patios encourage sociability between people of similar status while discouraging that with outsiders.

78. Lockhart, *The Nahuas*, 60–61.

79. Loreto López, "La casa," 158; Jefferey, "From Azulejos to Zaguanes," 320.

80. Loreto López, "La casa," 158.

81. Jeffery, "From Azulejos to Zaguanes," 315, says that the courtyard represents an Islamic element that used geometric forms and also the concept of centrality. Rapoport, *House Form and Culture*, 66, notes that Latin American buildings in general have an interior orientation that contrasts with the typically outward facing Anglo-Saxon house. He also notes that this practice derives from the Muslim tradition in urban architecture in which houses are inward looking.

82. Loreto López, "La casa," 158.

83. AJP no exp., 1846, Atlixco, proceso en contra María Guadalupe por herir; AJP no exp., 1826, Proceso en contra de Marcos de Santiago; AJP 1836 #179, Huejotzingo; AGN, Criminal, vol. 40, exp. 16, fol. 375–75v, Xochimilco, 1809; AGN Criminal vol. 52, exp. 6 fols. 247–59v, Temascaltepec, 1799; AGN Criminal vol. 203 exp. 10 fol. 404–432, Cuernavaca, 1816; AGN Criminal vol. 235 exp. 12 fol. 82–148, Coyoacán, 1802; AGN Criminal vol 253 exp. 6 fol. 161–226, Yautepec, 1816; AGN Criminal vol. 47 exp. 4 fol. 106–185, Cuernavaca, 1813; AGN Criminal vol. 130 exp. 9 fols. 334–482, Temascaltepec, 1799; AGN Criminal vol. 670 exp. 2 fol. 27–46, Mexico City, 1806.

84. Loreto López, "La casa," 158.

85. Cañeque, *The King's Living Image*, 138; Galban Ribera, *Catecismo de urbanidad civil*, 27.

86. Escoiquiz, *Tratado de las Obligaciones del Hombre*, 121–24; Anonymous, *Reglas de la buena crianza*,14; Cañeque, *The King's Living Body*, 137, also mentions this pattern of etiquette regarding stairs.

87. Diez de Bonilla, *Código completo*, 172. His recommendations are very similar to those of Escoiquiz.

88. AGN, Civil, legajo 206, no. exp., Mexico City, 1853.

89. De la Torre V. et al., "La vivienda," 116. Cope, *The Limits of Racial*, 30, writes that few plebeians in Mexico City could afford a home.

90. Morales and Gayón, "Viviendas," 345.

91. De la Torre V. et al., "La vivienda," 120.

92. Women living in accesorias were sometimes assumed to be prostitutes.

And sometimes they were, as in the case of María Gertrudis Ortega and María Josefa Romero, who used an accesoria in the Barrio Santa Ana for assignations with their male clients. AJTS Penales, vol. 9, exp. 20, fol. 202v, Mexico City, 1797.

93. Stern, *The Secret History of Gender,* 92; and Kanter, *Hijos del Pueblo,* 47.

94. De la Torre V. et al., "La vivienda," 118. Gonzalbo Aizpuru, *Vivir en Nueva España,* 227–28, writes that in New Spain the estrado did not follow the peninsular model of the raised platform but rather privacy was achieved with the use of folding screens.

95. Lira Vásquez, *Para una historia,* 107, 119–20.

96. Lira Vásquez, *Para una historia,* 114.

97. Escoiquiz, *Tratado de las Obligaciones,* 117–19; twentieth-century psychologists recognize a similar phenomenon. Argyle "The Syntaxes of Bodily Communication," 157, writes that conduct related to space can be used to indicate rank in other manners "by occupying seats or other areas which have symbolic value, for example sitting at the head of a table, or in one of the front seats."

98. Diez de Bonilla, *Código completo,* 96, 41.

99. AGN, Criminal, vol. 406, exp. 5, fol. 202–26v, Mexico City, 1804. He did, however, talk to her on a balcony.

100. Rossell, *La educación conforme,* 109. Diez de Bonilla, *Código completo,* 70, 113, writes that one's house is a reflection of oneself, and that both one's house and one's family should be orderly, regular, and clean. Galindo, *Parte segunda,* 38, also notes that if the saints portrayed in paintings are shown without clothes and in a provocative, dishonest way, this was sinful and not apt to inspire devotion.

101. Gonzalbo Aizpuru, *Introducción,* 188; and Hardendorft Burr, *Hispanic Furniture,* 107. Cruz, "Building Liberal Identities," 398, writes that the Spanish middle classes began to have more consumer goods in their homes in the eighteenth century.

102. Loreto López, "Familial Religiosity," 26–49.

103. Gonzalbo Aizpuru, *Introducción,* 189.

104. Rossell, *La educación,* 109.

105. Astete, *Tratado del buen govierno,* 55.

106. Astete, *Tratado del buen govierno,* 60–61, notes that instead the house was to be a place of work and any free time was to be spent in a chapel.

107. Astete, *Tratado del buen gobierno,* 183–84.

108. Astete, *Tratado del buen gobierno,* 217–18.

109. Cerda, *Libro intitulado,*10.

110. Lizana y Beaumont, *Instrucción Pastoral del Illmo*, 21; Galindo, *Parte segunda*, 154–56; Osuna, *Norte de los estados*, 94v; Astete, *Tratado del buen gobierno*, 55, 183–84; and Moles, *Doctrina Christiana*, 119.

111. See, for example, Galindo, *Parte segunda*, 154–56; Osuna, *Norte de los estados*, 94v; Astete, *Tratado del buen gobierno*, 55, 183–84; and Moles, *Doctrina Christiana*, 119.

112. One exception is AJP no. 4958, exp. 12, 1785, in which Capt. Ramón de Riveros describes how his Puebla neighbors watched at the windows when a woman insulted his daughter in front of their residence.

113. This contrasts with what Stansell, *City of Women*, 41, reports for New York where this association began to appear only in the early nineteenth century among the urban bourgeoisie.

114. Córdoba, *Jardín de las nobles donzellas*, part 2, chap. 3. Galindo, *Verdades morale*, 45, also says that women should not dress extravagantly to go out but rather stay home with their husbands. In a more contemporary study, Ross, "Fierce Questions and Taunts," 582, finds that "Household jurisdictions, and even physical spaces, were sharply divided by gender. Children's language showed their awareness of 'masculine' and 'feminine' household divisions."

115. De Arizmendi, *Sermones en las Festividades*, 20–21.

116. Astete, *Tratado del buen gobierno*, 148–49.

3. Behind Closed Doors

1. Van Deusen, *Between the Sacred and the Worldly*, 4–6, explains the gender dimensions and complications surrounding recogimiento in daily practice.

2. Moles, *Doctrina Christiana*, 150. Rapoport, *The Meaning of the Built Environment*, 129, reports that in West Africa, among the Dogomba, it was the doorframe of the portal to the compound whose embellishment and prominence was significant.

3. Galindo, *Verdades morales*, 147; see also de Rosales, *Caton Christiano*, 61.

4. Villa-Flores, *Dangerous Speech*, 117. Hall, *The Hidden Dimension*, 127, reports that Germans assign values to open or shut doors: "open doors are sloppy and disorderly," whereas closed doors protect the integrity of those within.

5. As cited in Loreto López, "Family Religiosity," 34.

6. Gonzalbo Aizpuru, *Introducción*, 178. In nineteenth-century New York City, Stansell, *City of Women*, 56, reports that "doors were seldom locked, even at night." Fraser, *The Architecture of Conquest*, 44, writes that in Matienzo's 1567 plan for indigenous house layouts "the front door of each house should open onto the street so that their activities could be monitored."

7. An example of suspicious activity can be found in the complaint of don Miguel Najera who rented the main rooms of his house to two women who proceeded to have men coming in at all hours of the night. Don Miguel went up to scold the women and found them in a tryst with men. AJTS, Penales, vol. 9, exp. 16, fol. 3–3v, Mexico City, 1792. Don Domingo Gutiérrez de la Torre, alcalde of the second cuartel, received a denunciation of suspicious activity in a house in front of the Colegio de San Gregorio. It was said that several women lived there and that they received men at all hours of the day and night. AJTS, Penales, vol. 8, exp. 20, fol. 2, Mexico City, 1798.

8. Astete, *Tratado del buen govierno*, 63.

9. AJP, paquete 6, Puebla, 1856, Proceso contra Magdaleno Juáres, heridor de su mujer Andrea Salazar. This correlation could also be true for men. María Gertrudis Rodríguez Corola, reported that she suspected her husband was in an affair because she found him enclosed in a room with a woman. AJTS, Penales, vol. 4, exp. 33, fol. 2, Mexico City, 1785.

10. AGN, Bienes Nacionales, vol. 292, exp. 1, Mexico City, 1790.

11. AJP, paquete 6, exp. 321, Puebla, 1856.

12. AGN, Criminal, vol. 11, exp. 9, fol. 61–77, Otumba, 1783.

13. AGN, Criminal, vol. 214, exp. 12, fol. 214–55, Cuautla Amilpas, 1779.

14. AGN, Criminal, vol. 630, exp. 16, fol. 385–403, Cuautitlan, 1771.

15. See discussion in Lipsett-Rivera, "The Intersection of Rape and Marriage," 559–90.

16. AGN, Criminal, vol. 431, exp. 7, fol. 245–257v, Atlixco, 1816.

17. AJTS, Penales, vol. 8, exp. 11, Mexico City, 1794.

18. AJTS, Penales, vol. 6 exp. 50, Mexico City, 1790.

19. AJP, paquete 6, Puebla, 1856, Proceso contra Antonio Herrera, heridor de su mujer, Severiana Figueroa.

20. AGN, Criminal, vol. 705, exp. 2, fol. 12–28, Tenango del Valle, 1763.

21. Taylor, *Honor and Violence*, 46.

22. Kanter, *Hijos de Pueblo*, 53.

23. AJTS, Penales, vol. 7, exp. 26, Mexico City, 1791.

24. AGN, Criminal, vol. 11, exp. 9, fol. 61–77, Otumba, 1783; the chile poultice might have its origins in more official punishments. Kanter, *Hijos del Pueblo*, 78, reports that an official ordered that the guards give a female prisoner an enema that she describes as "an unusual and humiliating punishment."

25. Rapoport, *House Form*, 80, writes that, "The compound in India or the Mexican or Moslem house put the threshold further forward than the Western house does, and the fence of the English house puts it further forward than the open lawn of the American suburb."

26. Ward, *A History of Domestic Space*, 133, states that "[t]he threshold marked the boundary between private and public terrain; moving indoors or out meant passing directly from one sphere to the other."

27. Lefebvre, *The Production of Space*, 210.

28. Stansell, *City of Women*, 56, writes that on warm summer nights the women living in New York City tenements would gather on their stoops and talk to each other. They would also hang out of windows and spend the evenings out of doors. Sloan, *Runaway Daughters*, 114, recounts how one couple courted in the woman's doorway. Taylor, *Honor and Violence*, 144.

29. Gonzalbo Aizpuru, *Vivir en Nueva España*, 197.

30. Gowing, *Domestic Dangers*, 98.

31. Hurl-Eamon, *Gender and Petty Violence*, 86.

32. One reference to communication between lovers through windows was found. Doña María Lino Ricardo de Iberri said that she spoke daily to Sergeant Miguel Ortiz at her window. AGN, Criminal, vol. 406, exp. 5, fol. 202–26v, Mexico City, 1804.

33. Viqueira Albán, *Propriety*, 100.

34. AGN, Inquisición, vol. 1373, exp. 13, fol. 173–223, Mexico City, 1792.

35. AJP, no. 2247, Puebla, 1846. proceso criminal contra Perfecta Vásquez. Hurl-Eamon, *Gender and Petty Violence*, 88, finds that some of the conflicts between neighbors in London were over the disciplining of children.

36. Nuñez, "The Interaction," 61–62.

37. AGN, Criminal, vol. 583, exp. 14, fol. 300–39, Mexico City, 1803.

38. AGN, Criminal, vol. 124, exp. 12, fol. 136, Santiago Tianguistengo, 1807.

39. AGN, Criminal, vol. 80, exp. 19, fol. 561–70, Tulancingo, 1811.

40. AGN, Criminal, vol. 582, exp. 15, fol. 341–42, Mexico City, 1802.

41. AGN, Criminal, vol. 27, exp. 8, fol. 230v, Teotihuacan, 1773.

42. AJP, no. 3390, Puebla, 1850, Causa en contra de Matías Ramírez, acusado de herir a María Simona Ochoa.

43. AGN, Criminal, vol. 41, exp. 25, fol. 389–389v, Xochimilco, 1741.

44. Gowing, *Domestic Dangers*, 98.

45. Rapoport, *House Form*, 80.

46. AJTS, Penales, vol. 7, exp. 77, Mexico City, 1792. Another example of using a window for an insult is more direct. María Berrios stuck her head out of a window and yelled to María Cevallos that she "era un chupa huesos" (that she sucked bones.) AJTS, Penales, vol. 4, exp. 15 Mexico City, 1785.

47. AJTS, Penales, vol. 7, exp. 59, Mexico City, 1792.

48. AJP no. 4958 exp. 12, Puebla, 1785.

49. AJTS, Penales, vol. 6, exp. 71, Coyoacán, 1791.

50. AGN, Criminal, vol. 139, exp. 9, fol. 139v-65v, Malinalco, 1799. Conversely, Marcelino Velasco was incensed when his amasia would not let him join a group inside her house. AJP, paquete 2, exp. 661, Puebla, 1836.

51. AJP, no. 7294, Puebla, 1800A. From there things deteriorated because Mariano objected to the group, saying "que aquello no era Fandango ni el iba a divertirlos" (this was not a party and he was not there to have fun), and as a result a fight broke out.

52. AGN, Bienes Nacionales, legajo 220, exp. 34, Mexico City, 1798. AGN, Criminal, vol. 116, exp. 11, fol. 202–20, Mexico City, 1803.

53. AJTS, Penales, vol. 6, exp. 31, Mexico City, 1790.

54. AJTS, Penales, vol. 12, exp. 11, Mexico City, 1849.

55. AGN, Criminal, vol. 713, exp. 5, fol. 188–202, Mexico City, 1802.

56. AJTS, Penales, vol. 12, exp. 13, Mexico City, 1831.

57. AGN, Civil, legajo, 130, parte 3a, exp. 7, Mexico City, 1832.

58. Galindo, *Excelencias de la castidad y virginidad,* 5–5v. Doña Susana Soriano complained that her husband would not allow her to go even to mass so that she would have to obey his precepts rather than those of the Catholic Church, AGN, Bienes Nacionales, legajo 470, exp. 17, fol. 4–9, Mexico City, 1836. Doña María de los Remedios Omaña had a similar complaint about her husband—he had not allowed her to go to mass for two years, AGN, Bienes Nacionales, legajo 470, exp. 19, fol. 3–11, Mexico City, 1836. Don Manuel Tapia would not allow his wife to go to mass saying that she had to ask his permission, AGN, Bienes Nacionales, legajo 717, exp. 56, Fol. 1–9v, Tochimilco, 1852. In order to get out of her imprisonment in the Casa de la Misericordia, doña María Manuela Billavicencio had to agree to behave in a number of ways, including not leaving the house without her husband's permission, AGN, Bienes Nacionales, legajo 1090, exp. 14, Mexico City, 1776.

59. Mannarelli, *Private Passions,* 101–2.

60. AJP, no. 4993, exp. 32, Amozoque, 1785.

61. AGN, Bienes Nacionales, legajo 874, exp. 8, Chalco, 1833.

62. AGN, Bienes Nacionales, vol. 88, exp. 6, Mexico City, 1832.

63. AJTS. Penales, vol. 12, exp. 50, fol. 2–3, Mexico City, 1804.

64. AGN, Criminal, vol. 130, exp. 9, fols. 334–482, Temascaltepec, 1799.

65. AGN, Bienes Nacionales, legajo 717, exp. 83, Atotonilco el Grande, 1853. Feliciano Pacheco reported a somewhat similar situation but in less detail. She told of previous assaults by her amasio that she did not report to the authorities because he did not let her out of the house, AJP, paquete 2,

Puebla, 1856, José Trinidad Sánchez, heridor de Feliciana Pacheco. Doña Claudia Carvallido complained that her husband shut himself into a room with her and tried to kill her. Her neighbors called the patrol and saved her, AGN, Indiferente de Guerra, Leg. 37a, no exp., no folio, Mexico City, 1800, Querella de Da. Claudia Carvallido contra su Marido D. Jose María Villalobos. María Olaya Pineda reported that her husband would shut her into a room and pass his lover off as his wife instead of her, AJTS, Penales, vol. 7, exp. 49, fol. 2–8, Mexico City, 1792.

66. AGN, Criminal, vol. 141, exp. 25, fol. 539–548, Chalco, 1812.

67. AGN, Criminal, vol. 252, exp. 9, fol. 439–447, Amecameca, 1806.

68. AJP, paquete 1, Puebla, 1856, Jose María Cordoval, estupro de María de la Cruz Mendical.

69. AGN, Criminal, vol. 670, exp. 2, fol. 27–46, Mexico City, 1806.

70. AGN, Criminal, vol. 10, exp. 20, fol. 296, Ecatepec, 1819.

71. Osuna, *Norte de los estados*, 154.

72. Van Deusen, *Between the Sacred and the Worldly*, 72.

73. Dávila Mendoza, *Hasta que la muerte nos separe*, 107.

74. Gutmann, *The Meanings of Macho*, 214–15.

75. AJP, paquete 5, Puebla, 1856, Manuel Flores heridor de su mujer Manuela Quintero. In another similar case, María Antonia Cisneros came back from an errand to a drunk husband who refused to believe that she had gone out for this purpose. Accusing her of infidelity, he knifed her in the chest. AJP, paquete 2, no exp., Puebla, 1835, Proceso criminal contra José María Roseta por herir a su esposa María Antonia Cisneros con un cuchillo.

76. AGN, Criminal, vol. 190, exp. 19, fol. 322–33, Calimaya, 1770.

77. AGN, Criminal, vol.206, exp. 20, fol. 236–52, Tenango del Valle, 1802

78. AGN, Inquisición, vol. 1292, exp. 11, fol. 87–92, Mexico City, 1788, "bastantemente libertinosa amiga de estarse en la calle." Interestingly, José Ruiz described his wife as totally free when for four days she went where she wished, AJP, paquete 2, exp. 15, 1775, Puebla. In another case, Pedro Coronel got mad at his wife for being out too long, and when she responded with insults rather than trying to mollify him, he bit her in the mouth, AJP, paquete 4, 1856, Puebla, Pedro Corona heridor de su esposa María Josefa Sánchez. See also, AJP, paquete 3, exp. 689, 1836, Puebla.

79. AGN, Criminal, vol. 716, exp. 11, fol. 141–50, Mexico City, 1762.

80. AGN, Civil. Vol. 2045, exp. 11, Mexico City, 1794.

81. AGN, Criminal, vol. 34, exp. 11, fol. 411–32v, Tetepango, 1764.

82. AGN, Criminal, vol. 42, exp. 15, fol. 426–19, Pachuca, 1802.

83. AJP, no exp., Puebla, 1846, contra Julian Torija, ebrio consuetidinario.

84. AJP, paquete 2, Puebla, 1856, José Trinidad Sánchez, heridor de Feliciana Pacheco.

85. AGN, Criminal, vol. 530 exp. 3, fol. 49–111 Mexico City, 1820.

4. Beyond the Door

1. Waldenberger, "Barrio Gardens," 233.

2. Vives, *Instrucción de la mujer cristiana*, 93. He also warned that girls should not leave the house unless on an errand for their parents. See also Diez de Bonilla, *Código completo*, 73–74.

3. Gómez de Terán, *Infancia ilustrada*, 310–11; and Astete, *Tratado del buen govierno*, 165.

4. Astete, *Tratado del buen govierno*, 165; Rossell, *La educación conforme*, 52–53; and Vives, *Instrucción de la mujer cristiana*, 69.

5. Van Deusen, *Between the Sacred and the Worldly*, 82–83.

6. AGN, Criminal, vol. 48, exp. 13, fol. 239–46, Xochimilco, 1780.

7. AGN, Bienes Nacionales, legajo 292, exp. 19, Mexico City, 1790.

8. AGN, Civil, legajo 206, no. exp., Mexico City, 1853. For examples of incidents when a spouse ejected either wife or husband during a fight, see also: AGN, Criminal, vol. 8, exp. 20, fol. 302–56, Teotihuacan, 1803; and AGN, Bienes Nacionales, legajo 292, exp. 26, Mexico City, 1790.

9. AJP, paquete 6, exp. 206, 1856, Chietla. The words she used were "ni él ni su mujer tenían govierno en su casa."

10. AJTS, Penales, vol. 6 exp. 30, Mexico City, 1790.

11. AGN, Criminal, vol. 65, exp. 8, fol. 460–83, Tulancingo, 1820.

12. Boyer, "Honor among Plebeians," 166–69.

13. Boyer, "Honor among Plebeians," 169.

14. AGN, Criminal, vol. 11, exp. 18, fol. 182–85, Otumba, 1748.

15. Gowing, *Domestic Dangers*, 98, however, reports that when several couples shared one house there were incidents in which fights occurred on the stairway.

16. AGN, Bienes Nacionales, legajo 470, exp. 17, Mexico City, 1836.

17. AJP, no. 17, Puebla, 1775, contra Francisco Xavier Navarro.

18. AGN, Criminal, vol. 262, exp. 12, fol. 160–202, Cuernavaca, 1803.

19. AJTS, Penales, vol. 9, exp. 4, Mexico City, 1797.

20. AGN, Criminal, vol. 682, exp. 3, fol. 127–60, San Juan del Río, 1782.

21. AJP, exp. 65, no. 6802, Puebla 1797A. For studies of houses of deposit, see Penyak, "Safe Harbors and Compulsory Custody," 83–99; Arrom, *The

Women of Mexico City; and Muriel, *Los recogimientos de mujeres*. Another case, although in this instance, of plebeian folk, of a man waiting in the corridor for the women with whom he had been *tratando de amores* is found in AGN, Criminal, vol. 530, exp. 5, fol. 148–78, Mexico City, 1820.

22. AGN, Criminal, vol. 406, exp. 5, fol. 202-226v Mexico City, 1804.

23. AJP, exp. 194, no. 6071, 28 diciembre 1793, Puebla, 1793B.

24. AGN, Criminal, vol. 95, exp. 1, fol. 1–82, Pachuca, 1792.

25. AGN, Civil, legajo 110, part 2c, exp. 2, Mexico City, 1790.

26. González Reyes, "Familia y violencia sexual," 107.

27. See Boyer, "Honor among Plebians"; Lipsett-Rivera, "A Slap in the Face of Honor"; and Graham, "Honor among Slaves."

28. AGN, Judicial, vol. 11, exp. 8, Mexico City, 1816. Mannarelli, *Private Passions*, 66, recounts two similar examples of a wife complaining that her husband had brought his lover into their marital home.

29. AGN, Bienes Nacionales, legajo 370, exp. 42, Mexico City, 1839.

30. AGN, Civil, vol. 2045, exp. 12, Puebla, 1794.

31. AJTS, Penales, vol. 12, exp. 1, fol. 2–3, Mexico City, 1801.

32. Haag, "The 'Ill-Use of a Wife,'" 458; Stansell, *City of Women*, 35, 81; Tomes, "A Torrent of Abuse," 335; and Ross, "Fierce Questions," 592.

33. AGN, Criminal, vol. 570, exp. 7, fol. 75–81, Mexico City, 1795.

34. AJP, paquete 2, 5 fol., Puebla, 1836, proceso criminal contra José Manuel Ramírez por herir a su mujer.

35. AJP, paquete 4, Puebla, 1856, Proceso contra Soledad Bernal, heridora de María de la Luz Rizo. Conversely, some Mexicans did not want to get involved. Lorenzo Cayetano Gómez heard shouting and violence from the next house but later told authorities that he did not like to get involved so he stayed home, AGN, Criminal, vol. 38, exp. 16, fol. 305–36, Cuernavaca, 1809.

36. AJP, no exp., Puebla, 1846, causa en contra de Pedro Vásquez. In another case, the casera came when José María Pérez hit his wife, the casera called the guards, AJP, no exp., Puebla, 1846, Heridas de Soledad Suárez. Also see AJP, paquete 2, exp. 663, Puebla, 1836; AJP, paquete 3, exp. 689, Puebla, 1836; and AGN, Criminal, vol. 118, exp. 13, fol. 473–81, Mexico City, 1807.

37. AGN, Criminal, vol. 682, exp. 6, fol. 203–39, Mexico City, 1780–82.

38. AGN, Bienes Nacionales, legajo 717, exp. 83, Atotonilco el Grande, 1853.

39. AGN, Criminal, Vol. 530, Exp. 5, Fol. 148–78, Mexico City, 1820.

40. AGN, Criminal, vol. 203, exp. 10, fol. 404–32, Cuernavaca, 1816.

41. AGN, Criminal, vol. 46, exp. 14, fol. 342–95, Cuernavaca, 1810.

42. AGN, Criminal, vol. 46, exp. 3, fol. 89–125, Cuernavaca, 1806.

43. AGN, Criminal, vol. 47, exp. 4, fol. 106–85, Cuernavaca, 1813.

44. AGN, Criminal, vol. 80, exp. 4, fol. 124–46, Tulancingo, 1809.

45. AJP, no. 3307, Puebla, 1850. Being drunk was actually a common complaint that Mexican husbands lodged against their wives.

46. AGN, Criminal, vol. 124, exp. 12, fol. 136, Santiago Tianguistengo 1807. Kanter, *Hijos del Puebla*, 71–78, reports on this incident in greater detail.

47. Shoemaker, *The London Mob*, 80.

48. AGN, Criminal, vol. 717, exp. 3, fol. 196–229v, Mexico City, 1806. People also went to mass on other days. Take, for example, doña Francisca Ursula, who left mass on a Friday and was accosted in full view of the neighborhood by Phelipa de Jesús, a known gossip, AJTS, Civil, vol. 113, no. exp., no fol., Coyoacán, 1756.

49. AJP, Puebla, 1836, proceso contra María Juana Cabrera por morder a Sebastiana Torres.

50. AGN, Criminal, vol. 149, exp. 5, fol. 150–55, Zinacantepec, 1809.

51. AGN, Criminal, vol. 54, exp. 11, fol. 1616–197, Tetepango, 1778.

52. AGN, Criminal, vol. 41, exp. 25, fols. 389–89v, Xochimilco.

53. AJTS, Penales, vol. 12, exp. 50, fol. 2–3, Mexico City, 1804.

54. AGN, Criminal, vol. 27, exp. 14, fols. 495–99v, Teotihuacan, 1802. This incident is discussed in more detail in Lipsett-Rivera, "A Slap in the Face of Honor," 185–86. A translation and transcription of this document is available in Lipsett-Rivera "Scandal at the Church," 216–23.

55. AGN, Criminal, vol. 80, exp. 10, fols. 290–358, Tulancingo, 1808.

56. AJP, no.616, 1846, Huauchinango, proceso criminal contra María Juliana.

57. AJP, paquete 2, exp. 663, Puebla, 1836.

58. AJP, paquete 5, Puebla, 1856, Francisca Molina, heridora grave de Manuela Sánchez.

59. AGN, Criminal, vol. 65, exp. 8, fol. 460–83, Tulancingo, 1820.

60. Stern, *Secret History*, 92.

61. Stern, *Secret History*, 211; Shoemaker, *The London Mob*, 132, also explains how mobs often imitated punishments even including the common practice of reprieve. Hernández, *Implicated Spaces*, 119, 142–43, notes that Guatemalan men also followed this practice.

62. AGN, Bienes Nacionales, legajo 1128, exp. 1, Xonacatepec, 1788.

63. AGN, Criminal, vol. 127, exp. 7, fol. 248–66v, Huichapan, 1805.

64. AGN Criminal vol. 8 exp. 20 fol. 302–56, Teotihuacan, 1803.

65. AGN, Criminal, vol. 216, exp. 9, fol. 337–47, Metepec, 1792.

66. AJTS, Penales, vol. 12, exp. 10, fol. 2–8, Tlalpan, 1833.

67. AGN, Criminal vol. 203 expx. 9 fols. 366–403, Cuernavaca, 1798.

68. AJP, paquete 2, no exp., San Salvador el Verde, 1836.

69. Taggart, *Nahuat Myth*, 79–80. See also Burkhart, *The Slippery Earth*, passim.

70. Jeffery, "From Azulejos to Zaguanes," 313–14.

71. Burkhart, *The Slippery Earth*, 63.

72. AGN, Criminal, vol. 28, exp. 1, fol. 1–80, Teotihuacan, 1799.

73. For a larger discussion of the place of the devil in Mexican society, see: Lipsett-Rivera, "Mira Lo que Hace el Diablo," 201–19; Cervantes, *The Devil in the New World*; and Sousa, "The Devil and Deviance."

74. AGN, Criminal, vol. 80, exp. 19, fol. 561–70, Tulancingo, 1811.

75. See my discussion in Lipsett-Rivera, "Mira Lo que Hace el Diablo"; and also Penyak, "Criminal Sexuality in Central Mexico," 234–35.

76. AJP, no exp., Izúcar, 1846, estupro de María Martín por Cesario Ceferino.

77. AJP, paquete 4, no exp., Proceso en contra de Amado Díaz, Huaquechula, Rancho de Teacalco, 1856.

78. See in particular: AJP, no exp., Juicio en contra de Ambrosio Bravo, Acatlán, 1850; AGN, Criminal, vol. 47, exp. 7, fol. 192–232, Cuernavaca, 1818; AJTS, Penales, vol. 12, exp. 20, Coyoacán, 1845; and AGN, Criminal, vol. 194, exp. 17, fol. 260–79, Texcoco, 1778. In a variant on this scenario, Mariano Gutiérrez and Pedro Medino dragged a woman from her house into the barranca in order to rape her. AGN, Criminal, vol. 2787, exp. 5, fol. 71–193, Cuernavaca, 1807. It was also the practice of the serial rapist Fernando Manuel to grab women at the river and take them to the monte where he raped them. AGN, Criminal, vol. 518, exp. 16, fol. 471–86, Amatepec, 1818. Joseph López took Luisa Francisca into the "obscuridad del Varranquita" in order to rape her. AGN, Criminal, vol. 624, exp. 1, fol. 1–37, Taxco, 1756. Francisco Sánchez took his stepdaughter of about seven or eight years old to the barranca and raped her. AJP, no exp., Puebla, 1826, Causa en contra de Francisco Sánchez por estupro sobre Juana Manuela de la Luz.

79. Foster, "Dreams," 109.

80. AJP, exp. 42, no. 6144, Puebla, 1794A.

81. AGN, Criminal, vol. 278, exp. 7, fol. 239–62, Xalostoc, 1796.

82. AGN, Criminal vol. 139, exp. 16 fol. 268–94, Malinalco, 1757.

83. AGN Criminal, vol. 705, exp. 9. fol. 69–79, Temascaltepec, 1783.

84. AGN, Criminal, vol. 2, exp. 2, fol. 31–69, Chalco, 1791–2.

85. AGN Criminal, vol. 184, exp. 10, fol. 241–79, Huichapan, 1808; AJP, paquete 2, no exp., San Salvador el Verde, 1836, Number proceso criminal contra el indígena José Bernardino Islas Antonio,.

86. Hunt, "Regulating Heterosocial Space," 2.

87. Hurl-Eamon, *Gender and Petty Violence*, 83.

88. Muchembled, *La violence au village*, 118–19.

89. Silva Dias, *Power and Everyday Life*, 61.

90. Pérez, *Habitat, familia y comunidad*, 327.

91. Castañeda, "La memoria de las niñas violadas," 45, 47.

92. Taggart, *Nahuat Myth*, 79, 83–84.

93. Muchembled, "Satanic Myth and Cultural Reality," 149.

94. Francisco Fabián y Fuero, *Colección de providencias diocesanas*, 451–52.

95. Simeón de Salazar, *Flores Citlalpapoca*, 9.

96. Taggart, *Nahuat Myth*, 79, 83–84.

97. AGN, Criminal, vol. 184, exp. 17, fol. 408–501v, Actopan, 1816.

98. AGN, Inquisición, vol. 1373, exp. 13, fol. 173–223, Mexico City, 1792.

99. AJTS, Penales, vol. 6, exp. 29, Mexico City, 1790. For a similar case see AJP, paquete 2, no. 4587, Puebla, 1856, Antonio Sánchez (profugo) por estupro en Cesaria Hernández.

100. AGN, Criminal, vol. 624, exp. 1, fol. 1–37, Taxco, 1756.

101. AGN, Criminal, vol. 62, ezp. 7, fol. 207–44, Tulancingo, 1803.

5. The Body in Daily Life

1. Cañeque, *The King's Living Image*, chap. 4, shows how the elite used clothes and body language to show their rank, but also connects how these codes worked spatially.

2. In Turner, *The Body and Society*, the author argues that many analytical frameworks are limited because they do not recognize the role of the body. He claims the importance of "embodiment" as a factor in sociological works.

3. In fact, although bodies may not vary much across time or place, human attitudes and culture surrounding the body are infinitely variable and complex. There is a huge literature and dense analysis particularly within sociology but also within anthropological writings. One of the best overviews of the ideas foundational to this field, I believe, it to be found in Entwistle, *The Fashioned Body*.

4. Entwistle, *The Fashioned Body*, 12.

5. Gallant, "Honor, Masculinity," 360; and Gallant, "Turning the Horns," 703.

6. Farr, "The Pure," 408. Taylor, *The Archive*, 46, writes that gestures have meaning particular to a culture.

7. Leach, "Magical Hair," 141–48; Greenberg, *Honor and Slavery*, 22, states that it is important to try to understand the "full meaning [of an act] in the language of honor." He argues that historians must look beyond the surface to see the symbolic content of actions.

8. Muchembled, *La violence au village*, 143.

9. Greenberg, *Honor and Slavery*, 15.

10. Greenberg, *Honor and Slavery*, 16; and Muchembled, *La violence au village*, 144. Interestingly, Diez de Bonilla, *Código completo*, 167, writes for his nineteenth-century audience that women should not use veils because others would want to read their faces.

11. Farr, "The Pure," 407; and Hurl-Eamon, *Gender and Petty Violence*. Shoemaker, *The London Mob*, 169, is rather mystified by female violence and so professes that it does not have rules. But his assertion comes undoubtedly from the fact that he has not really studied this type of violence.

12. Farr, "The Pure," 407.

13. Turner, *The Body and Society*, 38, 126. He states, "sociology of the body turns out to be crucially a sociological study of the control of sexuality, specifically female sexuality by men exercising patriarchal power."

14. Gallant, "Turning the Horns," 708.

15. Hurl-Eamon, *Gender and Petty Violence*, 65.

16. Hurl-Eamon, *Gender and Petty Violence*, 80

17. Spierenburg, "Knife Fighting," 115; and Muchembled, *La violence au village*, 167.

18. Farr, "The Pure," 411. Spierenburg, "Knife Fighting," 115, also calls these "negative rituals."

19. Synnott, *The Body Social*, 1.

20. Le Goff, "Head or Heart?" 13.

21. Falk, *The Consuming Body*, 54.

22. MacRae, "The Body and Social Metaphor," 64.

23. Osuna, *Norte de los estados*, 90–91v. Cerda, *Libro intitulado*, 323v., 338v, writes that husbands must give their wives shoes, clothes, and food as though their bodies were their own.

24. MacLachlan, *Spain's Empire in the New World*, 9. Grosz, *Space, Time, and Perversion*, 106, comments on this common image adding, that the laws are often likened to the nerves, the army to the arms, the commercial side to its legs or stomach. She continues that although this representation of state as

body is very common in many texts, it rarely provides a gender to the metaphorical body and thus no genitalia. See also Turner, *The Body and Society,* 144–45, 175–76. Farr, "The Pure," 394, 397, writes that Jean Bodin uses this same metaphor, and that Bodin associates the commoners with the liver, which was apparently the source of sensual passion.

25. MacRae, "The Body and Social Metaphor," 72.

26. Osuna, *Norte de los estados,* 90–91v. Cerda, *Libro intitulado,* 323v, writes "el hombre es cabeça y principio de donde la muger procedió" (man is the head from which woman emerges).

27. De Herrera, *Espejo de la perfecta casada,* 114–15, as cited by Boyer, "Women," 257.

28. Osuna, *Norte de los estados,* 92v.

29. This model and its workings is explained in greater detail in Lipsett-Rivera, "Marriage and Family Relations."

30. AGN, Civil, legajo 110, parte 2b, exp. 12, Mexico City, 1836.

31. D'Aubeterre Buznego, *El pago de la novia,* 101–2.

32. Muchembled, *La violence au village,* 167. Le Goff, "Head or Heart?" 14, writes, "The symbolic value of the head became unusually strong in the Christian system." See also Taylor, *Honor and Violence,* 46.

33. López Austin, *The Human Body and Ideology,* 171.

34. Diez de Bonilla, *Código completo,* 66, 104, 152–53.

35. AGN, Civil, lejajo 206, no exp., Toluca, 1853.

36. Escoiquiz, *Tratado de las obligaciones,* 114–16; Anonymous, *Reglas de la buena crianza,* 14; Martin *Governance and Society,* 98; Taylor, Magistrates *of the Sacred,* 230–31; and Gutiérrez, *When Jesus Came,* 183. Shoemaker, *The London Mob,* 15–16, notes that with the greater crush of people it became harder to distinguish who was superior or inferior, so the bodily language of deference became attenuated. For example, the curtsy became a bob and men just touched their hats instead of actually lifting them off their heads. Essentially, Londoners developed a shorthand version of deference.

37. Escoiquiz, *Tratado,* 114–16. See also Galban Ribera, *Catecismo de urbanidad,* 19–20.

38. Moles, *Doctrina para niños,* 112–14; Anonymous, *Reglas de la buena crianza,* 8–9; Diez de Bonilla, *Código completo,* 66.

39. Diez de Bonilla, *Código completo,* 66.

40. López Austin, *The Human Body and Ideology,* 172.

41. Bell, *On Human Finery,* 31.

42. Berdan, *The Aztecs of Central Mexico,* 47.

43. Amar y Borbón, *Discurso sobre*, 90, writes that excessive adornment on women's heads was prejudicial to their morality.

44. Entwistle, *The Fashioned Body*, 7. Tattoos are one of the ways that people adorn their bodies. I have not found any evidence of this practice in my documents, but Martin Nesvig (personal communication) found an account in the Inquisition papers of a man who had had a horse tattooed on his body in order to be a better equestrian.

45. I have found a few descriptions of male costume, including their hats, when women, particularly rape victims, described their assailants. See for example: AGN, Criminal, vol. 116, exp. 4, fols. 53–69v, Teposcolula, 1802; AGN, Criminal, vol. 713, exp. 5, fol. 188–202, Mexico City, 1802; and AGN, Criminal, vol. 80, exp. 19, fol. 561–70, Tulancingo, 1811.

46. Anonymous, *Reglas de la buena crianza*, 14. Diez de Bonilla, *Código completo*, 152–53, writes that taking off the hat is an old custom that does not mean respect but had to be done. This practice seems to be commented upon more when it is omitted. See also D'Aubeterre Buznego, *El pago de la novia*, 52. According to Wagner, *Manners, Customs, and Observances*, 64–65, the gender difference in doffing hats comes from the fact that when warriors removed their helmets they showed that they trusted in their safety because of their host's protection. Because women were not soldiers they did not need to show their trust in this manner. Muchembled, *La violence au village*, 144, 167, says that hats had their own semiological code. Taylor, *Honor and Violence*, 184, describes grabbing a hat as an insult.

47. See also Galindo, *Verdades morales*, 49. Cerda, *Libro intitulado*, 9, says that mothers must teach their daughters to go to mass with their heads covered. In some other cultures, it was a big insult to pull off the caps that covered women's hair. See, for the case of Holland, Spierenberg, "How Violent Were Women?" 9; for England see Shoemaker, *The London Mob*, 55; and for France see Farr, "The Pure," 411.

48. Synnott, *The Body Social*, 103. Bartlett, "Symbolic Meanings," 45, writes of the ways that various European peoples used hair to denote their ethnicity.

49. Turner, "The Social Skin," 18, when writing about the Kayapó of Brazil, states: "The hair of the head thus focuses the dynamic and unstable quality of the frontier between the 'natural,' bio-libidinous forces of the inner body and the external sphere of social relations. In this context, hair offers itself as a symbol of the libidinous energies of the self and of the never-ending struggle to constrain within acceptable forms their eruption into social space."

50. Rosenthal, "Raising Hair," 1–2.

51. Rosenthal, "Raising Hair," 2.

52. Diez de Bonilla, *Código completo,* 77–78.

53. Pardo, "How to Punish Indians," 96.

54. López Austin, *The Human Body and Ideology,* 170, 221.

55. De Trujillo, *Libro Llamado Reprobación de Trajes,* 19, 92–94v. Galindo, *Verdades morales,* 14–15, complains that the soldiers were wearing feminized clothing. Bartlett, "Symbolic Meanings of Hair," 44–45, 50–52, writes that in Ireland, hair cut short meant that the wearer was a servant so there was an association between aristocrats and long hair. In Bavaria, the law forced peasants to wear their hair short. He writes extensively about the fashion for long hair among the elites of medieval Europe and the clerical reaction against it.

56. Clendinnen, "The Cost of Courage," 56. They also were relegated to base, dishonorable employment for the rest of their lives and could not marry.

57. Rosenthal, "Raising Hair," 2.

58. Rosenthal, "Raising Hair," 6.

59. Gutiérrez, *When Jesus Came,* 205; and Gibson, *The Aztecs Under Spanish Rule,* 144. Bartlett, "Symbolic Meanings," 47, writes that the Christian kings of reconquest Spain imposed particular hairstyles on the Moors in order to distinguish them from their Christian subjects.

60. Pardo, "How to Punish Indians," 98.

61. AGN, Criminal, vol. 29, exp. 13, fol. 345–85, Xochimilco, 1790. In contemporary usage the term *balcarrotas* has come to mean some pretty impressive sideburns.

62. Bell, *On Human Finery,* 47. Farr, "The Pure," 401, says that moralists began to consider exposed hair as impious in the eighteenth century. Bartlett, "Symbolic Meanings," 54, writes that for medieval wives it was considered very inappropriate to wear their hair loose because it was associated with virginity—thus wearing their hair loose was a metaphor for breaking free of the bonds of marriage through adultery.

63. Galindo, *Verdades morales,* 49; and Osuna, *Norte de los estados,* 143v.

64. Astete, *Tratdo del buen gobierno,* 210; and Trujillo, *Libro Llamado,* 79–79v. See also Gómez de Terán, *Infancia ilustrada,* 311. Farr, "The Pure," 402, notes that French moralists also objected to curled hair, which they associated with debauchery and prostitutes.

65. As cited in López Austin, *The Human Body and Ideology,* 278. Clendinnen, *Aztecs,* 193, writes that Otomí women, whom the Aztecs considered very inferior morally, decorated their hair with feathers! See also Sayer, *Mexican Costume,* 68.

66. Burkhart, *The Slippery Earth*, 90. Farr, "The Pure," 401–2, notes that the French shared this metaphor using exposed and unruly hair as an allegorical symbol for chaos, disorder, and adultery.

67. Pardo, "How to Punish Indians," 92.

68. Pardo, "How to Punish Indians," 86–92. Gose, *Invaders as Ancestors*, 139, notes an example of head shaving as punishment in colonial Peru.

69. Taylor, *Magistrates of the Sacred*, 233; Frye, *Indians into Mexicans*, 77–78.

70. Pardo, "How to Punish Indians," 98–99.

71. Farr, "The Pure," 404–5.

72. Gutiérrez, *When Jesus Came*, 203–6; and Socolow, "Women and Crime," 49.

73. AGN, Criminal, vol. 278, exp. 7, fol. 239–62, Xalostoc, 1796; AGN, Civil, vol. 2045, exp. 11, Mexico City, 1794.

74. Taylor, *Magistrates*, 234–35.

75. AJTS, Ramo Penales, vol. 4, exp. 3, Mexico City, 1788.

76. AGN, Criminal, vol. 222, exp. 15, fol. 283–313v, Coatepec, 1771.

77. Anonymous, *Reglas de la buena crianza*, 14.

78. Escoiquiz, *Tratado de las Obligciones*, 112. See also Diez de Bonilla, *Código completo*, 61.

79. Cerda, *Libro intitulado*, 9–10v, 242–43; see also Rosales, *Caton Christiano*, 67. Spierenburg, *Written in Blood*, 171, writes of a similar etiquette for eighteenth-century Dutch women who "never [look] around, refusing to be distracted by any movement or sound." It was understood that such distractions were tricks to attract her attention, but an honest and honorable young woman would not fall for such tricks.

80. Martin, *Governance and Society*, 99; Lipsett-Rivera, "*De Obra y Palabra*," 515–18.

81. AJTS, Penales, vol. 4, exp. 3, Mexico City, 1788; AGN, Criminal, vol. 222, exp. 15, fol. 283–313v, Coatepec, 1771; AGN, Criminal, vol. 38, exp. 16, fol. 305–36, Cuernavacca, 1809; AGN, Criminal, vol. 118, exp. 13, fol. 473–81, Mexico City, 1807; AGN, Bienes Nacionales, leg. 663, exp. 9, Tacuba, 1812; YL-PC, Box 5, series 2, folder 72, Puebla, 1745; AJP, paquete 3, exp. 689, Puebla, 1836; AJP exp. 3325, Puebla, 1850; AJP, no. 4345, 31 fol., Puebla, 1776; AJP, no. 179, 16 fol., Puebla, 1836; AJP, paquete 4, Puebla, 1856, proceso contra Joaquina Rojas; AGN, Criminal. vol. 570, exp. 7, fol. 75–81, Mexico City, 1795; AJP, no exp., Puebla, 1846, proceso contra María Justa Palacios; AJP, exp. 616, Puebla, 1846; AJP, paquete 4, no exp., Puebla, 1856, proceso contra Juana María Bautista y Josefa Bárbara, 1856; AJP, exp. 3390,

Puebla, 1850; AJP, exp. 1287, Puebla, 1850; AJTS, Penales vol. 4, exp. 14, Mexico City, 1785; AJTS, Penales, vol. 4, exp. 26, Mexico City, 1785; AJTS, Penales, vol. 6, exp. 71, Mexico City, 1791; AJTS, Penales, vol. 9, exp. 2, Mexico City, 1797; AJTS, Penales, vol. 11, exp. 16, Mexico City, 1750; AJTS, Penales, vol. 11, exp. 68, Mexico City, 1752; AJTS, Penales, vol. 10, exp. 57, Mexico City, 1772; AJTS, Penales, vol. 3, exp. 2, Mexico City, 1777; AJTS, Civil, vol. 141, no exp., Mexico City, 1779; AJTS, Civil vol. 113, no exp., Mexico City, 1756; AJTS, Civil, vol. 110, no exp., Mexico City, 1754; and AJP, exp. 1287, Puebla, 1850.

82. Anonymous, *Reglas de la buena crianza*, 8–9. This advice was echoed by Amar y Borbón, *Discurso sobre la educación*, 242–43, as well as in instructions for a school for girls. See also AGI, Audiencia de México, legajo 724, exp. 16, fol. 68; and Diez de Bonilla, *Código completo*, 24, 37, 50.

83. De Salazar, *Flores Citlalpapoca*, passim.

84. Cerda, *Libro intitulado*, 10, 17v, 442. Vives, *Instrucción*, 94, 95, also advised women that when they were in the streets they should make their faces shameful and not look at men nor look to see if they were being observed. See also Diez de Bonilla, *Código completo*, 50.

85. Stansell, *City of Women*, 93.

86. Argyle, "The Syntaxes of Bodily Communication," 157.

87. López Austin, *The Human Body and Ideology*, 305.

88. Moles, *Doctrina Christiana*, 132; and Diez de Bonilla, *Código completo*, 133–34.

89. Astete, *Tratado del buen gobierno*, 217–18; Trujillo, *Libro Llamado*, 80; and Galindo, *Verdades morales*, 334–35.

90. Escoiquiz, *Tratado de las Obligaciones*, 112–14. The anonymous author of *Reglas de la buena crianza*, 11–12, gave almost identical advice: "1. No camines apresurado ni con pesadez, ni artificio o ligereza sino con medida, gravedad y decencia. 2. Quando camines no has de inclinar ni mover el cuerpo, no has de tener las manos ni los brazos pendientes; no golpees fuertemente el suelo con los pies, ni los arrastres, subiendo alguna escalera, ni subas dos escaleras de una vez" (1. Do not walk quickly or slowly, nor with artifice or nimbleness but rather with measured steps, seriousness and decency. 2. When you walk do not lean or move your body, don't incline your hands or arms; don't stomp or drag your feet when going up stairs, do not take two steps at once).

91. Diez de Bonilla, *Código completo*, 69, makes the connection between a fast walk and servants, a slow walk with laziness or for women with vanity.

92. Gómez de Terán, *Infancia ilustrada*, 311. Spierenburg, *Written in Blood*, 171–72, comments on similar strictures for early modern Holland.

93. Moles, *Doctrina Christiana*, 127.

94. Cerda, *Libro intitulado*, 17v.

95. Cordóba, *Jardín de las nobles donzellas*, part 2, chap. 9; Vives, *Instrucción*, 95, had similar advice: "En su andar, la mujer no vaya muy presurosa, ni muy despacio" (When walking, women must not either hurry or tarry).

96. Sahagún, *Florentine Codex*, Book 10, 100; Mendieta, *Historia eclesiástica Indiana*, 118; Zorita, *Life and Times in Ancient Mexico*, 148; and Burkhart, *The Slippery Earth*, 137.

97. Fluegel, *The Psychology of Clothes*, 83.

98. Fluegel, *The Psychology of Clothes*, 74; Entwistle, "The Dressed Body," 140; Steele, *Fashion and Eroticism*, 14–15.

99. Fluegel, *The Psychology of Clothes*, 75, writes "certain garments can become symbolic of inflexibility of character, severity of moral standard, and purity of moral purpose."

100. Arthur, "Dress and the Social Control of the Body," 1.

101. Bell, *On Human Finery*, 142.

102. Vives, *Insrucción*, 94; and Diez de Bonilla, *Código completo*, 114.

103. AGN, Criminal, vol. 47, exp. 7 fol. 192–232, Cuernavaca, 1818; AGN, Criminal, vol. 139, exp. 16, fol. 268–94, Malinalco, 1757; AJTS, Penales, vol. 7, exp. 59, fol. 2–4, Mexico City, 1792; and AGN, Criminal, vol. 206, exp. 20, fol. 236–51, Tenango del Valle, 1802.

104. AJTS, Penales, vol. 9, exp. 4, Mexico City, 1797; and AGN, Criminal, vol. 184, exp. 10, fol. 241–79, Huichapan, 1809.

105. AGN, Criminal, vol. 624, exp. 1, fol. 1–37, Taxco, 1756.

106. AGN, Criminal, vol. 10, exp. 20, fol. 296–351v, Ecatepec, 1819. I give more details of these cases and the concept of *malicia* in Lipsett-Rivera, "The Intersection of Rape and Marriage," 559–90.

107. AGN, Criminal, vol. 47, exp. 7, fol. 192–232, Cuernavaca, 1818.

108. AGN, Criminal, vol. 62, exp. 17, fol. 379–436, Tulancingo, 1804.

109. AJP, no exp., Puebla, 1846, contra Francisco Grijalbo por herir a su esposa.

110. AGN, Criminal, vol. 713, exp. 5, fol. 188–202, Mexico City, 1802. Another man took this further, lifting the naguas and biting a woman, AGN, Criminal, vol. 29, exp. 7, fol. 115–18v, Xochimilco, 1808.

111. Shoemaker, *The London Mob*, 57.

112. AJTS, Penales, vol. 12, exp. 50, fol. 2–3, Mexico City, 1804.

113. Osuna, *Norte de los estados*, 124; de Talavera, *Reforma de trages ilustrada*,10v; and Astete, *Tratado del buen gobierno*, 150, 207. Silva Dias, *Power*

and Everyday Life, 55, writes that in Brazil in 1705, moral authorities considered the wearing of silk as an enticement to sin. Referring more generally to silk in Western culture, Entwistle, "The Dressed Body," 143, writes that soft fabrics, such as silk, were often eroticized. Interestingly, the symbolism of these fabrics was inverted when it came to male priests. De Rosales, *Caton Christiano*, 81, writes that when the priest wore silk and gold, it represented Christ at the time of his birth, "vestido de la ropa de la Santisima Humanidad" (clothed in the dress of sainted humanity).

114. Astete, *Tratado del buen govierno*, 61, 72–74, 210; Galindo, *Excelencias*, 45–46v. Farr, "The Pure," 395–96, writes that French moralists made a connection between clean clothes and higher, honorable spirit, and as an external sign of the pure soul on the interior.

115. Talavera, *Reforma de trages*, 11; Astete, *Tratado*, 152–53, 245; Vives, *Instrucción*, 46–51, 96; Gómez de Terán, *Infancia ilustrada*, 16, 309–10; Galindo, *Parte segunda*, 154–56, 162; and Diez de Bonilla, *Código completo*, 104.

116. Turner, *The Body and Society*, 177, 181. Entwistle, *The Fashioned Body*, 84, argues that the denial of the body as advocated by religious teachings actually draws attention to it.

117. Moles, *Doctrina Cristiana*, 127; Galindo, *Verdades morales*, 5; Vives, *Instrucción*, 94; and de Cordóba, *Jardín de las nobles donzellas*, part 2, chap. 1. Not surprisingly, as Farr, "The Pure," 400, 406, notes, since the fashion apparently originated in France, French moralists also denounced this way of exposing breasts and necks.

118. Galindo, *Verdades morales*, 13–14.

119. Lizana y Beaumont, *Instrucción Pastoral del Illmo*, 27–28.

120. *Colección de providencias*, 121. See also Lizana y Beaumont, *Instrucción Pastoral*, 8–9, 10, 19–20.

121. Lizana y Beaumont, *Instrucción Pastoral*, 1–2.

122. AGN, Bienes Nacionales, legajo 210, exp. 40, Mexico City, 1799.

123. Astete, *Tratado*, 199–200, 214; Vives, *Instrucción*, 57–59; Osuna, *Norte de los estados*, 126v; and Trujillo, *Libro Llamado*, 86–87, 91. According to Pointon, "Women and their Jewels," 21, in moral discourse, jewels symbolized a superfluous character.

124. Bell, *On Human Finery*, 23; Barnes and Eicher, "Introduction," 1. In Brazil, different fabrics were identified with different social groups and classes, Silva Dias, *Power and Everyday Life*, 59.

125. Cordóba, *Jardín de las nobles donzellas*, part 2, chap. 9; Amar y Borbón, *Discurso sobre la educación*, 209, 214; Galindo, *Excelencias*, 45; and Diez de Bonilla, *Código completo*, 116.

126. Katzew, "Casta Painting," 8–29.

127. Bell, *On Human Finery*, 19.

128. AGN, Criminal, vol. 375, exp. 3, fol. 77–171, Puebla, 1809.

129. AJTS, Penales, vol. 3, exp. 23, fol. 2–5v, Mexico City, 1779, "un chusco de plaza."

130. AGN, Criminal, vol. 480, fol. 184–2020, Puebla, 1799.

131. AGN, Civil, legajo 130, parte 3A, exp. 14, Mexico City, 1822.

132. Entwistle, "The Dressed Body," 133. Hall, *The Hidden Dimension*, 147, argues that this notion of clothes as boundary is cultural; in Northern Europe clothes cannot be touched without permission, whereas in other areas this prohibition is not as strong.

133. Falk, *The Consuming Body*, 54; Fluegel, *The Psychology of Clothes*, 15; Turbin, "Refashioning the Concept of Public/Private," 45.

134. Curcio-Nagy, *The Great Festivals*, 20; Cañeque, *The King's Living Image*, 122, also makes this point.

135. Fluegel, *The Psychology of Clothes*, 34.

136. Bell, *On Human Finery*, 39.

137. Anonymous, *Reglas de la buena crianza*, 16–17.

138. Taylor, *Honor and Violence*, 46.

6. The Head, Honor, and Aggression

1. Taylor, *Drinking, Homicide and Rebellion*, 80, states that most homicides in his sample were committed with either knives followed by rocks, clubs or fists.

2. Taylor, *Honor and Violence*, 48–49, 120; also cited holding a stone or a stick as symbolic of a propensity for violence. Uribe-Uran, "Colonial *Baracunatanas*," 52, writes that there were patterns in the choice of weapons in Colombia as well: "Machetes and knives were women's weapons of choice, whereas men used these as well as their fists and feet. Clubs and rocks were used only on occasion. In a few instances, men engaged in exceedingly cruel behavior, such as throwing burning coal on the victim's face, or in one case, damaging the victim's internal sexual organs. Poison, a subtle and handy method, seems to have been used in just one of the cases under consideration."

3. AJP, paquete 3, Izúcar, 1856, Tomás Montellanos, heridor de su esposa María Crecencia.

4. AGN, Criminal, vol. 119, exp. 7, fol. 85–95, Actopan, 1815.

5. Sloan, *Runaway Daughters*, 150.

6. AGN, Criminal, vol. 91, exp. 14, fol. 313–34, Tlalmanalco, 1787.

7. AJP, exp. 1382, 1850, Puebla. Pieces of pottery were sometimes called

a stone or *piedra* when associated with pulquerías. The pieces from broken jars used to drink pulque are called *piedras*.

8. AJP, no exp., Puebla, 1846, causa en contra de Pedro Vásquez.

9. AJP, exp. 2957, 1850, Tehuacán.

10. AJP, exp. 205, no. 6124, 1794A, Puebla; and AGN, Bienes Nacionales, legajo 470, exp. 17, fol. 4–9, Mexico City, 1836.

11. Boyer, *Lives of the Bigamists*, 133–34, 147.

12. Galindo, *Parte segunda*, 159, 162–63, 398–400; Cerda, *Libro intitulado*, 416–17v.

13. AJP, exp. 44, no. 6037, Puebla, 1793B.

14. AGN, Bienes Nacionales, legajo 1090, exp. 14, Mexico City, 1776.

15. AGN, Judicial, vol. 32, exp. 51, fol. 454–64v, Mexico City, 1809; AGN, Civil, leg. 92, parte 2, no exp., 1848, divorce of José María Arce and Manuela Velásquez; AGN, Civil, leg. 92, parte 2, no exp., Mexico City, 1848, divorce of don Francisco Coste and doña Guadalupe Manresa; AGN, Bienes Nacionales, leg. 717, exp. 63, Mexico City, 1853; AGN, Bienes Nacionales, leg. 1128, exp. 1, Xonacatepec, 1788; and AGN, Clero Regular y Secular, vol. 197, exp. 20, fol. 358–67, Mexico City, 1768.

16. AGN, Clero Regular y Secular, vol. 197, exp. 20, fol. 358–67, Mexico City, 1768.

17. AGN, Bienes Nacionales, leg. 874, exp. 7, Ixtacalco, 1833.

18. AJP, no. 5535, San Juan de los Llanos, 1791.

19. AGN, Criminal, vol. 122, exp. 18, fol. 395–402v, Calimaya, 1783; and AGN, Clero Regular y Secular, vol. 197, exp. 20, fol. 363–64, Mexico City, 1768.

20. AJP, exp. 1050, Puebla, 1850.

21. AGN, Criminal, vol. 624, exp. 2, fol. 39–40v, Mexico City, 1756; AGN, Bienes Nacionales, leg. 76, exp. 11, Mexico City, 1856; AGN, Bienes Nacionales, leg. 76, exp. 45, Mexico City, 1856; AGN, Judicial, vol. 32, exp. 50, fol. 422–53v, Yagualicam, 1809; AGN, Civil, leg. 92, parte 2, no exp., Huayacocotla, 1848, divorce of Josefa Mayorga and Martín Lugo; AGN, Civil, leg. 92, parte 2 no exp., Cadereyta, 1848, divorce of doña Margarita Llata and Eusebio Bolaños; AGN, Bienes Nacionales, leg. 370, exp. 42, Mexico City, 1839; AGN, Bienes Nacionales, leg. 470, exp. 31, Mexico City, 1836; AGN, Bienes Nacionales, leg. 1045, exp. 35, Mexico City, 1832; AGN, Criminal, vol. 43, exp. 4, fol. 63–71, Pachuca, 1770; AGN, Criminal, vol. 556, exp. 10, fol. 119–122, Mexico City, 1798; AGN, Criminal, vol. 557, exp. Exp. 7b, fol. 192–202, Mexico City, 1782; AGN, Criminal, vol. 118, exp. 13, fol. 473–81, Mexico City, 1807; AGN, Criminal, vol. 614, exp. 18, fol. 112–22, Tula, 1785; AGN,

Criminal, vol. 716, exp. 15, fol. 154–68, Mexico City, 1765; AGN, Clero Regular y Secular, vol. 197, exp. 20, fol. 358–67, Mexico City, 1768; AGN, Civil, vol. 1469, exp. 19, Mexico City, 1794; and AGN, Criminal, vol. 118, exp. 13, fol. 473–81, Mexico City, 1807.

22. AJP, paquete 3, Izúcar, 1856, Genevevo Robledo, heridor de Rita Romero.

23. AJP, paquete 5, Puebla, 1856, Manuel Valencia, heridor de Francisca Sánchez.

24. AGN, Criminal, vol. 119, exp. 7, fol. 85–95, Actopan, 1815.

25. AGN, Criminal, vol. 712, exp. 1, fol. 3–27, Mexico City, 1805.

26. AGN, Criminal, vol. 118, exp. 5, fol. 158–83, Actopan, 1808.

27. AJP, paquete 4, Puebla, 1856, José María Ortega, heridor de María de Jesús Castillo. See also AJP, paquete 1, no exp., Puebla, 1836, proceso criminal contra Paulino de Yto, in which this scenario occurs between brother and sister. Also AGN, Civil legajo 119, exp. 4, Mexico City, 1838, in which one woman attacked another over treatment of some children. And AJP, paquete 5, Puebla, 1856, José Guadalupe Sánchez, heridor de María Simona Ochoa.

28. AJTS, Penales, vol. 3, exp. 61, fol. 1, Mexico City, 1784.

29. AJP, paquete 2, exp. 44, Puebla, 1775.

30. AJP, paquete 4, Puebla, 1856, Joaquina Rojas, heridora de Concepción Torres; AGN, Criminal, vol. 597, exp. 6, fol. 156, Mexico City, 1736; AGN, Criminal, vol. 11, exp. 9, fol. 61–77, Otumba, 1783; AJP, paquete 1, no exp., Puebla, 1836, proceso criminal contra María Lugarda Ignacio por herir en la frente con una piedra a Francisca Carranza; and AJP, paquete 3, Izúcar, 1856, María Felipa de Jesús, heridora de Margarita de la Paz.

31. AJP, paquete 1, no exp., Puebla, 1836, proceso criminal contra Juana Isidora de León por herir en la cabeza con una piedra a Agustina Salcedo; and AJP, exp. 3333, Puebla, 1850.

32. AGN, Criminal, col. 267, exp. 9, fol. 93–103, Naucalpan, 1771.

33. Chasteen, "Violence for Show," 52; Spierenburg, "Knife Fighting," 116; Taylor, *Honor and Violence*, 45, 210; and Gallant, "Honor, Masculinity," 363.

34. Gorn, "Gouge and Bite," 18–43.

35. It is not a universal form of assault, however; Hurl-Eamon, *Gender and Petty Violence*, 70, reports that it was entirely absent from her sample.

36. AGN, Criminal, vol. 18, exp. 11, fol. 419–27, Malinalco, 1797.

37. AGN, Criminal, vol. 47, exp. 4, fol. 106–85, Cuernavaca, 1813.

38. AJTS, Penales, vol. 3, exp. 2, fol. 2–3v, Mexico City, 1785. There is another case between husband and wife in which the wife seems to have been

hit in the face but the document does not provide a lot of details, AJP, no exp., Izúcar, 1846.

39. AJP, no exp., Puebla, 1836, causa en contra de Manuela Chica por herir a Manuela Suáres.

40. AGN, Criminal, vol. 131, exp. 27, fol. 425–80, Tacubaya, 1802.

41. AGN, Criminal, vol. 206, exp. 18, fol. 219–27, Tenango del Valle, 1771.

42. Spierenburg, *Written in Blood*, 58.

43. Hurl-Eamon, *Gender and Petty Violence*, 79.

44. Shoemaker, *The London Mob*, 53.

45. AGN, Inquisición, vol. 1049, exp. 9, fol. 76–79, Mexico City, 1768.

46. AGN, Civil, leg. 39 part 5a, no exp., no fol., Mexico City, 1854.

47. AJP, exp. 3319, Puebla, 1850.

48. AJTS, Penales, vol. 4, exp. 15, fol. 3–3v, Mexico City, 1785.

49. Gallant, "Honor, Masculinity," 363. See also Spierenburg, "Knife Fighting."

50. Fluegel, *The Psychology of Clothes*, 40.

51. Greenberg, *Honor and Slavery*, 15.

52. Spierenberg, "How Violent Were Women?" 15.

53. Spierenburg, "How Violent Were Women?" 18.

54. Spierenburg, "Knife Fighting," 118.

55. AJTS, Penales, vol. 7, exp. 5, fol. 2–6, Mexico City, 1791.

56. AGN, Bienes Nacionales, legajo 717, exp. 100, fol. 1–4v, Mexico City, 1853.

57. AJP, paquete 2, Puebla, 1856, José Trinidad Sánchez, heridor de Feliciana Pacheco. See also AJP, no. 3873, Puebla, 1763M. María Josepha del Castillo complained that her husband had cut her face but does not give the context so it is hard to know why he did so.

58. AJP, no. 3329, Puebla, 1850.

59. AGN, Criminal, vol. 375, exp. 3, fol. 77–171, Puebla, 1809.

60. AGN, Criminal, vol. 459, exp. 5, fol. 237–83, Puebla, 1817–1820.

61. AJP, paquete 4, Puebla, 1856, Mariano Mendiola, heridor de Rafaela y Dolores Arroyo.

62. AJP, paquete 6, exp. 38, Acatlan, 1856; AJP, exp. 3180, Puebla, 1850; and AJP, paquete 1, exp. 18, Izúcar, 1856.

63. AJP, no exp., 1846, Puebla, Mariano Gómez, heridor de María del Carmen García.

64. AGN, Criminal, vol. 12, exp. 9, fol. 276–28v, Metepec, 1744.

65. AJP, exp. 2249, Puebla, 1846.

66. AJP, paquete 5, Puebla, 1856, Miguel García, heridor de Soledad Mellado.

67. AJTS, Penales, vol. 3, exp. 62, fol. 3–4, Mexico City, 1776.

68. AJP, paquete 2, no exp., Izúcar, 1856, Gertrudis, heridora de María Juana Faustina.

69. AJP, paquete 4, Puebla, 1856, Catarina Mendoza, heridora de Angela Martínez.

70. AJP, paquete 1, no exp., Puebla, 1856, María de Jesus Arroyo, heridora de Dolores Peres (complice María Josefa García.); AJP, exp. 3348, Puebla, 1850; and AJP, paquete 5, Puebla, 1856, Juana Martínez, heridora de Francisca Romero.

71. Spierenburg, *Written in Blood*, 55.

72. AJP, exp. 29, no. 6535, Puebla, 1795B.

73. AGN, Criminal, vol. 80, exp. 10, fol. 290–358, Tulancingo, 1808.

74. AGN, Criminal, vol. 194, exp. 17, fol. 260–79, Texcoco, 1778.

75. Shoemaker, *The London Mob*, 57.

76. This law was published in the *Recopilación de las Leyes de los Reinos de las Indias*, as law 31, book 6, title 1. Reference in Lozano Armendares, *La criminalidad*, 101–2.

77. CEHM-Condumex, Don Pedro Garibay, Bando dado en México el 19 de enero, 1809. Lozano Armendares, *La criminalidad,* 101–5, found some instances of arrests for carrying prohibited weapons but mostly the issue arose when people were arrested for assault or homicides.

78. Astete, *Tratado del buen gobierno*, 211.

79. Van Deusen, *Between the Sacred and the Worldly*, 65.

80. Clendinnen, *Aztecs*, 193; Sayer, *Mexican Costume*, 68; Sahagún, *Florentine Codex*, 101.

81. Villa-Flores, *Dangerous Speech*, 94–95.

82. Diez de Bonilla, *Código completo*, 24, 50.

83. AJP, no exp., Puebla, 1846, contra María Luisa Torres y María Andrea Meza por heridas.

84. AJP, paquete 1, no exp., Puebla, 1834, proceso contra María de la Luz Ruiz.

85. AJP, paquete 5, Huejotzingo, 1856, Rafaela Pérez, heridora de Pascuala Martínez.

86. AGN, Criminal, vol. 119, exp. 30, fol. 477–88v, Actopan, 1806.

87. AJP, paquete 4, Puebla, 1856, Pedro Corona heridor de su esposa María Josefa Sánchez.

88. AJTS, Penales, vol. 12, exp. 10, fol. 2–8, Tlalpan, 1833.

89. AGN, Criminal, vol. 641, exp. 24, fol. 75–364, Mexico City, 1806.

90. AGN, Criminal, vol. 184, exp. 10, fol. 241–79, Huichapan, 1809.

91. Hurl-Eamon, *Gender and Petty Violence*, 72.

92. AGN, Criminal, vol. 29, exp. 7, fol. 115–18v, Xochimilco, 1808.

93. AJP, paquete 6, no exp., Puebla, 1856, Petra Briseño heridora de Anselma Hernández.

94. AJP, paquete 4, Puebla, 1856, Juana María Bautista y Josefa Barbara, heridoras mutuas.

95. AJP, paquete 6, no exp., Puebla, 1856, proceso criminal contra María de la Luz Romero por herir a Candelaria Cortes.

96. AJP, exp. 179, 1836, Huejotzingo.

97. AJTS Penales, vol. 8, exp. 11, Mexico City, 1794.

98. AJP, Puebla, 1836, Proceso criminal contra María Juana Cabrera por morder a Sebastiana Torres, en una mano; AJP, exp. 3180, Puebla, 1850; AJP, paquete 6, San Juan Aparicio, 1856, María de la Cueba Santa, heridora de María Teodora Aguilar; AJP, paquete 1, no exp., Puebla, 1856, Luis Miguel (reo profugo) por heridor de su esposa.

99. Escoiquiz, *Tratado*, 134–37; Anonymous, *Reglas de la buena crianza*, 10, 28–29.

100. Diez de Bonilla, *Código completo*, 22.

101. Hurl-Eamon, *Gender and Petty Violence*, 72. Shoemaker, *The London Mob*, 53, also writes about showing contempt through spitting among other acts.

102. AJTS, Penales vol. 7, exp. 77, 1792.

103. AJP, no. 3390, 18 fol., Puebla, 1850, Causa en contra de Matías Ramírez acusado de herir a María Simona Ochoa.

104. AGN, Criminal, vol. 177, exp. 13 fol. 245–61, Tultitlan, 1763.

105. AJP, paquete 3, Puebla, 1856, proceso contra Marcelino Carrion; AJP paquete 2, exp. 3346, Puebla, 1836; AGN, Civil, legajo 39, parte 5ª, no exp., no. fol., Mexico City, 1854.

106. AJP, paquete 3, Atlixco, 1856. Marcelino Carrion, heridor de su esposa María Petra de la Luz.

107. AGN, Criminal, vol. 206, exp. 20, fol. 236–51, Tenango del Valle, 1802.

108. AGN, Criminal, vol. 139, exp. 16, fol. 268–94 Malinalco, 1757.

109. AJTS, Penales, vol. 7, exp. 59, fol. 2–4, Mexico City, 1792.

110. AGN, Criminal, vol. 53, exp. 21, fol. 286–292, Tula, 1740.

111. AGN, Criminal, vol. 184, exp. 10, fol. 241–279, Huichapan, 1809.

112. AGN, Criminal, vol. 11, exp. 9, fol. 61–77, Otumba, 1783.

113. Clendinnen, *Aztecs*, 192.

114. Kanter, *Hijos del Pueblo*, 78.

115. AGN, Criminal, vol. 40, exp. 16, fol. 375–429v, Xochimilco, 1809.

116. AGN, Bienes Nacionales, legajo 874, exp. 7, fol. 1–35v, Ixtacalco, 1833.

117. AGN, Criminal, vol. 29, exp. 13, fol. 345–85, Xochimilco, 1790.

118. AJTS, Penales, vol. 4, exp. 14, Mexico City, 1785.

119. AGN, Bienes Nacionales, legajo 292, exp. 26, Mexico City, 1790.

120. Spierenburg, *Written in Blood*, 10.

7. Power, Sex, Hair, and Clothes

1. Bell, *On Human Finery*, 19.

2. Anonymous, *Reglas de la buena crianza*, 16–17.

3. Hurl-Eamon, *Gender and Petty Violence*, 75.

4. Entwistle, "The Dressed Body," 134, is referring only to clothes but this statement is also true of hair.

5. Entwistle, "The Dressed Body," 133.

6. AGN, Civil, vol. 1469, exp. 19, Mexico City, 1794.

7. AGN, Bienes Nacionales, leg. 292, exp. 28, Mexico City, 1790. In two other cases, women make similar complaints: AGN, Civil, legajo 118, exp. 7, Mexico City, 1827; and AGN, Civil, legajo 169, exp. 1, fol. 1–68v, Mexico City, 1762.

8. Osuna, *Norte de los estados*, 92v; Galindo, *Parte segunda*, 160; Ferrer, *Suma moral*, 418.

9. AGN, Criminal, vol. 41, exp. 21, fol. 320–42, Coyoacán, 1810.

10. AJTS, Penales, vol. 6, exp. 31, Mexico City, 1790.

11. AGN, Criminal, vol. 715, exp. 1, fol. 2–11v, Mexico City, 1772.

12. AGN, Bienes Nacionales, vol. 88, exp. 6, Mexico City, 1832.

13. AGN, Criminal, vol. 190, exp. 19, fol. 322–33, Calimaya, 1770. Some wives believed that they were the equivalent of an unpaid servant who looked after their husband's clothes; doña María Josefa Mijares, for example, complained that she served only to care for her husband, "much like a slave," AGN, Judicial, vol. 11, exp. 8, Mexico City, 1816.

14. AGN, Bienes Nacionales, lejago 1126, exp. 1, fol. 1–2v, Ayocingo, 1788.

15. AGN, Bienes Nacionales, lejajo 717, exp. 102, fol. 2–4, Mexico City, 1853.

16. AGN, Clero Regular y Secular, vol. 197, exp. 20, fol. 358–67, Mexico City, 1768. Juan Antonio de Zepeda, castizo, said that his wife María Josepha de Loreto Martínez would not wash his clothes, AGN Judicial, vol. 32, exp. 51, fol. 454–64v, Mexico City, 1809. Don Juan José Domínguez Sotomayor, professor of surgery in the court, complained that his wife did not do household

tasks so much so that he had to eat out and get someone outside of his home to care for his clothes, AGN, Civil, legajo 92, parte 2, no exp., Mexico City, 1848, divorcio de José María Arce y Manuela Velásques.

17. AGN, Criminal, vol. 641, exp. 17, fol. 107–111v, Mexico City, 1785.

18. Sánchez, *El Padre de familias*; Dávila Mendoza, *Hasta que la muerte*, 68, reports that many women complained that their husbands took their bed-clothes and left them naked.

19. AGN, Criminal, vol. 716, exp. 15, fol. 177–88, Mexico City, 1766.

20. AJP, no. 7241, Puebla, 1800A.

21. AGN, Bienes Nacionales, legajo 370, exp. 42, Mexico City, 1839.

22. AGN, Bienes Nacionales, legajo 1128, exp. 1, fol. 1–1v, Mextitlan, 1788.

23. AGN, Bienes Nacionales, legajo 470, exp. 17, fol. 4–9, Mexico City, 1836; and AGN, Criminal, vol. 624, exp. 2, fol. 39v-40, Mexico City, 1756.

24. AGN, Civil, legajo 199, part 2, exp. 4, fol. 2–5, Mexico City, 1846.

25. According to Gonzalbo Aizpuru, *Las mujeres en la Nueva España*, 204, for some women their clothes represented their dowry. Francois, *A Culture of Everyday Credit*, 17–23, writes about the uses of clothes as objects for pawning and keeping households afloat.

26. AJTS, Civil, vol. 107, no. exp., Mexico City, 1751–52.

27. AGN, Criminal, vol. 41, exp. 33, fol. 468–68v, Xochimilco, 1775.

28. AJP, no. 4020, Puebla, 1767. In this case, it was doña Josepha who asked for such a report when don Joseph Armeria wounded her.

29. Haslip-Vicra, *Crime and Punishment*, 33–34. María Clara Mota, a widow, reported that she had gone to ask the master tailor José if she could rent some clothes to attend a salon when she ran into trouble, AGN, Criminal, vol. 41, exp. 33, fol. 468–68v, Xochimilco, 1775.

30. AGN, Criminal, vol. 456, exp. 6, fol. 125–26, Mexico City, 1783.

31. AJTS, Penales, vol. 9, exp. 7 fol. 2–5v, Mexico City, 1797.

32. AJTS, Penales, vol. 8, exp. 25, fol. 2–3v, Mexico City, 1795; and AGN, Bienes Nacionales, legajo 717, exp. 100, fol. 1–4v, Mexico City, 1853.

33. AGN, Criminal, vol. 611, exp. 6, fol. 125–380, Ixmiquilpan, 1752.

34. AJTS, Penales, vol. 3, exp. 72, fol. 1, Mexico City, 1783.

35. AGN, Bienes Nacionales, legajo 292, exp. 25, fol. 1–7, Tezontepec, 1790; AJP, exp. 200, Puebla, 1794A; AJTS, Penales, vol. 7, exp. 74, fol. 2–2v, Mexico City, 1792; AJTS, Penales, vol. 12, exp. 48, fol. 2–3v, Mexico City, 1832; AJTS, Penales, vol. 3, exp. 67bis, fol. 1–7 Mexico City, 1782; AGN, Bienes Nacionales, lejajo 854, exp. 4, fol. 3–21, Mexico City, 1807; AGN, Criminal, col. 577, exp. 7b, fol. 192–202, Mexico City, 1782; AJP, exp. 87, no. 6814 Puebla, 1797A; NS AGN, Criminal, vol. 641, exp. 17, fol. 107–11v, Mexico City, 1785.

36. AGN, Criminal, vol. 613, exp. 7, fol. 157–64, Mexico City, 1755.

37. AGN, Criminal, vol. 716, exp. 11, fol. 141–50, Mexico City, 1762.

38. AGN, Bienes Nacionales, legajo 1045, exp. 34, fol. 1–3v, Mexico City, 1832.

39. AGN, Criminal, vol. 632, exp. 9, fol. 271–90, Mexico City, 1779.

40. AGN, Clero Regular y Secular, vol. 192, exp. 2, fol. 18–27, Mexico City, 1760.

41. AGN, Bienes Nacionales, legajo 1128, exp. 1, fol. 1–4v, Texcoco, 1788.

42. AGN, Bienes Nacionales, legajo 470, exp. 15, fol. 2–13v Mexico City, 1836.

43. AGN, Criminal, vol. 142, exp. 15, fol. 468–477 Chalco, 1812.

44. AGN, Criminal, vol. 716, exp. 15, fol. 154–168, Mexico City, 1765.

45. Sloan, *Runaway Daughters*, 120.

46. AGN, Criminal, vol. 364, exp. 3, fol. 72–128, Chietla, 1803.

47. AGN Inquisición, vol. 1373, exp. 13, fol. 173–223, Mexico City, 1792. The expression *quimon bretaña* comes from the Japanese word "kimono," a piece of cotton cloth of about six and a half meters long and is a very fine cloth, printed and painted. The best ones came from Japan.

48. AJTS, Penales, vol. 8, exp. 11, Mexico City, 1794.

49. AGN, Criminal, vol. 105, exp. 10, fol. 307–10, Ixmiquilpan, 1792.

50. AGN, Criminal, vol. 29, exp. 11, fol. 204–49, Xochimilco, 1743.

51. AGN, Criminal, vol. 706, exp. 8, Tula, 1804.

52. Sloan, *Runaway Daughters*, 124.

53. AGN, Civil, legajo 23, arte 3, exp. 6, fol. 1–15, Iztacalco, 1817.

54. AJP, paquete 6, exp. 189, Puebla, 1856.

55. AGN, Bienes Nacionales, legajo 717, exp. 56, fol. 1–9v, Tochimilco, 1852.

56. AGN, Civil, vol. 1600, exp. 16, no fol., Mexico City, 1752.

57. AJTS, Penales, vol. 7, exp. 13, fol. 1–2, Mexico City, 1791.

58. AGN, Criminal, vol. 583, exp. 14, fol. 300–39, Mexico City, 1803.

59. AJP, exp. 4346, Puebla, 1776.

60. Haslip-Viera, *Crime and Punishment*, 33–34.

61. AGN, Criminal, col. 206, exp. 18, fol. 219–27, Tenango del Valle, 1771.

62. AGN, Criminal, vol. 50, exp. 10, fol. 63, Xochimilco, 1777.

63. AJP, paquete 1, no exp., Puebla, 1856, Antonio Flores, heridor de María Soledad Martínez.

64. AJP, paquete 6, Puebla, 1856, María Rosa, heridora de María de la Luz.

65. AJP, paquete 6, exp. 206, Chietla, 1856.

66. AJP. paquete 2, Puebla, 1856, Pascual Reyes, heridor de María de la Luz Mirón, su esposa.

67. AJTS, Penales, vol. 4, exp. 14, Mexico City, 1785.

68. AGN, Criminal, vol. 221, exp. 1, fol. 1–48, Metepec, 1804.

69. AGN, Bienes Nacionales, legajo 292, exp. 26, fol. 1–46v, Mexico City, 1790.

70. AJP, paquete 3, exp. 689, Puebla, 1836.

71. AGN, Criminal, vol. 41, exp. 21, fol. 320–42, Coyoacán, 1810.

72. AGN, Criminal, vol. 265, exp. 25, fol. 285–300, Tacuba, 1802.

73. AJP, paquete 4, Puebla, 1856, Juana Maria Bautista y Josefa Barbara, heridoras mutuas.

74. AGN, Civil, legajo 119, exp. 4, Mexico City, 1838.

75. AJTS, Penales, vol. 6, exp. 71, fol. 1–2v, Coyoacán, 1791.

76. AJTS, Penales, vol. 11, exp. 16, fol. 2–2v, Mexico City, 1750.

77. AGN, Criminal, vol. 583, exp. 14, fol. 300–39, Mexico City, 1803.

78. AJP, exp. 29, no. 6535, Puebla, 1795B.

79. Hurl-Eamon, *Gender and Petty Violence*, 76.

80. Hurl-Eamon, *Gender and Petty Violence*, 75–76.

81. Sloan, *Runaway Daughters*, 125.

82. Muchembled, *La violence au village*, 168.

83. Johnson, "Dangerous Words," 127–28. Muchembled, *La violence au village*, 191, also notes that because so often men's hair was covered by hats, people pulled their beards.

84. Diez de Bonilla, *Código completo*, 52.

85. AJTS, Civil, vol. 113, no. exp., no fol., Coyoacán, 1756.

86. AJTS, Civil, vol. 141, no exp., no fol., Milpa Alta, 1779.

87. AGN, Criminal, vol. 27, exp. 8, fol. 230–36v, Teotihuacan, 1773.

88. AGN, Clero Regular y Secular, vol. 145, exp. 10, fols. 278–306, Aculco, 1785.

89. AGN, Civil, vol. 113, no exp., Mexico City, 1805.

90. AGN, Criminal, vol. 29, exp. 13, fol. 345–85, Xochimilco, 1790.

91. AJP, no. 1287, Puebla, 1850.

92. Diez de Bonilla, *Código completo*, 77–78.

93. AJP, exp. 87, no. 6814 Puebla, 1797A.

94. AGN, Criminal, vol. 670, exp. 2, fol. 27–46, Mexico City, 1806.

95. AGN, Criminal, vol. 42, exp. 15, fol. 426–519, Pachuca, 1802.

96. AGN, Criminal, vol. 41, exp. 25, fol. 389–389v, Xochimilco, 1741,

97. AGN, Criminal, vol. 11, exp. 9, fol. 61–77, Otumba, 1783.

98. Farr, "The Pure," 411.

99. AGN, Criminal, vol. 278, exp. 7, fol. 239–62, Xalostoc, 1796; and AGN, Civil, vol. 2045, exp. 11, no fol., Mexico City, 1794.

100. AGN, Criminal, vol. 130, exp. 9, fol. 334–482, Temascaltepec, 1799.

101. AJP, exp. 616, Huauchinango, 1846.

102. AGN, Criminal, vol. 131, exp. 27, fol. 351–61v, Tacubaya, 1727.

103. AGN, Criminal, vol. 41, exp. 33, fol. 468–468v, Xochimilco, 1775.

104. AGN, Criminal, col. 119, exp. 29, fol. 441–74, Actopan, 1753.

105. AJTS, penales, vol. 11, exp. 64, fol. 1, Coyoacán, 1752.

106. AJP, paquete 3, exp. 689, Puebla, 1836.

107. AGN, Criminal, vol. 8. exp. 20. fol. 302–56, Teotihuacan, 1803.

108. AGN, Bienes Nacionales, legajo 470, exp. 17, fol. 4–9, Mexico City, 1836.

109. AJTS, Penales, vol. 3, exp. 2, fol. 2–2v, Coyoacán, 1777.

110. AJTS, Penales, vol. 9, exp. 7, fol. 2–5v, Mexico City, 1797.

111. AJTS, Penales, vol. 4, exp. 36, fol. 1–3, Mexico City, 1785; AGN, Civil, legajo 76, no exp., Huichapan, 1805, Manuela Salvador (alias la Meti) contra Antonio Chávez, su esposo; AGN, Bienes Nacionales, legajo 874, exp. 7, fol. 1–35v, Ixtacalco, 1833; AGN, Bienes Nacionales, legajo 76, exp. 16, Mexico City, 1855; AGN, Criminal, vol. 50, exp. 15, fol. 248–248v, Xochimilco, 1780; and AGN, Bienes Nacionales, legajo 470, exp. 12, Mexico City, 1836.

112. Spierenberg, "How Violent Were Women?" 23; Muchembled, *La violence au village,* 191.

113. Muchembled, *La violence au village,* 191.

114. AJP, no. 3325, Puebla, 1850.

115. Shoemaker, *The London Mob,* 68.

116. AJP, exp. 2249, Puebla, 1846; AJP, paquete 2, no exp., Puebla, 1856, Andrea Mendoza, heridor del Sargento Domingo Trejo; AJTS, Civil, vol. 10, no exp., no fol., Coyoacán, 1754.

117. AJP, no. 1287, Puebla, 1850.

118. AGN, Civil, legajo 206, no. exp., Mexico City, 1853.

119. AJTS, Penales, vol. 6, exp. 71, fol. 1–2v, Coyoacán, 1791; AJTS, Penales, vol. 4, exp. 14, Mexico City, 1785; AGN, Criminal, vol. 222, exp. 25, fol. 283–323v, Coatepec, 1772; AGN, Criminal, vol. 193, exp. 12, fol. 135–39, Texcoco, 1735; AGN, Criminal, vol. 265, exp. 25, fol. 285–300, Tacuba, 1802; AGN, Criminal, vol. 194, exp. 19, fols. 397–410, Texcoco, 1800; AGN, Criminal, vol. 80, exp. 14, Tulancingo, 1815; AGN, Criminal, vol. 80, exp. 14, fol. 466–91, Tulancingo, 1815; AGN, Criminal, vol. 570, exp. 7, fol. 75–81, Mexico City, 1795; AJP, no exp., Puebla, 1846, contra María Justa Palacios, heridora de María de la Luz Mejia; AGN, Criminal, vol. 18, exp. 18, fol. 552, 554v., Malinalco, 1807; AJP, paquete 4, Puebla, 1846, Juana María Bautista y Josefa Barbara, heridoras mutuas; AJP, exp. 3390, Puebla, 1850; AJP, exp. 29, no. 6535, Puebla, 1795B.

120. AGN, Criminal, vol. 91, exp. 14, fol. 313–34, Tlalmanalco, 1787.

121. AJTS, Penales, vol. 10, exp. 57, Mexico City, 1772.

122. AGN, Criminal, vol. 338, exp. 20, fol. 333–39, Puebla, 1789.

123. AGN, Criminal, vol. 262, exp. 11, fol. 160–201, Cuernavaca, 1803.

124. AGN, Criminal, vol. 48, exp. 13, fol. 239–46, Xochimilco, 1780.

125. AGN, Criminal, vol. 38, exp. 16, fol. 305–36, Cuernavaca, 1809.

126. AGN, Bienes Nacionales, legajo 663, exp. 9, fol. 1–8, Tacuba, 1812.

127. AGN, Criminal, vol. 582, exp. 15, fol. 341–42, Mexico City, 1802.

Bibliography

Archives

Archivo General de la Nación (AGN), Criminal, Civil. Bienes Nacionales, Inquisición, Judicial, Mexico City, Mexico.

Archivo de General Indias (AGI). Audiencia de México, Seville, Spain.

Archivo Judicial del Tribunal Superior del Distrito Federal (AJTS), Penales, Civil, Mexico City, Mexico.

Archivo Judicial de Puebla (AJP), Puebla, Mexico.

De Arizmendi, Padre Fray Baltasar. *Sermones en las Festividades de María Santísima Predicados en diversos lugares.* Manuscript, tomo 1, Biblioteca Nacional, Madrid, Spain, (eighteenth century).

Yale Library, Puebla Collection, New Haven, Connecticut.

Published Works

Amar y Borbón, Doña Josefa. *Discurso sobre la educación física y moral de las mugeres.* Madrid: Imprenta de D. Benito Cano, 1790.

Anonymous. *Reglas de la buena crianza civil y christiana Utílisimas para todos, y singularmente para los que cuiden de la educación de los Niños, a quienes las deberían explicar, inspirándoles insensiblemente su practica en todas ocurrencias.* Puebla: Oficina de Don Pedro de la Rosa, 1802.

Argyle, Michael. "The Syntaxes of Bodily Communication." In *The Body as a Medium of Expression,* edited by Jonathan Benthall and Ted Polhemus, 143–61. London: Allen Lane, 1975.

Arrom, Silvia. *The Women of Mexico City, 1790–1857.* Stanford: Stanford University Press, 1985.

Arthur, Linda B. "Dress and the Social Control of the Body." In *Religion, Dress and the Body,* edited by Linda B. Arthur, 1–7. New York: Berg, 1999.

Astete, Padre Gaspar de. *Tratado del buen govierno de la familia y estado de las viudas y doncellas.* Burgos: Juan Baptista Varedio, 1603.

Bailey, Joanne. "I Dye [*sic*] by Inches: Locating Wife-Beating in the Concept of Privatization of Marriage and Violence in Eighteenth Century England." *Social History* 31, no. 3 (2006): 273–94.

Bartlett, Robert. "Symbolic Meanings of Hair in the Middle Ages." *Transactions of the Royal Historical Society,* 6th series, no. 4 (1994): 43–60.

Beezley, William. *Mexican National Identity: Memory, Innuendo and Popular Culture.* Tucson: University of Arizona Press, 2008.

Bell, Quentin. *On Human Finery.* London: Hogarth, 1976.

Berdan, Frances. *The Aztecs of Central Mexico: An Imperial Society.* New York: Holt, 1982.

Bourdieu, Pierre. *Outline of a Theory of Practice.* Translated by Richard Nice. Cambridge: Cambridge University Press, 1977.

Boyer, Richard. "Honor among Plebeians: *Mala Sangre* and Social Reputation." In Johnson and Lipsett-Rivera, 152–78.

———. *Lives of the Bigamists: Marriage, Family and Community in Colonial Mexico.* Albuquerque: University of New Mexico Press, 1995.

———. "Respect and Identity: Horizontal and Vertical Reference Points in Speech Acts." *The Americas* 54, no. 4 (1998): 491–509.

———. "Women, *La Mala Vida* and the Politics of Marriage." In *Sexuality and Marriage in Colonial Latin America,* edited by Asuncion Lavrin, 252–86. Lincoln: University of Nebraska Press, 1989.

Burkhart, Louise. *The Slippery Earth: Nahua-Christian Moral Dialogues in Sixteenth-Century Mexico.* Tucson: University of Arizona Press, 1989.

Cámara Muñoz, Alicia. *Arquitectura y sociedad en el siglo de oro: Idea, traza y edificio.* Madrid: Ediciones El Arquero, 1990.

Cañeque, Alejandro. *The King's Living Image: The Culture and Politics of Viceregal Power in Colonial Mexico.* New York: Routledge, 2004.

Caro Baroja, Julio. *La ciudad y el campo.* Madrid: Alfaguara, 1966.

Castañeda, Carmen. "La memoria de las niñas violadas." *Encuentro,* 5.2, no. 1, (1984): 41–56.

Cerda, Juan de la. *Libro intitulado vida política de todos los estados de mugeres: En el qual dan muy provechosos y Christianos documentos y avisos, para criarse y conservarse debidamente las mugeres en sus estados.* Alcalá de Hénares, Casa de Juan Gracian, 1599.

Certeau, Michel de. *The Practice of Everyday Life.* Translated by Steven Rendall. Berkeley: University of California Press, 1984.

Cervantes, Fernando. *The Devil in the New World: The Impact of Diabolism in New Spain.* New Haven: Yale University Press, 1994.

Chambers, Sarah C. *From Subjects to Citizens: Honor, Gender, and Politics in Arequipa, Peru, 1780–1854.* University Park: The Pennsylvania State University Press, 1999.

Chasteen, John. "Violence for Show: Knife Dueling on a Nineteenth-Century Cattle Frontier." In *The Problem of Order in Changing Societies: Essays on Crime and Policing in Argentina and Uruguay, 1750–1940,* edited by Lyman Johnson, 47–64. Albuquerque: University of New Mexico Press, 1994.

Clendinnen, Inge. *Aztecs: An Interpretation,* New York: Cambridge University Press, 1991.

———. "The Cost of Courage in Aztec Society." *Past and Present* 107, no. 56 (1985): 44–89.

Colección de providencias diocesanas del obispado de la Puebla de los Angeles, hechas y ordenadas por su Señoria Ilustrísima el Sr. Dr. D. Francisco Fabian y Fuero. Puebla: Imprenta del Real Seminario Palafoxiano, 1770.

Cope, R. Douglas. *The Limits of Racial Domination: Plebeian Society in Colonial Mexico City, 1660–1720.* Madison: University of Wisconsin Press, 1994.

Córdoba, Martín de. *Jardín de las nobles doncellas.* N.p., N.p, 1542.

Cruz, Jesus. "Building Liberal Identities in Nineteenth-Century Madrid: The Role of Middle Class Material Culture." *The Americas* 60, no. 3 (2004): 391–410.

Curcio-Nagy, Linda. "Giants and Gypsies: Corpus Christi in a Colonial Mexican City." In *Rituals of Rule, Rituals of Resistance: Public Celebrations and Popular Culture in Mexico.* Edited by William Beezley, William French, and Cheryl Martin, 1–26. Wilmington DE: Scholarly Resources, 1994.

———. *The Great Festivals of Colonial Mexico City: Performing Power and Identity.* Albuquerque: University of New Mexico Press, 2004.

D'Aubeterre Buznego, María Eugenia. *El pago de la novia, Matrimonio, vida conyugal y prácticas transnacionales en San Miguel Acuexcomac, Puebla.* Zamora: El Colegio de Michoacán, 2000.

Dávila Mendoza, Dora. *Hasta que la muerte nos separe: El divorcio eclesiástico en el arzobispado de México, 1702–1800.* Mexico City: El Colegio de México, Universidad Iberoamericana, Universidad Católico Andrés Bello, 2005.

Diez de Bonilla, Manuel. *Código completo de urbanidad y buenas maneras, según los usos y costumbres de las naciones más cultas, extractado de las mejores obras escritas sobre la materia en especial de la titulada Galatea del Señor Melchor Rioja*. N.p., N.p., 1879; first published in 1844 in Paris by Charles Bouret).

Entwistle, Joanne. "The Dressed Body." In *Real Bodies: A Sociological Introduction*, edited by Mary Evans and Ellie Lee, 133–150. London: Palgrave, 2002.

———. *The Fashioned Body: Fashion, Dress, and Modern Social Theory*. Cambridge: Polity Press, 2000.

Escoiquiz, Don Juan de. *Tratado de las Obligaciones del Hombre*. Madrid: Imprenta Real, 1803.

Fabián y Fuero, Francisco. *Colección de providencias diocesanas del Obispado de Puebla de los Angeles*. Puebla: Imprenta del Real Seminario Palafoxiana, 1770.

Falk, Pasi. *The Consuming Body*. London: Sage, 1994.

Farr, James R. "The Pure and Disciplined Body: Hierarchy, Morality, and Symbolism during the Catholic Reformation." *Journal of Interdisciplinary History* 21, no. 3 (Winter 1991): 391–414.

Ferrer, Vicente. *Suma Moral para examen de curas y confesors en que a la luz del sol de las escuelas Santo Thomás, se desvanecen los perniciosos extremos de laxedad y rigor*. Valencia: Oficina de Joseph Thomas Lucas, 1736.

Fluegel, John Carl. *The Psychology of Clothes*. London: Hogarth, 1950.

Foster, George. "Dreams, Character and Cognitive Orientation in Tzintzuntzán." *Ethos* 1, no. 1 (April 1973): 106–21.

Francois, Marie Eileen. *A Culture of Everyday Credit: Housekeeping, Pawnbroking, and Governance in Mexico City, 1750–1920*. Lincoln: University of Nebraska Press, 2006.

Fraser, Valerie. *The Architecture of Conquest, Building in the Viceroyalty of Peru, 1535–1635*. Cambridge: Cambridge University Press, 1990.

Frye, David. *Indians into Mexicans: History and Identity in a Mexican Town*. Austin: University of Texas Press, 1996.

Galban Ribera, Mariano. *Catecismo de urbanidad civil y cristiana para uso de las escuelas*. Mexico City: Tipografia de la V.E. Hijos de Murguia, 1880.

Galindo, Pedro. *Excelencias de la castidad y virginidad. Dividese en dos partes*. Madrid: Matheo de Espinosa y Arteaga, 1681.

———. *Parte segunda del directorio de Penitentes, y practica de una buena y prudente confesion*. Madrid: Antonio de Zafra, 1680.

———. *Verdades morales en que se reprehendan y condenan los trages vanos, superfluos, y profanos; con otros vicios, y abusos que oy se usan: mayormente los escotados deshonestos de las mugeres*. Madrid: Francisco Sáenz, 1678.

Gallant, Thomas. "Honor, Masculinity, and Ritual Knife Fighting in Nineteenth-Century Greece." *The American Historical Review* 105, no. 2 (April 2001): 359–63.

———. "Turning the Horns: Cultural Metaphors, Material Conditions, and the Peasant Language Resistance in Ionian Islands (Greece) During the Nineteenth Century." *Comparative Studies in Society and History* 36, no. 4 (1994): 702–19.

García Márquez, Gabriel. *Crónica de una muerte anunciada*. Buenos Aires: Editorial Suramericana, 1981.

Gibson, Charles. *The Aztecs under Spanish Rule: A History of the Indians of the Valley of Mexico, 1529–1810*. Stanford: Stanford University Press, 1964.

Gómez de Terán, Doctor Don Juan Elias. *Infancia ilustrada y niñes instruida en todo género de virtudes Christianas, Morales, y Políticas, que conducen a la Santa Educación y buena crianza de los niños*. Madrid: Oficina de Antonio Marín, 1735.

Gonzalbo Aizpuru, Pilar. "Familias y viviendas en la capital del virreinato." In *Casas, vivienda y hogares en la historia de México*, edited by Rosalva Loreto López, 75–107. Mexico City: El Colegio de México, 2001.

———. *Introducción a la historia de la vida cotidiana*. Mexico City: El Colegio de México, 2006.

———. *Las mujeres en la Nueva España. Educación y vida cotidiana*. Mexico City: El Colegio de México, 1987.

———. *Vivir en Nueva España: Orden y desorden en la vida cotidiana*. Mexico City: El Colegio de México, 2009.

González Reyes, Gerardo. "Familia y violencia sexual: Aproximaciones al estudio del rapto, la violación y el estupro en la primer mitad del siglo XVIII." In *Familia iberoamericana. Historia, identidad y conflictos*, edited by Pilar Gonzalbo Aizpuru, 93–115. Mexico City: El Colegio de México, 2001.

Gorn, Elliott J. "'Gouge and Bite, Pull Hair and Scratch': The Social Significance of Fighting in the Southern Backcountry." *American Historical Review* 1, no. 90 (1985): 18–43.

Gose, Peter. *Invaders as Ancestors: On the Intercultural Making and Unmaking of Spanish Colonialism in the Andes*. Toronto: University of Toronto Press, 2008.

Gowing, Laura. *Domestic Dangers: Women, Words, and Sex in Early Modern London*. Oxford: Clarendon Press, 1996.

Greenberg, Kenneth S. *Honor and Slavery*. Princeton: Princeton University Press, 1996.

Grosz, Elizabeth. *Space, Time, and Perversion: Essays on the Politics of Bodies*. New York: Routledge, 1995.

Gutiérrez, Ramón. *When Jesus Came, the Corn Mothers Went Away: Marriage, Sexuality, and Power in New Mexico, 1500–1846.* Stanford: Stanford University Press, 1991.

Gutmann, Matthew C. *The Meanings of Macho: Being a Man in Mexico City.* Berkeley: University of California Press, 1996.

Haag, Pamela. "'The Ill-Use of a Wife': Patterns of Working-Class Violence in Domestic and Public New York City, 1660–1880." *Journal of Social History* 25, no. 3 (1992): 447–78.

Hall, Edward T. *The Hidden Dimension.* Garden City NJ: Doubleday, 1966.

Hardendorft Burr, Grace. *Hispanic Furniture from the Fifteenth through the Eighteenth Century.* 2nd ed. New York: Archive Press, 1964.

Haslip-Viera, Gabriel. *Crime and Punishment in Late Colonial Mexico City, 1692–1810.* Albuquerque: University of New Mexico Press, 1988.

Hernández, Leonardo Fabricio. "Implicated Spaces, Daily Struggles: Home and Street Life in Late Colonial Guatemala City, 1750–1824." PhD diss., Brown University, 1999.

Herrera, Fray Alonso de. *Espejo de la perfecta casada.* Granada: Blas Martínez, 1636.

Holler, Jacqueline. "Conquered Spaces, Colonial Skirmishes: Spatial Contestation in Sixteenth-Century Mexico City." *Radical History Review* 99, no. 3 (2007): 107–20.

Hunt, Alan. "Regulating Heterosocial Space: Sexual Politics in the Early Twentieth Century." *Journal of Historical Sociology* 15, no. 1 (2002): 1–34.

Hurl-Eamon, Jennine. *Gender and Petty Violence in London, 1680–1720.* Columbus: The Ohio State University Press, 2005.

Jeffery, R. Brooks. "From Azulejos to Zaguanes: The Islamic Legacy in the Built Environment of Hispano-America." *Journal of the Southwest* 45, no. 1–2 (2003): 289–327.

Jímenez Muñoz, Jorge H. *La traza del poder: Historia de la política y los negocios urbanos en el distrito federal de sus orígenes a la desaparición del Ayuntamiento, (1824–1928).* Mexico City: Dedalo, 1993.

Johnson, Lyman. "Dangerous Words, Provocative Gestures, and Violent Acts: The Disputed Hierarchies of Plebeian Life in Colonial Buenos Aires." In Johnson and Lipsett-Rivera, *The Faces of Honor,* 127–51.

Johnson, Lyman, and Lipsett-Rivera, Sonya, eds. *The Faces of Honor: Sex, Shame and Violence in Colonial Latin America.* Albuquerque: University of New Mexico Press, 1998.

Kagan, Richard. *Urban Images of the Hispanic World, 1493–1793.* New Haven: Yale University Press, 2000.

Kanter, Deborah. *Hijos del Pueblo: Gender, Family, and Community in Rural Mexico, 1730–1850*. Austin: University of Texas Press, 2008.

Katzew, Ilona. "Casta Painting: Identity and Social Stratification in Colonial Mexico." In *New World Orders: Casta Painting and Colonial Latin America*, edited by Ilona Katzew, 8–29. New York: Americas Society Art Gallery, 1996.

Lauderdale Graham, Sandra. *House and Street: The Domestic World of Servants and Masters in Nineteenth-Century Rio de Janeiro*. Austin: University of Texas Press, 1988.

———. "Honor among Slaves." In Johnson and Lipsett-Rivera, *The Faces of Honor*, 201–28.

Leach, Edmund R. "Magical Hair," *Journal of the Royal Anthropological Institute of Great Britain and Ireland* 88, no. 2 (July–Dec. 1958): 147–64.

Lefebvre, Henri. *The Production of Space*. Translated by Donald Nicholson-Smith. Oxford: Blackwell, 1991.

Le Goff, Jacques. "Head or Heart? The Political Use of Body Metaphors in the Middle Ages." In *Fragments for a History of the Human Body, Part Three*, edited by Michel Feher, 13–26. New York: Zone, 1989.

Lejeune, Jean-François. "Dreams of Order: Utopia, Cruelty and Modernity." In *Cruelty & Utopia: Cities and Landscapes in Latin America*, edited by Jean-François Lejeune, 30–63. New York: Princeton Architectural Press, 2005.

Lipsett-Rivera, Sonya. "*De Obra y Palabra*: Patterns of Insults in Mexico, 1750–1856." *The Americas* 54, no. 4 (1998): 511–39.

———. "The Intersection of Rape and Marriage in Late-Colonial and Early-National Mexico." *Colonial Latin American Historical Review* 6, no. 4 (Nov. 1997): 559–90.

———. "Language of Body and Body as Language: Religious Thought and Cultural Syncretism." In *Religion in New Spain*, edited by Susan Schroeder and Stafford Poole, 66–82. Albuquerque: University of New Mexico Press, 2007.

———. "Marriage and Family Relations in Mexico during the Transition from Colony to Nation." In *State and Society in Spanish America during the Age of Revolution*, edited by Victor Uribe-Uran, 121–48. Wilmington DE: Scholarly Resources, 2001.

———. "Mira Lo que Hace el Diablo: The Devil in Mexican Popular Culture, 1750–1856." *The Americas* 59, no. 2 (2002): 201–19.

———. "Scandal at the Church: José de Alfaro Accuses Doña Theresa Bravo and Others of Insulting and Beating His *Castiza* Wife, Josefa Cadena (Mexico, 1782)." In *Colonial Lives: Documents on Latin American History*,

1550–1850, edited by Richard Boyer and Geoffrey Spurling, 216–23. New York: Oxford University Press, 2000.

———. "A Slap in the Face of Honor: Social Transgression and Women in Late-Colonial Mexico" In Johnson and Lipsett-Rivera, *The Faces of Honor,* 179–200.

Lira Vásquez, Carlos. *Para una historia de la arquitectura mexicana.* Mexico City: Universidad Nacional Autónoma Metropolitana, Azcapotzalco, 1990.

Lizana y Beaumont, Francisco Javier. *Instrucción Pastoral del Illmo. Señor Don Francisco Xavier de Lizana y Beaumont, Arzobispo de México del Consejo de S. M. & C. Sobre la costumbre de llevar las Señoras el pecho y brazos desnudos.* Mexico City: Oficina de Doña María Fernández de Jauregui, Calle de Santo Domingo, 1808.

Lockhart, James. *The Nahuas after the Conquest: A Social and Cultural History of the Indians of Central Mexico, Sixteenth through Eighteenth Centuries.* Stanford: Stanford University Press, 1992.

Lombardo de Ruiz, Sonia. "El desarrollo urbano de México-Tenochtitlan," *Historia Mexicana* 22, no. 2 (1972): 121–41.

López Austin, Alfredo. *The Human Body and Ideology. Concepts of the Ancient Nahuas.* Vol. 1. Translated by Thelma Ortiz de Montellano and Bernard Ortiz de Montellano. Salt Lake City: University of Utah Press, 1988.

Loreto López, Rosalva. "La casa, la vivienda y el espacio doméstico en la Puebla de los Ángeles del siglo XVIII." In *Casas, vivienda y hogares en la historia de México,* edited by Rosalva Loreto López, 147–206. Mexico City: El Colegio de México, 2001.

———. "Familial Religiosity and Images in the Home: Eighteenth-Century Puebla de los Angeles, Mexico," *Journal of Family History* 22, no. 1 (1997): 26–49.

Lozano Armendares, Teresa. *La criminalidad en la ciudad de México 1800–1821.* Mexico City: Universidad Nacional Autónoma de México, 1987.

MacLachlan, Colin. *Spain's Empire in the New World: The Role of Ideas in Institutional and Social Change.* Los Angeles: University of California Press, 1988.

MacRae, Donald G. "The Body and Social Metaphor." In *The Body as a Medium of Expression,* edited by Jonathan Benthall and Ted Polhemus. London: Allen Lane, 1975.

Macias-González, Victor. "Hombres de mundo: La masculinidad, el consumo, y los manuales de urbanidad y buenas maneras." In *Orden social e identidad de género, México, siglos XIX y XX,* edited by María Teresa Fernández Aceves, Carmen Ramos Escandón, and Susie Porter, 267–97. Guadalajara: CIESAS Guadalajara, 2006.

Mannarelli, María Emma. *Private Passions and Public Sins: Men and Women in Seventeenth-Century Lima*. Translated by Sidney Evans and Meredith D. Dodge. Albuquerque: University of New Mexico Press, 2007.

Maravall, José Antonio. *Poder, honor y élites en el siglo XVII*. Madrid: Siglo Veintiuno Editores, 1979.

Martin, Cheryl E. *Governance and Society in Colonial Mexico: Chihuahua in the Eighteenth Century*. Stanford: Stanford University Press, 1996.

Mendieta, Jerónimo de. *Historia eclesiástica Indiana*. Mexico City: Editorial Porrua, 1971.

Moles, Don Joaquín. *Doctrina Christiana para niños y adultos, a la mente de San Carlos Boromeo, y del catolicismo romano*. Madrid: Imprenta de Pantaleon Aznar, 1769.

Morales, María Dolores, and María Gayón. "Viviendas, casas y usos de suelo en la ciudad de México, 1848–1881." In *Casas, vivienda y hogares en la historia de México*, edited by Rosalva Loreto López, 339–55. Mexico City: El Colegio de México, 2001.

Morse, Richard. "Some Characteristics of Latin American Urban History." *American Historical Review* 67, no. 2 (1962): 317–38.

Muchembled, Robert. "Satanic Myth and Cultural Reality." In *Early Modern European Witchcraft: Centres and Peripheries*, edited by Bengt Ankarloo and Gustav Henningsen, 139–60. Oxford: Clarendon Press, 1990.

———. *La violence au village: Sociabilité et comportements populaires en Artois du XVe au XVIIe siècle*. Turnhout: Editions Brepols, 1989.

Muriel, Josefina. *Los recogimientos de mujeres: Respuesta a una problemática social novohispana*. Mexico City: Universidad Nacional Autónoma de México, 1974.

Nuñez, Fernando. "The Interaction of Space and Place: The Mexican Mixture." In *Space and Place in the Mexican Landscape. The Evolution of a Colonial City*, edited by Malcolm Quantrill, 1–73. College Station: Texas A&M University Press, 2001.

Osuna, Fray Francisco de. *Norte de los estados en que se da regla de bivir a los mancebos: y a los casados; y a los viudos; y a todos los continentes; y se tratan muy por estenso los remedios del desastrado casamiento; enseñando que tal a de ser la vida del cristiano casado*. Sevilla, n.p., 1531.

Pardo, Osvaldo. "How to Punish Indians: Law and Cultural Change in Early Colonial Mexico." *Comparative Studies in Society and History* 48, no. 1 (2006): 79–109.

Parker, David. "Law, Honor and Impunity in Spanish America: The Debate over Dueling, 1870–1920." *Law and History Review* 19, no. 2 (2001): 311–45.

Penyak, Lee Michael. "Safe Harbors and Compulsory custody: *Casas de depósito* in Mexico, 1750–1865." *Hispanic American Historical Review* 79, no. 1 (1999): 83–99.

———. "Criminal Sexuality in Central Mexico, 1750–1850." PhD diss., University of Connecticut, 1993.

Pérez, María Teresa. "*Habitat, familia y comunidad en Popayán (Colombia), 1750–1850.*" PhD diss., Université de Montreal, 2009.

Peristiany, J. G. *Honor and Shame: The Values of Mediterranean Society.* Chicago: University of Chicago Press, 1966.

Peristiany, J. G., and Julian Pitt-Rivers. *Honor and Grace in Anthropology.* New York: Cambridge University Press, 1992.

Piccato, Pablo. "Politics and the Technology of Honor: Dueling in Turn-of-the-Century Mexico." *Journal of Social History* 33, no. 2 (1999): 331–54.

Pitt-Rivers, Julian. *The Fate of Shechem, or The Politics of Sex: Essays in the Anthropology of the Mediterranean.* Cambridge: Cambridge University Press, 1977.

Pointon, Marcia. "Women and their Jewels." In *Women and Material Culture, 1660–1830,* edited by Jennie Batchelor and Cora Kaplan, 11–30. London: Palgrave MacMillan, 2007.

Rapoport, Amos. *House Form and Culture.* Englewood Cliffs: Prentice-Hall, 1969.

———. *The Meaning of the Built Environment.* Tucson: The University of Arizona Press, 1990.

Rivera-Ayala, Sergio. *El Discurso colonial en textos Novohispanos: Espacio, cuerpo y poder.* Woodbridge, Suffolk, UK: Tamesis, 2009.

Rosales, Padre Jerónimo de. *Caton Christiano y catecismo de la doctrina cristiana para la educación y buena crianza de los niños y muy provechosos para personas de totos estados.* Mexico City: Imprenta Nueva de la Biblioteca Mexicana, 1761.

Rosenthal, Angela. "Raising Hair." *Eighteenth-Century Studies* 38, no. 1 (2004): 1–16.

Ross, Ellen. "Fierce Questions and Taunts: Married Life in London, 1876–1914." *Feminist Studies* 8, no. 3 (1982): 575–602.

———. "Survival Networks: Women's Neighbourhood Sharing in London Before World War I." *History Workshop* 15, no. 1 (Spring 1983): 4–27.

Rossell, Doctor don Manuel. *La educación conforme a los principios de la religión christiana, leyes y constumbres, de la nación española en tres libros dirigidos a los padres de familia.* Madrid: Imprenta Real, 1786.

Rybczynski, Witold. *Home: A Short History of an Idea.* New York: Viking, 1986.

Sahagún, Bernardino de. *Florentine Codex; General History of the Things of New*

Spain, edited and translated by Charles E. Dibble and Arthur J. O. Anderson. Salt Lake City: University of Utah Press, and the School for American Research, 1953.

Salazar, Br. Don Nicolás Simeón de. *Flores Citlalpapoca. Directorio de Confessores que ofrece a los principiantes y nuevos ministros de el Sacramento.* Puebla: Imprenta de la viuda de Miguel de Ortega, 1715.

Sánchez, Padre Matías. *El Padre de familias, Brevemente instruido en sus muchas obligaciones de padre.* Madrid: n.p., 1786.

Sayer, Chloë. *Mexican Costume.* London: British Museum Publications, 1985.

Sennett, Richard. *The Conscience of the Eye: The Design and Social Life of Cities.* New York: Alfred Knopf, 1990.

Shoemaker, Robert B. *The London Mob: Violence and Disorder in Eighteenth-Century England.* London: Hambledon, 2004.

———. "The Taming of the Duel: Masculinity, Honour, and Ritual Violence in London, 1660–1800." *Historical Journal* 45, no. 3 (2002): 525–45.

Silva Dias, Maria Odila. *Power and Everyday Life: The Lives of Working Women in Nineteenth-Century Brazil.* Translated by Ann Frost. New Brunswick: Rutgers University Press, 1995.

Sloan, Kathryn A. *Runaway Daughters: Seduction, Elopement, and Honor in Nineteenth-Century Mexico.* Albuquerque: University of New Mexico Press, 2008.

Socolow, Susan. "Women and Crime: Buenos Aires 1757–97." *Journal of Latin American Studies* 12, no. 1 (1980): 39–54.

Sousa, Lisa. "The Devil and Deviance in Native Criminal Narratives from Early Mexico." *The Americas* 59, no. 2 (2002): 161–79.

Spain, Daphne. *Gendered Spaces.* Chapel Hill: University of North Carolina Press, 1992.

Spierenberg, Pieter. "Knife Fighting and Popular Codes of Honor in Early Modern Amsterdam." In *Men and Violence: Gender, Honor, and Rituals in Modern Europe and America,* edited by Pieter Spierenberg, 103–27. Columbus: Ohio State University Press, 1998.

———. "How Violent Were Women? Court Cases in Amsterdam, 1650–1810." *Crime, Histoire & Sociétés* 1, no. 1 (1997): 9–28.

———. *Written in Blood: Fatal Attraction in Enlightenment Amsterdam.* Columbus: The Ohio State University Press, 2004.

Stansell, Christine. *City of Women: Sex and Class in New York, 1789–1860.* Urbana: University of Chicago Press, 1983.

———. "Women, Children and the Uses of the Streets: Class and Gender Conflict in New York City, 1850–1860." *Feminist Studies* 8, no. 2 (1982): 309–35.

Steele, Valerie. *Fashion and Eroticism: Ideals of Feminine Beauty from the Victorian Era to the Jazz Age.* New York: Oxford University Press, 1985.

Stern, Steve. *The Secret History of Gender: Women, Men, and Power in Late Colonial Mexico.* Chapel Hill: University of North Carolina Press, 1995.

Synnott, Anthony. *The Body Social: Symbolism, Self and Society.* London: Routledge, 1993.

Taggart, James. *Nahuat Myth and Social Structure.* Austin: University of Texas Press, 1983.

Talavera, Hernando de. *Reforma de trages ilustrada por el maestro Bartolomé Ximenez, regente del estudio de letras umanas a Villanueba de los Infantes.* Baeça: Juan de la Cuesta, 1638.

Taylor, Diana. *The Archive and the Repertoire: Performing Cultural Memory in the Americas.* Durham: Duke University Press, 2003.

Taylor, Scott K. *Honor and Violence in Golden Age Spain.* New Haven: Yale University Press, 2008.

Taylor, William B. *Drinking, Homicide and Rebellion in Colonial Mexican Villages.* Stanford: Stanford University Press, 1979.

———. *Magistrates of the Sacred: Priests and Parishioners in Eighteenth-Century Mexico.* Stanford: Stanford University Press, 1996.

Tomes, Nancy. "A Torrent of Abuse: Violence between Working-Class Men and Women in London." *Journal of Social History* 11, no. 3 (1978): 328–46.

Torre V., Guadalupe de la, Sonia Lombardo de Ruiz, and Jorge González Angulo A. "La vivienda en una zona al suroeste de la Plaza Mayor de la ciudad de México (1753–1811)." In *Casas, vivienda y hogares en la historia de México,* edited by Rosalva Loreto López, 109–46. Mexico City: El Colegio de México, 2001.

Torres Septién, Valentina. "Notas sobre urbanidad y buenas maneras de Erasmo al Manual de Carreño." In *Historia de la educación y enseñanza de la historia,* edited by Pilar Gonzalbo Aizpuru, 89–111. Mexico City: El Colegio de México, 1998.

Trujillo, Fray Thomas de. *Libro Llamado Reprobación de Trajes, Con un Tratado de Limosnas.* Navarra: n.p., 1563.

Twinam, Ann. *Public Lives, Private Secrets: Gender, Honor, Sexuality, and Illegitimacy in Colonial Latin America.* Stanford: Stanford University Press, 1999.

Tuan, Yi-Fu. *Space and Place. The Perspective of Experience.* Minneapolis: University of Minnesota Press, 1977.

Turner, Bryan S. *The Body and Society: Explorations in Social Theory.* London: Sage, 1996.

Turner, Terence S. "The Social Skin." In *Reading the Social Body*, edited by Catherine B. Burroughs and Jeffrey David Ehrenreich, 15–39. Iowa City: University of Iowa Press, 1993.

Undurraga Schüler, Verónica. "Cuando las afrentas se lavaban con sangre: honor, masculinidad y duelos de espadas en el siglo XVIII chileno." *Historia* 41, no. 1 (2008): 165–88.

Uribe-Uran, Victor M. "Colonial *Baracunatanas* and Their Nasty Men: Spousal Homicides and the Law in Late Colonial New Granada." *Journal of Social History* 35, no. 1 (2001): 43–72.

Van Deusen, Nancy E. *Between the Sacred and the Worldly: The Institutional and Cultural Practice of Recogimiento in Colonial Lima*. Stanford: Stanford University Press, 2001.

Villa-Flores, Javier. *Dangerous Speech: A Social History of Blasphemy in Colonial Mexico*. Tucson: University of Arizona Press, 2006.

Viqueira Albán, Juan Pedro. *Propriety and Permissiveness in Bourbon Mexico*. Translated by Sonya Lipsett-Rivera and Sergio Rivera Ayala. Wilmington DE: Scholarly Resources, 1999.

Vives, Juan Luis. *Instrucción de la mujer cristiana*. 4th ed. Buenos Aires: Espasa-Calpe, 1948 (original publication 1528).

Wagner, Leopold. *Manners, Customs, and Observances: Their Origin and Signification*. London: William Heinemann, 1894.

Waldenberger, Suzanne. "Barrio Gardens: The Arrangement of a Woman's Space." *Western Folklore* 59, no. 3–4 (2000): 232–45.

Walker, Charles F. "The Upper Classes and their Upper Stories: Architecture and the Aftermath of the Lima Earthquake of 1746." *Hispanic American Historical Review* 83, no. 1 (2003): 53–82.

Ward, Peter. *A History of Domestic Space: Privacy and the Canadian Home*. Vancouver: UBC Press, 1999.

Wood, J. Carter. "Locating Violence: The Spatial Production and Construction of Physical Aggression." In *Assaulting the Past: Violence and Civilization in Historical Context*, edited by Katherine D. Watson, 20–37. Cambridge: Cambridge Scholars, 2007.

———. *Violence and Crime in Nineteenth-Century England: The Shadow of Our Refinement*. London: Routledge, 2004.

Zorita, Alonso de. *Life and Times in Ancient Mexico: The Brief and Summary Relation of the Lords of New Spain*. Translated by Benjamin Keen. New Brunswick: Rutgers University Press, 1963.

Index

Cope, R. Douglas, 53

Córdoba, Martín de, 65, 160–61

corral (livestock pen), 56, 84

countryside, 106; sexualization of, 25–26, 41, 59; and violence against women, 32, 124–27, 204–5, 271n78

court files, 4, 8–9, 16, 250

courtship, in *zaguánes*, 93–94

covacha (space under a stairway), 53

Coyoacán, D.F.: clothes-tearing incidents in, 232; hair-pulling incidents in, 235, 243, 244; house invasion in, 40

coyote (mixed mestizo and indigenous ancestry), 77

credit, and honor, 186

criminal punishment, 124

Crónica de una Muerte Anunciada (Chronicle of a Death Foretold) (Garcia Márquez), 8

crossroads, 126

cuartos (rented rooms), 51, 53

Cuautitlan, Mor., sexual assaults in, 76

Cuautla Amilpas, Mor., sexual assaults in, 76

Cuernavaca, Mor.: domestic violence in, 112, 119; exemplary violence in, 125

cultural behavior: and architecture, 1–2; and gender, 22–23; internalizing of, 28–29; as means of transmitting knowledge, 3; research on, 4–5

culture, and daily life, 1

Curcio-Nagy, Linda, 169

daily life, and culture, 1

D'Aubeterre Buznego, María Eugenia, 146

décolleté, 165–66

devil, 127, 131–32

Diez de Bonilla, Manuel: etiquette book by, 57; on the head, 148; on spitting, 203; on table manners, 234, 237; on use of the eyes, 159–60, 199; on women's behavior, 107, 153, 162

disobedience, and violence against women, 101

divorce. *See* ecclesiastical divorce

dogs, and personal space, 17, 255–56n31

domestic violence: and attacks on head, 173–74, 182–83; and authority, 176–79; and elites, 243–44; and hair pulling, 242–43; and home, 257n19; in imitation of official punishment, 204; intervention in, 26, 60, 97, 105, 111, 117–20, 129, 266–67n65, 269nn35–36; patterns of, 174–76; and power relations, 176–78; and pulling off pants, 231

domestic world, components of, 41

doors, 72; being half-closed, 79–80; and morality, 40, 55–56, 63–64, 69–71, 263n2, 263n4, 263n112; observing the street from, 84, 86, 88–89; opening and closing of, 73–74, 263n6, 264n7; and sexual assault, 75–76, 78–82

duels, 6, 185

Ecatepec, Mex., child rape in, 98

ecclesiastical divorce, 5, 22, 46, 129; and clothes, 218; and men, 179–80

elites: and abusive enclosure, 96, 266–67n65; and control of space, 37; and domestic violence, 178, 243–44; homes of, *48*; and honor, 13; influence on plebeian culture by, 10; mistresses brought into the home by, 117; as originators of social behavior, 251

enclosure, 94–99; as imprisonment, 266–67n65; and obsessive control over women, 266n58. See also *recogimiento*

entresuelo (space between floors), 53

Erasmus, 5, 254n8

Escoiquiz, Juan de, 160; etiquette manual by, 148

Esperanza (informant), 146

estrado (women's area), 51, 60, 114, 262n94

ethnicity, and appearance, 154–55, 167, 247, 275n48, 276n59

etiquette, 2–3; and behavior, 137; and staircases, 57; for walking, 160, 278nn90–91, 279n95

etiquette manuals, 5, 69, 171, 250, 253n2, 254n8; about dueling, 6; for behavior in interior spaces, 61; by Escoiquiz, 148; on spitting, 203; for staircase use, 57; and thresholds, 82, 84. *See also* Diez de Bonilla, Manuel

excrement, throwing of, 187, 189

exemplary violence, 26, 105–6, 124–25, 129

exterior spaces: as masculine, 65, 263n114; sexualization of, 33

eyes: gazing, 159–60, 198; gouging, 185; staring, 158, 199–200, 277n79, 278n82, 278n84

Fabian y Fuero, Francisco, 131, 166

face: attacks on, 184–87, 196; and sexuality, 198

face cutting, 173, 185, 190–98; and sexuality, 27; and violence against women, 284n57

families, 59–60; supplanting improvident husband, 221

Farr, James, 17, 143, 239

fashion, 165–69, 280n117

financial support: and authority, 214; lack of, 218–21; and male rights, 193

Fluegel, John Carl, 161, 190

Foster, George, 128

France, attacks on head in, 143

Fraser, Valerie, 44

furniture: and honor, 19; social meaning of, 31; and status, 2, 253n1, 253–54n3

Galindo, Pedro, 71, 95, 160, 165

Gallant, Thomas, 7, 142, 185

Garcia Márquez, Gabriel, 8

Garibay, Pedro, 197

gender: and body symbolism, 145, 273n23, 274n26; and hair, 153–54, 234; and home, 35, 64–65; and

honor, 14, 15; and humiliation, 9; and nighttime, 130–31; and space, 33–35, 256n4; and violence, 22–23, 255n20; and work, 65

genitals: attacks on, 27, 81, 91, 129–30, 138, 163, 204–7, 230; and size of vagina, 162–63; women attacking men's, 231

gestures, 27, 273n6. *See also* body language

Gómez de Terán, Juan Elías, 160

Gonzalbo Aizpuru, Pilar, 39, 73

González Reyes, Gerardo, 115

Gorn, Elliott, 185

Gowing, Laura, 84, 89

Granada, Luis de, 71

Greenberg, Kenneth, 141, 190–91

Gutmann, Matthew C., 99

hair, 151–57, 233–34, 247; and ethnicity, 275n48, 276n59; facial, 276n61; and identity, 27, 212–13; length of, 276n55; and morality, 276n62, 276n64, 277n66; and sexuality, 213, 237–40; and status, 28; symbolic attributes of, 275nn48–49. *See also* haircutting; hair pulling; head shaving

haircutting, 81, 122, 129; and humiliation, 236–37; and returning of cut hair, 239

hair pulling, 138, 157–59, 196, 211–12, 234–36, 246–48

Hall, Edward T., 17

handkerchiefs, 187

hats, 149

head: adornment of, 148, 275n43; attacks on, 143, 172–74, 176–77, 181; and attacks on women, 27; and body language, 147–48; lowering of, 235, 241; symbolism of, 142, 145, 147, 274n32

head coverings, for women, 149, *150*, 151, *152*, 275n47

head of household, respect for, 113–14, 115

head shaving, 156–57

Hernández, Leonardo Fabricio, 33

Herrera, Alonso de, 145

hierarchy: and the built environment, 34; in Nahua culture, 16; and personal space, 17–18

hitting, 211

home, 39–40; admission into, 112–13; attacks on boundaries of, 114–15; defense of, 258n32; and domestic violence, 257n19; and gender, 34–35, 64–65; inner sanctum of, 106; proper behavior in, 63, 262n106; respect for, 62, 262n99; and status, 34, 256n9. *See also* houses

honor, 12–19; and architecture, 25; and attack on clothes, 227; and body language, 2; and credit, 186; and doors, 80; and hair pulling, 235; and the head, 147, 148; and home, 40; and interior space, 61; language of, 142; of market vendors, 255n26; among Nahuas, 16; and patterns of violence, 172; and plebeians, 255n25; and rules of violence, 7; and sexuality, 240; and social position, 251; and status, 2; study of, 251

honor (honor attached to status), 13

honor systems, 7, 11–12, 141, 250

honra (honor attached to virtue), 13–15

household reputation: and expulsion from houses, 109; and visitors, 105

houses: expulsion from, 107–10; interior of, as female space, 106–7; perils of entering, 91–92; proximity to each other, 120; proximity to street, 82, *83*; rural, 60; social spaces in, 56; spatial organization of, 25–26, 54–57, 79; and status, 49; and violence against women, 115. *See also* doors; home; mansions; thresholds

house-scorning, 80–81

Huauchinango, Pue.: fights at water sources, 123; hair-pulling incidents in, 240

Huejotzingo, Pue., wife attacking husband in, 202

Huichapan, Hgo., violence in the countryside near, 124

humiliation, 28, 211–12; and attacks on genitals, 27; audiences for, 39, 106, 122, 125, 164; and women's clothing, 216–17; and gender, 9; and haircutting, 236–37; and hair pulling, 157, 241; as inversed honor code, 143, 273n18; and thrown excrement, 189

Hunt, Alan, 130

Hurl-Eamon, Jennine, 6, 10, 84, 131, 142, 201, 212, 232

husbands: lack of respect for, 99, 236, 243; murder of, 196. *See also* men

identity, and appearance, 247

imprisonment, 118–19. *See also* enclosure; *recogimiento*

incest, 97

in-laws, 99–100, 113–14, 119, 236; and rape, 238; supplanting role of improvident husband, 221

Innocent XI (pope), 166

insults, 265n46; audiences for, 120–21; and beard pulling, 234, 290n83; and expulsion from houses, 109; and hair pulling, 235–36; in markets, 123; and masculinity, 110, 177; and pulling clothes, 229; and spatial intrusions, 116; and spitting, 202–3, 286n101; staring as, 200; and thresholds, 89–91; unintentional, 92, 266n51

interior decoration, and morality, 62–63

interior spaces, 251, 61–63; and interaction, 56; invitation into and exclusion from, 91–92, 266n50; and morality, 82, 262n100; spatial organization of, 262n101; and status, 262n97

Islamic society: architecture of, 261n81; and order found at the center, 126; and spatial organization, 47, 114

Iztacalco, D.F., rape incident in, 225